MEMOIRS FROM MY CELL!
THE RESURRECTION OF
JOHN BELL JR!

By John Bell Jr.

Thank you for supporting!

God Bless

John Bell Jr

This is a work of Non-Fiction. Names, characters have been changed to protect identities.

ISBN: 978-1-7338693-0-0
ISBN: 1-7338693-0-1

COVER PAGES ROYALTY FREE IMAGES

COVER DESIGN: BRIANNA WILLIAMS

AUTHOR PHOTO: BRIAN TRU

EDITING: ZAKEISHIA (SECRET) BELL,
MICHELLE STEVENS (MOMMA)
JOHN E BELL JR.

WWW.COACHJOHNBELL.COM

Acknowledgements!

First, I would like to thank God, through my Lord and Savior Jesus Christ. None of this would've been possible without his mercy and grace. He didn't just save me, he invested in me and I intend to give him a full payoff on His investment.

Every poem, every chapter, every word was motivated by the Spirit of God, I can only take credit for listening when he spoke to me. There were times when I wanted to give up, and Your voice was loud and clear. I GOT YOU SON, TRUST ME! Thank you, Lord, for seeing the best in me.

I have to thank my support system, those people who made a conscious decision to stand beside me through thick and thin. There were times when the circumstances discouraged you, but you didn't walk away, you chose to stand by my side motivating me along the way.

I have to thank my Son, Chaz Seegars, my best friend, my wingman, my constant motivation. Your existence changed the direction of my life, I want to thank you for sticking by me even when life, people tried to influence you to do different. I also have to thank my cousin/brother Robert Martin, he gets a special shout out because he has been a blessing to my life. Every time I call on this man he never hesitated to aid and assist me. I will never be able to repay you for the love and support that you've given me, my brother from another mother.

I also want to thank the men who walked with me through HELL, everyone isn't built to survive that lifestyle, it wasn't easy, but we made it SOLDIERS!

It's a must that I acknowledge my siblings, two tough individuals who I love dearly. We all went through our own storms in life and survived every one of them, because we come from a cloth that was not meant to tear and cannot be duplicated, knowing the two of you survived your storms encouraged me to keep going when I really wanted to quit.

To my special Lady, MY WIFE, my friend, my editor, my encouragement, my motivator, my helpmate. Mrs. Bell thank you for being you, which helps me be a better me, thanks for your love and support along with your constant motivation. Since the day you came into my life you've been pushing me to be better, while being patient with me in the process. Most of all thank you being genuine and someone I can TRUST!

To my Girls, Brianna and Sydney…MY MONSTERS. The two of you have added a dimension to my life that I always wanted. You ladies give me motivation in times when I need it the most by simply being YOU! I love you ladies and I want you to know, I'M HERE!

To my brother- in -Law Aubrey, my utility knife, you are the person I can count on to get it done at the last minute. If an email, invoice, design, draft, or event set-up needs to be done you are my go-to in the clutch. Thank you lil bro for being that support I need, I GOT YOU!

To my parents, John E Bell Sr, and the fabulous Michelle Stevens. Dad thank you for stepping up and being who I needed you to be at the right time, your support helped me through one of the toughest storms in my life.

Momma, thank you for my being my rock, my strength, my support, my shoulder to cry on, my encourager, and my biggest fan. The love that you have for your children surpasses any love that I have ever felt or seen. God created you to be MY MOM, I wouldn't have survived the streets, or prison system if it wasn't for your prayers and support. You have totally loved beyond your limits when it comes to me. God couldn't have given me a better Friend/Mom! I love you from that place that only you and I share. Thank you for being aggressive with the editing and making sure this project is perfect.

Finally, I want to acknowledge those who tried to stop me, turned your back on me, betrayed me, those who did their best to slander me or speak failure on my name. If it wasn't for your obedience to the enemies plan, I wouldn't have gained the strength, knowledge, and wisdom from our experiences. You've taught me how to turn negative people/experiences into a positive push, which helped with my preparation to becoming a Man.

THANK YOU!

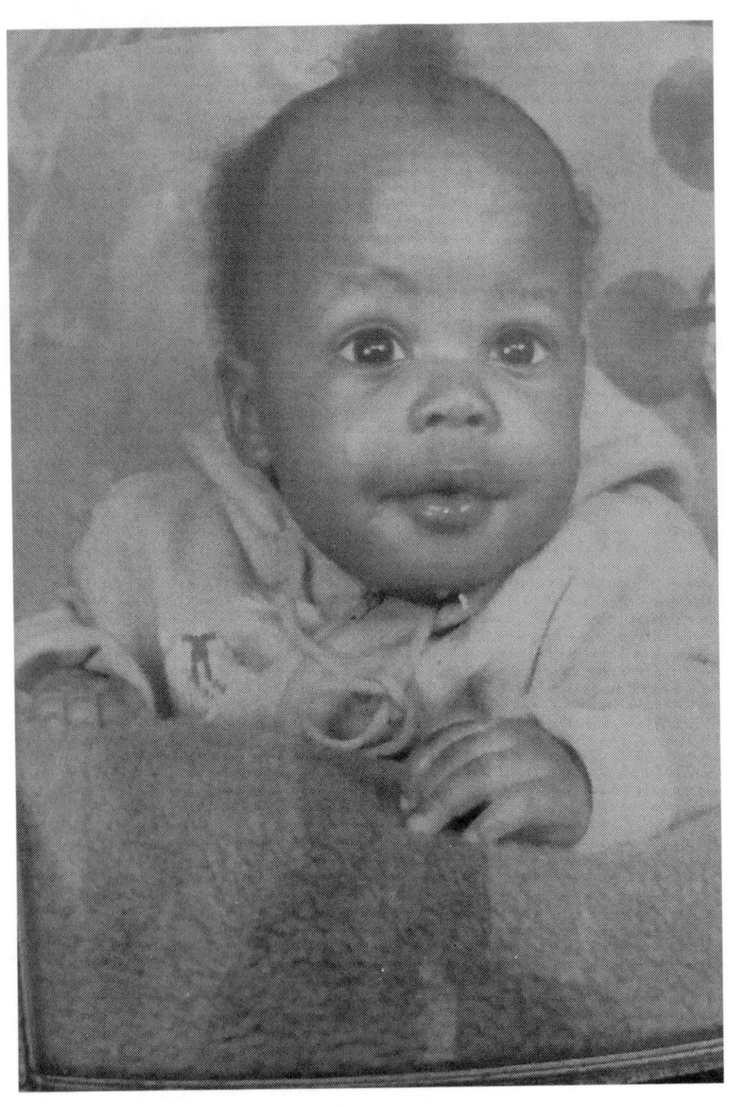

THE BABY BOY!
JOHN E BELL JR.
NOVEMBER 19, 1978

THE PARENTS!
MICHELLE BELL AND JOHN E BELL SR.

THE DREAMER WHO DROPPED THE BALL!

INTRODUCTION!

January 31st, 2002, I was apprehended by the Prince George's County police department for Distribution of a Controlled Dangerous Substance (CRACK). The consequences of my actions caused me to be sentenced to 188 months in Federal Prison. In the process of my punishment I experienced a lot of trials and tribulations which lead me to Christ. God placed this book on my heart, and I had no other choice but to share my experiences with you.

This book is about life, love, betrayal, deceit, dishonesty, family, generational curses, transformation, and most of all, Grace and mercy! It's also My testimony!

The things that I've grown through and survived; and I constantly thank God for His Grace and Mercy. He saw something in me to save me from myself.

No one said that life would be mistakes free, but I had to learn easy life lessons the hard way. Yet, I've grown to understand mistakes are made to mature yourself in areas that you were once weak and are often setbacks for a stronger comeback. It's important that you try not to repeat mistakes as they can become habits that will turn into a lifestyle.

It's better to learn from someone else's story rather than experience it for yourself. My journey is very relatable, learn from my lessons and process it as your blessing. "All the ways of a man are clean in his own eyes…" (Proverbs 16:2, KJV)

Lesson one: Don't be a fool and see someone else fail and think it can't happen to you, and you repeat the exact same mistake!

This book is my life and based upon 68 poems. It has biblical significance, as 6 represent Man, and 8 represents New beginnings! I started writing poems when I was incarcerated; I wrote my first poem May 2008. Every poem I wrote is a snapshot of my life, from the shedding of the old me to a man after God's own heart.

Welcome to the rebirth of John Edward Bell Jr! GOD BLESS

THIS STORY

This story is about Man who deceived, lied, and manipulated,
This story is about a Man who hurt innocent lives because what he saw in the mirror he hated.
This story is about a Man who lost soul in the currents of the enemy's storm,
This story is about a Man who fell from grace, chasing things he thought kept him warm.
This story is about a Man who was filled with lust, so from commitment...he always ran,
This story is about a Man who was told he couldn't and was deprived of knowing that he can.
This story is about Man who was lost in lies, in search of new life through religion,
This story is about a Man who found his soul, in the confines of a place called PRISON!

THIS STORY

Written at two o'clock in the morning on July 17, 2009 while I was lying in bed. Most of my writings took place in the morning; I seemed to be most creative then. Although tired, I was disciplined enough to get up in the middle of the night and write in the dark. The spirit of truth would guide my hand along the paper with one eye open, I'd try my best to decipher it in the morning.

This poem describes me, and what it took to get my soul back from the enemy. These were some of the things that God allowed me to see to experience the pain I caused others. I am truly apologetic for my adolescent mistakes, which is why I chose to change my lifestyle as well as the direction I choose to attack this beast (LIFE) the next time that I am blessed with the opportunity to be free.

A lot of lives were destroyed or altered because of the choices I made being in the streets. In no way form or fashion did I overlook or try to justify the things I've done. I am driven to do the will of God, and his will alone.

My focus moving forward is to connect with the youth in the streets in an attempt to stop them from putting on the shoes I just took off. If only these kids were able to get a glimpse of my past they would be scared straight, this is why I am telling my story! I survived what I have been through to be a testimony. IT'S MANDATORY and a part of my calling!

I understand communicating with the children, our future, I'll have to speak to them in a manner that's relatable to where they are now. Most of them won't understand me quoting scriptures. However, I want them to know my journey comes from a place of experience. I'm sharing what I know and what I have learned, not what I've heard.

I love God and I love the scriptures of the bible, eventually they got me through everything. This is also important for the future leaders to know because some things that I have been through would have crumbled a man. God gave me the strength to walk through the trials and the tribulations to become stronger from the things that I've had to endure.

He allowed the storm to come but I was safe inside the rain. When you read this story and certain things pertain to you, make the necessary changes so that you will not have to experience the things that I've had to in order to get back to the place where God can use you. It's time to save your life, by changing your life.

It all starts with you. Don't be the person that witness someone else's mistake and repeat it thinking you are different. That's insanity. You have to be crazy to see someone go through something and still make the same decisions that will put you in the same situation.

Learn from my mistakes or the situations that lie within the pages of this book. There is a lot of pain within these pages; don't let this end up being your story. Let my mistakes encourage you not to make the same ones. Life is precious, so put yourself in position to live a good one. I hope you enjoy the story!

INFLUENTIAL WOMAN

I came home from prison, to a woman that I had
questions about,
I tried to make the best of us, even though
my mind was full of doubts.
I vowed to Love our relationship, and treat
your kids like mine,
But you chose to love the things of the
world and leave our life behind.
I allowed your influence to push me, into a
world filled with sin,
In a world where I knew the stakes were high,
and I had a small chance to win.
I thought be leaving I'd hurt you, but in
turn I hurt myself,
Chasing things that were illusions,
thinking I'd find some wealth.
I can't blame you for my failures, regardless I
should have been strong,
It was my choice to make that decision, to do
the things I knew that were wrong.
I traveled a life unconscious, in a game of
indefinite assurance,
I wish I was stronger in that time of my life;
I wish I could resist your INFLUENCE.

INFLUENTIAL WOMAN

This poem represents how I set my mind to do the right thing, to not waiver on the goals that I set for himself, until the power of a woman's influence comes along and distracted me from keeping my promise to myself. The influence of a woman can break a man if he is not Grounded in Christ.

I came home in 1999, I had it set in my mind that I was going to do the right thing. No more jail cells, no more drug game, little did I know the enemy was waiting on me as well. He sent an attack on me that I was not prepared for, he sent it from a place that I never thought it would come from. IN MY HOUSEHOLD!

I had my mind made up to do the things that a father was supposed to do for a child. I had a son and she had two girls at the time, I vowed that I would do the things that I was told to do, I knew that it was God because He put us in each other's lives where we both had to help one another. I could be a good father figure to our children if I could stay focused, as long as I did not allow myself to get sidetracked by the praises of the people of my past.

I feel as though Marianne was supposed to be someone I dealt with for a season. She wasn't meant to be my girlfriend or someone I considered a friend. This woman was all for self and immediately I regretted going against my gut when everything unfolded. My gut said to leave this girl alone before we had sex. I never liked her in the past and now I see the reason why.

Giving her the benefit of the doubt, I decided to step out

of my comfort zone and pursue a sexual relationship with her, one-time lead to another, then another, then she started spending the nights at my apartment not really wanting to go home. I didn't fight it because she didn't ask any questions and she was down for whatever I said. She would just lay in my bed all day answering the phone when other women would call and give my messages when I came home. "PERFECT"!

I thought I had something sweet, the whole time this woman was a serious opportunist. Whenever she saw a way to get over or make her situation better, she took it. As a young man I couldn't look past the way her submission fed my adolescent ego. I had a woman in the bed every night and whenever I was ready to sleep with another woman. I would just take her home until I was ready to see her again and there were no questions asked. How about that for an 18-year-old who didn't have a damn clue.

I used to pick Marianne up from her mother's house and she would stay for weeks at a time. I never thought about why she wasn't home with her kids, and who was watching them, that was none of my concern because I was getting what I wanted. Anyone who spends that amount of time away from her kids with no remorse should not have been trusted from the beginning.

One night I had another female friend over, I was pursuing her for a minute, and I was going to make sure I got her tonight. Before I got the chance to get her in the bed, the police raided my apartment that night and took my buddy and I to jail.

I got out on bond a week later and Marianne and I decided to start a relationship, we were doing the best we could to stay on our feet, our parents were bringing us food and we were working at Nordstrom's warehouse together. I was doing my best not to go back to the streets, at the end of the day all I knew were the streets and that was the only way I would feel comfortable with the money I had coming in.

During my court hearing process, we decided to move into an apartment together despite everything. We were sticking together, and Marianne was showing strong signs of loyalty. She seemed like someone I could trust. I fell in love with her twin daughters and I could see myself raising those girls as my own, their father was murdered when they were newborns and I saw myself being placed in their lives to be that father figure they needed.

I had a 2-year-old son and she had 2- year old twins, so I would be a father of three. Not knowing how to be a father of my own but I decided that I was going to love them babies the best way I knew how.

At my final court hearing I was offered 3 years in prison, my lawyer said I would do 6 months in a program that would kill the rest of my time, I took the plea agreement and the court awarded me 30 days to self-surrender because it was my first conviction.

During those 30 days we got closer, the girls were calling me daddy and I felt like one too. It was like Marianne and I had an unspoken bond and there was no one else or their opinion that mattered outside of our bond.

The day came when I had to turn myself in and it was an emotional one, the girls didn't know what was going on and my son didn't either. We looked each other in the eyes, and we said a lot without speaking, Marianne said "I'LL BE HERE WHEN YOU GET BACK, I GOT YOU".

And that was all I needed to hear. She showed me that she could be loyal, so I didn't question her last words. Yet loyalty isn't what you do when someone's watching, Loyalty is what you do when that person can't see you.

During the time in the county jail she came to visit a lot but when I was shipped to Baltimore in route to Eastern shore MD, I didn't see her or speak to her as much.

I felt something wasn't right, but I was praying that I was just tripping. When I got to Eastern shore, I spoke with her on the phone and she assured me that she was still in my corner and I didn't have anything to worry about. I believed her, and my spirits were a little better. She came to see me and that was all I needed at the moment. We laughed, kissed and hugged in the visiting room and that made my suspicions go away.

No one wants to believe their mate is cheating or being disloyal, even if the signs say they are. I called home one day and spoke to my buddy Lee. During the conversation he told me he stopped by my house to check on Marianne and the girls and a guy was over there hiding in the bathroom. My pride wouldn't allow me to believe my friend.

When I spoke to her about it, she said that he was there for her roommate Mellissa. Her girlfriend was sneaky, I knew that from previous situations, another opportunist, so I believed what she said and kept it moving.

My sentence went by fast, 1 year and a day was given to the prison system because of my adolescent mistakes. I told myself I didn't need another lesson, that time was enough, and I was going to do the right thing come hell or hot water. I knew it would be rough coming home to Marianne, my son, and the girls, with 3 mouths to feed, I would be starting from scratch.

I went to Anne Arundel community College while I was in Boot Camp in Jessup MD, I was fortunate to earn my Fiber optic installation certificate, so I wasn't coming home empty handed. I didn't know a lot but I knew enough to get a job.

I came home April 15th, 1999, everyone was happy to see me. I was happy to be home and it felt good. Marianne and I sat down the first night and we spoke about the journey we had ahead of us and how we were going to be successful in accomplishing the goals we had set for our family. It seemed like a full proof plan and in my heart, I felt that we could achieve it with a little sacrifice and hard work.

We both had jobs, I was working at Harmony Memorial Cemetery while she was working for Calvin Klein. She was making more money than I was but at least I had something coming in for the time being. Everything was going good for the first couple of months and then in the blink of an eye, things changed for the worse. Marianne started holding back on sex. It was a strange feeling because it was the first time a woman had done that to me. I asked her about it, and she blew it off like it wasn't nothing, I worked a lot which made it easier to cope with.

Marianne started to treat me like I was less of a man, talking to me crazy, getting smart for no reason. I was looking at her during arguments thinking to myself, "How am I allowing this little girl to speak to me in this manner"? I took it for a while but the man in me wouldn't allow me to sit in these circumstances anymore.

I was always a lady's man and I never had a problem getting sex or companionship from women, but the first woman I chose to be faithful too turned out to the one that didn't deserve it. I didn't feel the love I wanted so, I decided to run to where I felt that I would feel loved, and that was the STREETS!

That's exactly what I did. When I ran away from Marianne, I ran right into the enemy's plan. I realized that he wanted me out of that house so I couldn't help raise those girls and be a consistent male role model in their lives.

I could've gone back to my mother's house, but my pride said that I would've looked like a failure and momma had to many rules for a man that just came home from rules. I called my cousin, Whitey.

He told me to come stay with him, He had a one-bedroom apartment 5 minutes from the area that I sold drugs in. The enemies plan was working.

He lured me right back in the environment that would place me around my weakness, which would push me back in the drug game, and lead me to Jail or the Graveyard. (MISSION ACCOMPLISHED). It only took one week with hanging around the neighborhood, seeing and hanging with old associates and friends, and it would be hard for me to resist. During the first week of being back around the homies I was missing days at work.

Eventually my Boss recognized my absence and fired me the next Friday. I saw it as a relief because I wanted to get back in the game and start hustling again, but it wasn't for survival, it was more for revenge. I called it REVENGE HUSTLING. I dived right in with one purpose, to show Marianne she carried the wrong one.

I called my connect and told him that I was BACK, and he said, I WAS WAITING ON YOU, who does that sound like by just reading that statement? He met me at the shell gas station and gave me enough drugs to make about $5,000 I told him I would give him the money as soon as possible. Before the words left my mouth, he told me to keep it and get on my feet.

From that point it was on, full steam ahead without a thought of turning back. The money came so fast it was scaring me, $1,000, $2,000, $3,000 before Friday and I still had the weekend. By the end of the month I had $5,000 saved up and $7,500 worth of drugs that was mine.

I remember telling myself one night as I was counting some money. I'm going to show off on Marianne when I see her. I planned a shopping trip for myself, new car, new watch, new clothes and plenty of partying.

I looked at the way the situation played out. The enemy used her influence to push me right back into the game. I didn't have a plan; I was hustling because I was hurt. My pride made me submit to the tricks of the enemy.

The enemy used my girlfriend to attack the little boy in me, and that attack was one that I was not prepared for. After 2 and a half years of being home, a year and a half in the drug game partying, living wild, my time was up. I got arrested again, DAMN!

The consequences of me not being prepared for that attack sent me straight to prison again but, this time I would be going for 15 years!

Man, if I would have known what I know now, I would have resisted the enemy's attack and went to my mother's house and got a job in order to get back on my feet. Now I sit in this prison cell feeling like I am "Defeated", feeling like I am never going to be able to bounce back and be the man that God wants me to be, the man that I WANT TO BE!

I feel like I am in prison physically and mentally. My thoughts were so caught up in what happened that I didn't want to think of anything else but revenge, not on just Marianne, but all women. I couldn't think of anything else but how I felt and the way I was getting treated.

Well, one thing that I know now, is when you say

that you are not going to be a certain way anymore, or you are not going to do certain things anymore, the enemy will come to see if you are going to keep your word and stand by what you said.

I came home saying that I was not going to sell drugs again and that I was going to make it work no matter what. Well the devil surely came to see if I was telling the truth and I failed hard and fast. When I finally sat down and spoke to God about what I had done, I realized that I couldn't be mad at her because she did not know she was being used for the devil's purpose.

I couldn't take my frustrations out on her or anybody else, I allowed the devil to destroy me then and I would be allowing him to destroy me for the long haul if I didn't forgive her.

I came home saying that I was not going to sell drugs again and that I was going to make it work no matter what, well the devil surely came to see if I was telling the truth, and I failed hard and fast. When I finally sat down and spoke to God about what I had done, I realized that I couldn't be mad at her because she did not know she was being used for the devil's purpose.

I couldn't take my frustrations out on her or anybody else, I allowed the devil to destroy me then and I would be allowing him to destroy me for the long haul if I didn't forgive her.

One thing about when you don't have a relationship with God, you only have one choice, and that's to be in full submission to the plans the enemy has for you. Fellas, if you have made a vow to yourself that you are not going to be who you used to be, and you are going to do whatever it takes to get on the right track, don't let the enemy use the woman you Love to be the woman that hurts you.

If she is trying to push you to fast, keep moving at your own pace. If she is continually complaining about what you're not doing but you are trying your best, then keep moving at a pace that's comfortable for you.

When you start to try to speed up, that's when you start to move to fast and you start to miss the blessings that God is trying to lay out for you. You will be in places that your woman wants you to be and not in the places that God wants you to be. You can't be blessed if you are not in the right place. If your woman is this type of woman, you either get rid of her or stay strong enough within the attacks until He reveals the real reason why you are there.

Don't be so fast to leave but be quick to listen. Establish that relationship with God that will allow you to hear his voice when you pray. Stand fast until He tells you to do something different.

I encourage any man or woman that is reading this chapter, if you feel as though God has told you to be with someone, or you feel as though you are in the right place. DON'T GIVE UP.

Don't let the way someone acts towards you, or the things someone says to you, make you step out of the will of God. I am giving you a WARNING. If you know it's the right thing to do then stand firm, knowing that God is going to raise his hand and bless your household!

People, you know if the situation that you are in is

right or not. Please don't allow the enemy to trick you into leaving when you know that you should be staying, and don't allow the enemy to trick you into staying when you know that you should be leaving!

If God is calling you to leave. He will replace what you left with something or someone better. If He's calling you to stay. He is going to bless your situation but, you must be patient. The devil will attack when he hears someone speaking about their situation with faith! Get prepared for the devil to try to attack what you love; He wants you to Love Him! Remember, HE COMES TO STEAL, KILL, AND
DESTROY! John 10:10

IT'S OVER

How did my life take this horrible turn, is the punishment worth my mistake?

I thought I'd get a hold of things, but it seems like it's too late.
My mind is racing with fear, and I'm trying to ignore the pain,
When I walk inside this courtroom, things will never be the same.
I was influenced by my circumstances, my environment was more than Tough,

I should've got out with the money I had, but greed said it wasn't enough.

How can I face my mom's disappointment, I should've stopped those tears in her eyes,

I lost serious pieces of my heart, every time I heard my mother cry.

I'm finally about to receive my fate for all the selfish things I've did,

It's time to accept the consequences, for the sins I thought I hid.

IT'S OVER

"Inmate BELL, Inmate BELL, it's time for court!" The officers voice screamed through the intercom on the wall. This is the day, the day that I stand before the judge and receive my fate. I was nervous because I knew that it wasn't going to be pretty. I was hoping and praying for the lighter sentence but, something deep down inside told me that wasn't going to be the case.

I was moving slow because I didn't want to see this judge today but, I've been waiting for 16 months now to get sentenced, it's time. After I finished getting my hygiene together, I said a quick prayer and I stepped out of my cell. Guys were looking out of their door windows giving words of encouragement to those who they knew were going to court, especially if they were going to get sentenced.

It's funny how we wouldn't have spoken to each other on the streets, yet because we're all going through a tough time we came together like brothers and it felt kind of surreal.

Some of the transportation marshals were cool, they would always ask how you were doing when you came out of court. Sometimes you'd be so shocked at what happened that you just need someone to talk to and the Marshals would be the first people you see. Basically, they've heard and seen it all so, it was always good to hear someone agree with you who's considered to be on the other side of the law.

On the way to the courthouse I looked out the back window of the van. There were four of us being transported in to be sentenced. Together, it would add up to 100 years if we all get the maximum of our sentences.

We arrived at the courthouse and I couldn't control my hands, they were shaking and sweating, I wasn't scared, I guess I was frustrated and disappointed with the fact that I allowed myself to be tricked by the drug game and I'm possibly about to give these people 15 years of my life.

We filed out of the van into the holding area, the shackles around my ankles were cutting into my Achilles, yet my mind was focused on this sentence so I didn't complain like I would usually do. They called the names by alphabetical order so; I was the first victim.

Bailiff: "All rise!"

The bailiff shouted as The Honorable Deborah Chase walked into the courtroom. She was supposed to be the fair one out of the federal Judges. I was hoping she would be yet prepared for the worst.

The procedure went fast, I was in sort of a trance, so I didn't hear a lot of the things that were said, yet when I came back to reality, I heard her speak.

Judge Chase: "Mr. Bell, I see that you have a lot of supporters in the courtroom today and I must admit that I have never seen so many people coming to support one man. There are multiple character letters on my desk that lets me know how many people looked up to you and depended on you. The example you set for these people has hurt your community more than you have helped.

How many of these young men in this courtroom think that you are the example of MAN? Looking at your criminal history you have a lot of charges that were thrown out, but the dates of the charges were extremely close and consistent. Which brings me to my next point, I don't think you take the judicial system seriously, I looked at my lawyer hoping he would say something, but he just sat there looking stupid like I was.

Well, Mr. Bell, you need to trust and believe that we are for real and we will not tolerate someone who thinks he can straddle the fence of right and wrong. You can't say that you are helping your community when you are contributing to the problem. With the size of your support system you could've made a positive impact on your community

I hope by the time you come home you'll realize the power a positive role model possesses. "Judge Chase said, as she looked me in the eye over her thick rimmed glasses. Then she handed me my sentence, I sentence you to 188 months and 5 years' probation!

"BANG" the judge banged her gavel and through tear filled eyes I got up to walk out of the courtroom. I had tears in my eyes because I had just become the father I tried not to be; I was leaving my child to fight the world by himself. I looked at my mother and my family and told them to be strong and not to worry. My son was too young to know what was going on all he saw was everyone crying and trying to figure out why. I looked at my lawyer and he dropped his head. He told me that if I took the plea agreement to the 5 years. I would be good, yet I just received 15 years and 8 months. Judge Chase was right, the Judicial system isn't a joke and she just made me a believer.

It's finally over, my thoughts ran rapid as I was being escorted out of the courtroom and reality started to set in. Is it real? Will this be my life for the next 15 years? How will I get through this and what lies behind these prison walls? Clink, the cell doors finally shut, and this journey has officially begun, I had to fight off the feelings of disappointment, sadness, and loneliness in order to focus on my journey ahead. I knew it wasn't going to be easy, but I had to find a way to overcome the odds. The Beginning of the Resurrection of John Bell Jr.

THEY'RE GONE

As I sit inside this prison cell, trying to reinvent myself
I see that my mom is my only support but where is everyone else?
I slowly let go of the moments I loved, when I was running wild in the streets
Am I able to win in the season of life, or will I have to accept defeat?
I don't know what happened to my family, I'm confused, where are my friends?
They say street people don't last that long, at some

point the relationship will end.
I must focus on my mission, and place my past on the shelf,
I've come to grips with fighting alone, I've always felt stronger by myself.

THEY'RE GONE

As I sat on this concrete slab covered with a plastic mat, I accepted the fact that this would be my bed until I am released. It's only been 3 years and I feel like I'm a memory already, my name doesn't get called at mail call or for visitation anymore. People don't pick up their phone when I call and I'm paying for the calls.

Where are my friends that I popped bottles with or blew stacks of money with? This is a tough reality check, people only love the NEED of you and when you can no longer provide what they need, you become a memory.

I come from a tight knit family where we love and support one another, yet at the time when I need them the most they're nowhere to be found. I think that's what bothers me the most, I can deal with the fact that friends/associates have fallen off, but FAMILY... that's hard to swallow.

I just knew at least one of the women I was sleeping with, giving her everything she wanted and needed would be right here by my side, especially the one that was supposed to be my lady. Yet here I am standing in this storm by myself irritated, upset, confused, and looking for revenge. I'm learning some valuable lessons right now, they're painful but much needed.

I see that if it wasn't for this prison sentence, I would've never seen people for who they really are, I would've continued to allow these people to trick me with this false love. It's crazy how the things that you were supposed to see gets looked over until you get to a place where you're forced to pay attention. I don't know how to feel, I want to be angry and vengeful, I want to disown my family just like they disowned me.

I must refocus because I won't make it if I continue to dwell on who's not here or supposed to be here. I must move on with my life because the only way I'll survive this sentence is by staying focused and letting the streets be the streets. When I get out of here, I'm making a vow to myself, other than my mother, son, and father I don't have anything to say to anyone else.

Maybe it's better this way, I guess this will make me stronger in the long run, not having no one to depend on can make you self-sufficient. I know I'm going to be successful when I get out of here, I don't know how it's going to happen, but I know it will happen. Now that everyone has deserted me, I won't have to bless anyone when I get on my feet. It's a selfish way of looking at things but, I must think about me because no one else is.

KARMA

How many times do you think you can hurt someone, before it starts to come back?
How many situations have you caused, what type of energy do you attract?

How many lives have you ruined; you've created wounds that probably won't heal?

Have you thought of the chaos you've caused; how do you know how your victims feel?

What makes a Man not want to be a Man, and desire the enemies plan?

Could you please help me see clearly, is it possible to even understand?
Well today karma has caught up with you, and I'm glad I was a part of karmas plan,
I felt amazing every time I punched you, your Karma came from on my hands!

KARMA

The doors opened at 6am. I made up my mind before I went to bed last night that I would run in the morning. Sometimes I would run when I had a lot on my mind, it was therapy for me. As I was walking out of my cell, I remembered that I had to wash clothes. I stopped to get my dirty clothes bag so I could get a spot at the washer because it gets crowded on Saturday mornings.

The housing unit was huge, 3 long floors lined with about 80 cells and multiple 3,4, and 8-man rooms. I really didn't like washing because of the crazy things that go on in the washing room at the early hours of the morning.

It was dark in the washing room hallway and guys would be gambling, fighting, smoking weed/cigarettes, hanging out telling war stories. I could handle those type of guys but, I hated walking up on guys having sex or paying debts with sexual favors. This was the hallway were everything illegal/disgusting would be going on. It sad because these activities were the way a lot of men coped with reality. I had to reserve a spot and pay the laundry man to wash my clothes so I could go on about my day. There's a hustle for everyone inside these prison walls and whatever a man has to do to survive, he'll do it.

I walked through the door of the laundry room hallway and immediately I smelled weed/cigarette smoke mixed with laundry detergent and dryer sheets. The hallway was lined with empty water bottles that use to be filled with homemade prison wine, sometimes the smell is unbearable, and the heat didn't make it any better.

Something in my gut told me that something wasn't right, I slowed my pace because it was darker than usual, and the hallways that's usually packed with inmates/convicts were empty. I heard the dryer humming and the washer spinning finishing its cycle, but in between the washer switching cycles I heard feet scuffling on the floor and it seemed like a fight was going on.

I started to turn back and then I heard: "STOP, I DON'T GET DOWN LIKE THAT!"
Immediately that caught my attention and I tried to turn around again and the voice got louder.

"I SAID STOP, LET ME GO!"

The second time I heard the voice I recognized who the voice belongs too, so I stepped back in the hallway and raced to the cell where I heard the scuffling, adrenaline was running wild just thinking about what I was about to see. I got to the entrance of the cell to see an inmate with his arm around Lil Barkley's neck and a knife to his abdomen. Lil Barkley was from Southeast D.C. He was 19 years old and he suffered from memory loss and he would have seizures a lot because of the PCP that he used almost his entire life.

He had a 15-year sentence for Carjacking and assault with intent to kill. He stood about 5'10, 210 pounds and he was strong as a bull. I liked the kid as soon as I met him because he had a crazy sense of humor and he would listen when I told him to do the right thing. The PCP really messed his head up and it was like talking to a 3-year-old at times. Lil Barkley couldn't process information as fast as everyone else and he was extremely sensitive and terrified of knives. He caught his case because he was given a gun and an order, and he carried out the order. It was supposed to be a simple job but, the passenger of the car resisted, andLil Barkley panicked and choked the woman almost to her death.

A pedestrian saw the entire thing and came to the lady's assistance and pulled a gun on Lil Barkley and he ran away. Police caught him at the subway station begging for change the next day.

I entered the cell and realized the guy was trying to rape Lil Barkley, I didn't warn him that I was behind him because my anger took over and all I saw was RED, I wanted to attack. I crept up on him and hit him in the ribs with all the power I had in me. It caught him off guard and he let Lil Barkley go and dropped the knife. Lil Barkley took advantage of the split second to get away and ran out of the cell with his back bleeding pulling his pants up.

He was crying so hard that his face was covered with tears, I HATED A BULLY and today this chump was going to feel how much I hated them. When he turned around, I saw that it was a new inmate that everyone said was going around trying to rape the younger guys. I didn't know his name I just knew he was from North Carolina and he was locked up for child Molestation.

I looked him in his eye as he winced in pain, getting hit with a body shot when you're not expecting it is tough to deal with, it's almost impossible to breathe. I didn't wait I attacked the creep. He tried to bend down and grab the knife, but it was a move I predicted, I was bigger than him and he saw the rage in my eyes, he knew his only hope was to get to that knife.

I wasn't having it. I stepped to the side and kicked him in his face as he kneeled attempting to grab the knife. His head snapped back and blood shot from his nose, the fear in his eyes was not rewarded with sympathy, I wanted to torture this punk for trying to take advantage of a young kid. He gained his balance and tried to apologize, "PLEASE LET ME GO, I'M SORRY I WON'T DO IT ANYMORE!" Pleaded the Pedophile.

With malice in my voice, I said, "SHUT UP SUCKA, HOW MANY OF THESE KIDS PLEADED FOR YOU TO LET THEM GO?"

I lunged at him again and he balled up in the corner screaming for help. The laundry room hallway was the spot for a lot of the illegal/crazy activity because it was in the back of the unit and the officer's desk was in the front. I called it NO MANS LAND. "SCREAM ALL YOU WANT, NO ONE IS COMING, I'M GOING TO BEAT YOU UNTIL I GET TIRED!" I said to him through clinched teeth.

I kicked him repeatedly in his ribs and head, I always wore my steal toe boots to the track and switched into my tennis shoes when I got there. Every kicked opened a gash on his head or knotted him up.

He lifted his head trying to plea at the wrong time but, the right time for me. I kicked him in his forehead and his eyes rolled back in his head as his body went limp against the wall. I knew he was unconscious, so I stomped his head a few times and then exited the cell. There were showers at the end of each tier. I washed the blood off my boots and walked out like nothing was wrong. There weren't any cameras in the entire prison, so I didn't have to worry about getting caught. he would have to tell, and it would be my word against his. I had no scars, so it would be hard to prove it was me.

I watched these younger guys come into the prison system without a clue thinking they know it all, most of them get tricked by prison life before they get a chance to understand how things go. 90% of the inmates are manipulators and they usually get what they want. I try my best to get a hold of the younger guys before prison life gets a hold of them. Most of them come in can't fight, read, write, or have that I HAVE A GUN mindset. Only a small percentage of the younger generation come in and get right on track, trying to get their GED or learn a trade. The object of the enemy is to destroy our young men, if he can replace the father with the son in the prison system, he wins the war.

I encourage the parents that's reading this chapter, there aren't a lot of guys like me in the system, most people will mind their business and allow your child to get taken advantage of. If you want your child to experience life and not have to walk this road, pay more attention to your child, be a parent and stop trying to be a friend. Life inside these prison walls is not a joke. IT'S NOT A GAME and these situations happen EVERYDAY and most of the times they get away with it.

I couldn't allow it to happen on my watch because I have a son. If you have one, do your best to keep them out of here. He has a better chance of winning if his road doesn't have to go through a prison cell.

SHOOTER

Dear Mr. Shooter Man, was this a part of your plan?
Did you think you'd lose most of your life, when you put that gun in your hand?
You didn't think you would see him again, that innocent person you killed
You say you weren't given an option, I'm sure he would've wanted to live,
Now you're stuck dealing with me, please don't make this hard on yourself.
In the streets you're feared and respected, but in here you're like everyone else,

SHOOTER

I was sitting on my bed looking at a magazine when my neighbor came on the tier and walked into his cell. His name was Whitey, he was a young kid from Simple City, a very aggressive neighborhood in South East, D.C. He was locked up for attempted murder and possession of a firearm, Whitey had 18 years and you couldn't tell him nothing. He was a Hot head and he scared a lot of the older guys with the looks on his face and the way he spoke. He was 5'5 157 pounds with a vicious napoleon complex. He had only been in the system for two years and he was bitter because of the length of his sentence.

A lot of young guys don't think about the consequences before they pull the trigger, they just point and shoot, not thinking about the innocent people/kids that get hit. Or the lives that are affected by their deaths or injuries. They never think about getting caught and having to do 20 or 30 years in the prison system. Most of them couldn't even began to defend themselves without that gun. They would come in with their face balled up like they were tough and the first time they got tested, they failed.

This life is different than the streets, you don't have a group of guys to help or a gun to solve your problems. It was every man for himself. Most of the young guys couldn't fight, Read, Write or spell, it was sad to see these young kids come into this system with so many strikes against them.

Whitey loves to play his music loud when he comes into his cell, he came in at 4pm from the weight pile and he'd be charged up. At this time, I would already have worked out and taking a nap, so I could go play basketball at 6pm, this was my chill time. We had several conversations about this music thing, he would get it for a couple of days and result back to playing it loud again. I liked the kid, so I gave him a break, usually I wouldn't repeat myself I would just react, but it was something about this youngster that made me want to change the way I looked at him.

"Whitey, Whitey," I called his name twice before I got out of my bed, slipping my boots on making sure I was prepared for any response I would get from him.

"Turn your music down homie!"

Whitey looked at me and laughed, I grabbed his headphones and Walkman and turned his music off. He turned around with rage in his eyes like he always does, he would have multiple bodies if looks could kill. "You should really think about your next move champ, because it could cost you your life if you make the wrong choice".

I looked Whitey in his eyes and spoke to whatever percentage of man that was inside of him. "Remember youngster you don't have that gun in here. "Why you always on me about my music?" Whitey replied with crazy look in his eyes. "Because you need to learn a little more about respect if you're going to make it out of here alive." I explained to him, "I respect you, but you must respect me!" Whitey said, as he tried to keep that killer look on his face.

"When you respect someone, you respect them enough to keep your word to them. We had a conversation about your music before and you gave me your word that we wouldn't speak about it again, yet here we are." I spoke with more passion rather than anger. Maybe because I saw so much of myself in this kid.

"BUT I'M A GROWN ASS MAN, how are you going to tell me when and how I can I play my music?" Whitey started out yelling but by the end of his statement he was speaking like he wanted an understanding versus starting a fire.

This was the time where I was able to teach the young guy something instead of putting my hands on him. "Youngster, you just got to the prison system and guys such as myself who have already been down for a while have set the environment, so we are able to coexist with whomever we allow to live on this tier. We're a little more laid-back soldier and after a few calendars go by you'll fall right in line.

Listen! A lot of young guys come in wild and aggressive, Hell I was one of them thinking I had to prove a point. I quickly learned a valuable lesson, Man won't respect who you're trying to be, He'll respect who you are. It takes a real man to listen when someone is trying to tell him something against what he believes to be true. You have to stop allowing every situation that you encounter be a challenge to your ego. I can assure you that you will not make it out of here if you don't change the way you look at life." I explained calmly.

Once he sat on the bed, I knew he was ready to listen, so I broke it down to him what a man was and what's expected from us as a dominant male. I asked him about his relationship with his dad and he said, he never met him, all he knew was he'd been locked up for 19 years and he still had 7 to go. We spoke about his kids and religion and he asked me would I be open to speak with him when he needs to talk. I said of course and don't hesitate to ask questions.

We both agreed to keep our word to each other, no more loud music and I would speak to him when he wanted to talk. Not all the youngsters were crazy, some of them just needed a little more guidance. Someone to talk to them who wasn't scared. Inside they are still kids looking for that hug they never got from their dads. After this conversation with Whitey I made a vow to myself that I would try to save as many of these young men as possible, after all I couldn't turn my back on something I unconsciously help create.

I felt as though these younger guys were just a product of the examples I've set. A child can only do what they're taught or emulate what they see. There were so many young guys who looked up to me when I was home, and as we speak, they're all drug dealers, dead, or on their way to prison they became what their environment tricked them into thinking they should be. I feel obligated/guilty, so I'll do my best to give back, even if it's just sitting down listening, I WILL!

I LOST IT ALL

When I opened my eyes in the morning, I ask myself who will I be?
Will be an asset to my community, or be an example of the things that I see?
Will I fail at the finish line, or stumble as the horn goes off?
Will I find my way through the storms of life, or continue to walk around lost?
Will I be a man who leaves a legacy, will my decisions kill my seed?

Will I be tricked by the things I want, and overlook the things that I need?
Will I lose life and blow my chance to live, or commit to a life that's stable?
A man does his best to make sure his kids eat, but in return he takes food off the table.

I LOST IT ALL

"Come on Man!" Randy said impatiently "I'm coming let me put my shirt on playa" I hollered back at Randy as I walked out of my cell. Randy was from St Clair county in East St. Louis, one of the most dangerous cities in St. Louis. He was the leader of the Vice Lords, a well-known gang that's spread across both coasts. He was a good guy underneath the anger and bitterness, I guess you can say half of us were.

The things he has seen and experienced gave him a heart of stone. He was given Life plus 56 years for murder and Conspiracy to commit murder on a rival gang member and tampering with a government witness.

Randy was the only child in a single parent household. His pops was a gang member who got killed in a shootout with the police. At a young age Randy had to be the man of the house and make decisions of a man at 13 years old. He never had a childhood, too embarrassed to play amongst the other kids in fear of being talked about because of the clothes that he wore. It was all his mother could afford with the income she had coming in.

She was an unlicensed nurse and she cared for sick patients who couldn't get out of their bed, she had a problem with her nerves in her right hand which kept her from passing the physical part of the test that would've awarded her a license.

Life changed for Randy the day his mom couldn't make the payment on the apartment. Come to find out the landlord had been generous because Randy's mom was the neighborhood nurse. Yet she was 3 months behind and, the line had to be drawn somewhere. Randy came home with his friends one day and there was a big sign on his door saying, EVICTION NOTICE.

Randy was scared, embarrassed, and upset at the same time. His friends didn't clown Randy because he was the biggest and toughest out of the crew and they didn't want to upset him. At that age Randy was 6"0 190 pounds of Hate, anger, and Rage. Randy's Mom came home and saw the notice on the nightstand with the other mail. They lived in a rundown building on the east side of St. Louis. The building would've been shut down if the right people would've come to inspect but, the area was so bad it kept the inspectors out.

Ethel called the landlord as randy listened from the other room. Listening to the conversation Randy heard that if his mom could come up with two months rent it would stop the eviction. The rent was 575 so she would need a miracle to stop the eviction within the next few days.

Randy sat on his bed confused, before his pops died, he told Randy that he would soon be faced with some tough decisions because of the environment they lived in, if you were a male in that area nine times out of ten you were affiliated with a gang. He weighed his options and decided to become what his environment has been wanting him to be since he was 10 years old. Luther, (the head of the Gangster Disciples) a rival gang on the South end of the projects. He was trying to recruit Randy since his father died.

Randy's father was well known and respected, but when he lost his life in a shootout with corrupt cops everyone, VICE LORDS and GANGSTER DISCIPLES showed up at his funeral to show their respects. He killed 2 dirty cops in the standoff and that freed the city up, because those two cops were extorting robbing and illegally arresting gang members and assaulting their women.

Randy always turned Luther down because he was to young and his dad continued to tell him every time he saw the look in his eye, "IT'S NOT YOUR TIME", When it comes to being your own man, don't follow no one, and that's what randy did. Randy was always fighting; the local drug boys would always come get him when some little kid was talking trash and they would pay randy to beat the little kid up. He started to get into fights with older and bigger kids and He would win convincingly.

Randy's attitude was fueled by anger and pain, trying to figure out why his life was so rough at such a young age. Randy decided to join the Vice Lords because his dad died a well-respected member of the Vice Lords. He told Sankey, the (head of the Vice Lords) that he would join on one condition, he was going to start his own crew within the gang.

There was no resistance, Sankey wanted to expand anyway, Randy started his own crew from the friends he ran with since he was young, they called themselves LIL TOUGHY. They started out selling weed, they used the startup money they got from Sankey to buy a couple of pounds.

Randy told them his situation at home, so all proceeds went to Randy and his mom. By the end of the month Randy had the rent money and 4 months cushion. His mother didn't even question him when he walked in with over $3,500 in his hand. She shed a few tears, told him to be careful, then took the money and paid the rent

Within the next 5 months Randy's crew was holding their own. They were getting pick up jobs from the big drug dealers, collecting huge debts in other part of ST. Louis. You had to be crazy to walk in rival gang members turf asking for debts to be paid that belongs to someone else. Randy and his crew were crazy enough, and the entire St. Louis knew it.

Eight months had gone by and Randy and his crew were 15 strong between the ages of 15 to 19. They dropped the name Lil Toughie and picked up The Tough Guys. Randy said the name change sounds more masculine and it demands respect. Randy and his team were robbing, selling weed and dope along with doing pickups for the Big Drug dealers who were scared to ask for their money. Randy loved them because he could charge whatever he wanted for the job because he knew they were scared and wouldn't do anything if they told him they were keeping the money. In the beginning, he was charging 10% then he saw the opportunity to make an extra dollar, Randy started charging half of what he picked up.

As the years flew by Randy had lost his mom when he was 20 years old. Just when things were picking up, he had bought them a new house, and a new car. Randy even told his mom to stop working. She loved the fact that Randy was really stepping up as far as being a provider, but she was content with the fact that she knew what he was doing but he wasn't getting his hands dirty while doing it, he was a lot smarter than his dad. When Ethel passed it crushed Randy, he became heartless and he started to get back in the streets doing Kidnappings holding dudes for ransom, his mom was the only person who could keep Randy calm when he had a fit of rage.

It was Randy's birthday and he wanted to show out for his day. He rented A Night Club on Collinson Ave in East St. Louis. He really did it up for his 21st birthday. He had the best women, the biggest drug boys, the flyest cars, banners with his face on it draped on the walls throughout the club. It truly was known that this was the head of the TOUGH GUYS NIGHT!

Randy and his crew were pulling in millions at this point and it was no secret that if you wanted or even thought about getting some money in East St. Louis you had to go through Randy, or you wouldn't be successful.

Admission was free, the drinks were free, and

everyone took advantage of Randy's generosity. The club was packed 45 minutes after the doors opened and it was filled with THE TOUGH GUYS, who were now 100 strong with 50 potential recruits. Randy and his top lieutenants were in V.I.P laughing and popping bottles. Cassy walked in the club and everyone would stop and stare. Cassy is a stallion from Illinois. Cassy was 5'8 155 pounds with blue eyes and long black hair, she would shut the club down when she came through. Everyone knew who she was, so they looked but didn't think to touch.

Yet there is always one. As Cassy was walking back to V.I.P from the bathroom. She got in eyesight of Randy, one of the older Vice Lords from Sankey's team spotted her and pursued. Randy was locked in on his woman's every move and he saw when the Old Head made his move, so Randy made his. Randy's team was so tight that when he moved, they moved, Sankey's lieutenant name was Rawls. He was loyal to the Vice Lord code but, hated the fact that Randy was allowed to establish his own team and own rules within the organization without earning his stripes.

Randy's dad was a legend and Rawls respected that fact but, he didn't like the way Randy and his team moved and he envied the TOUGH GUYS.

Randy had to pick up a debt from Rawls one day. Rawls loved snorting dope;he would go to Illinois to purchase large quantities from the Soft Side. Soft Side is what they called the small parts of Illinois. A lot of gangsters would go over to the SOFT SIDE make an agreement to get drugs and pay later, (CONSIGNMENT) and never pay the guys. Yet when they heard about Randy and his crew the guys sent a word that they needed THE TOUGH GUYS assistance. Randy gladly accepted and his first pickup was Rawls. No one knew that Rawls was a dope head,and Sankey didn't condone his top guys using because they were around product a lot. They also handled the counting of the money.

Randy called Sankey and told him that he needed to speak with Rawls. Sankey didn't ask any questions he gave Randy the number. When Rawls answered the phone Randy just asked him could they talk in person, Rawls accepted the offer not knowing that Randy and his team were doing money grabs for the SOFT GUYS.

They met in the parking lot of Randy's old apartment building, that's where Randy and his team set up shop for their business. Rawls got out the car and greeted Randy with the special handshake that represented the Vice Lords.

Randy didn't waste no time and told Rawls that he came to collect. Rawls looked confused at first and then he burst out laughing. Sankey was hiding in the cut because he found it odd that Randy wanted to meet with his top guy without his presence. Randy told Rawls with a straight face that he wasn't playing and if he didn't comply it would be bloodshed.

The decision would be justified because Rawls was breaking the rules, NO TOP GUY CAN USE DRUGS! Randy had 10 men lurking in the background at the meeting, the bill was $40,000 and Rawls had just done a pickup from one of the drug houses, so he had the money in the trunk. Rawls was Livid, He couldn't believe his cover was blown, and he was about to give the LIL NIGGA, as he called

Randy,

$40,000 in cash for a debt he wasn't expecting to pay.

Sankey saw the entire situation but never said anything. Rawls never got over that day and he was waiting to disrespect Randy, and this was his chance. Rawls zeroed in on Cassy, Randy Zeroed in on Rawls. Awild woman was dancing crazy and cut Randy off which gave him a slight delay. Rawls had gotten to Cassy before Randy. Rawls grabbed her on the butt and grinded his penis on her thigh. Cassy was shocked because she never thought she would be disrespected like that. She turned around to see Rawls licking his lips holding his penis in his hands.

Cassy lift her hand to smack him and she saw a bottle come crashing down on Rawls head. Seeing it was Randy she stepped back and got out of the way. Randy beat Rawls to the floor with the bottle, Randy's team wanted to stop him but the last time one of his members tried to stop him while he was handling business, Randy shot him in both knees and both of his hands. Randy was in Rage; he swung the bottle so hard that blood was splashing on the walls across the room. He was covered in blood and he would've beaten Rawls for hours if someone didn't yell POLICE ARE HERE.

Randy broke his trance and walked to the office, the club owner paid Randy for protection, so Randy basically owned the spot. He took all his clothes off and jumped in the club owners personal shower. Randy had clothes there because he always played the club instead of going to hotels.

Randy showered and switched clothes within minutes. The police saw Rawls and locked the club down as they released people one by one, searching everyone for bruises that could put them at the fight. Randy was no stranger to the police, and because they were corrupt, they knew what he and his team were capable of and they were terrified. As Randy got to the door, they were wheeling Rawls body out on the stretcher with a white sheet that was stained with blood covering his head.

That meant Rawls didn't survive the beaten, Rawls was pronounced dead at the scene of the crime. Randy and his men walked out of the club and headed toward the entourage of S.U. V's they traveled in, they heard a woman hollering extremely loud, "WHY, WHY".

They turned around and saw the lady talking to the homicide detective, When she spotted Randy shouted. "THAT'S HIM, THAT'S THE ANIMAL THAT BEAT MY HUSBAND TO DEATH." with a look of fear on her face.

Randy was shocked and confused at the same time, Randy panicked, and he ordered the hit right there on the scene, one of the S.U. V's was parked behind the police car where the woman was standing. The passenger door flew open and bullets started spraying.

The cop saw it coming so he jumped out of the way before the gun was in the air. The lady was hit six times, none of the bullets hit her in places where it was life threatening. Randy jumped in his truck and sped out of the parking lot of the club. Two weeks later, they raided Randy's house and locked him up, charging him with First Degree Murder, Conspiracy to Commit Murder on a witness and Police officer.

Randy was sentenced to Life plus 56 years for his crime. When he went to trial and everyone that he kidnapped, robbed or extorted were in the courtroom waiting to testify against him, they wanted to make sure he never came home. When I met Randy, he had been locked up for 18 years and he was just getting to the compound at Petersburg V.A. We got close because of basketball and he couldn't read that well so he would try to read his mail until he became frustrated and then he would pass it to me. This happened to me a lot, it was sad to see these grown men in here who couldn't read or write but, they knew how to shoot guns, Dope and stab each other really well.

Well, Randy gave me the letter and we headed out to walk the track. This was our normal routine after lunch on Saturdays. The letter didn't have any name on it so I opened it, it smelled good, like it was sprayed with perfume. Women did that to keep their memory fresh in our minds and we loved and appreciated it. I read the letter out loud and Randy wanted to stop. He always wanted me to go to the bottom first to see who it's from so he could visualize them saying it in person. It was from Cassy, she started out with an apology for keeping a secret from him, then went on to say they had twin boys and they were just like him.

She also attached a newspaper clipping and that was the end of the letter. Randy JR and Ronnie, the heads of the Tough Guy Gang were feared in all of St. Louis, Randy JR got into a beef with some rival gang members and they shot him to death at a block party. In retaliation, Ronnie killed the gunman's mother, daughter, and wife and let the gunman live, the worse torcher in the world, to lose the most important people in your life because of something you did.

Ronnie got double life plus 20, as I was reading the last paragraph Cassy wrote on the paper, I hope you don't have grandkids, because the world can't take any more monsters from your bloodline. I looked at Randy as He dropped his head. He tried to hide it by cursing Cassy out for hiding this information from him for all these years, that was his defense mechanism. I didn't say anything else because it was obvious, He was really going through it. It's hard to function when you get bad news and can't do anything about it.

Reading this letter and newspaper clipping really gave me a different perspective of life. The enemies plan is to destroy our households by tricking the minds of the man in the house. He places an obligation on the male from the first day he comes out of the womb but doesn't give an example to show him how to fulfill it. A large percentage of the environment we grow up in teaches us to be tough. Young males aren't taught/ shown how to deal with their emotions, so they walk through life covering up their issues which causes them to be aticking time bomb. Never really having a chance or no one to vent too or show them how to deal with their emotions.

The product you see in society today that's killing and robbing within the community are the percentage of males that I'm speaking about in this chapter. A lot of us don't know the damage we do to our communities by putting broken products (KIDS) into society. When we adapt and accept the lifestyle our environment presents to us, we in turn present that to our kids.

It's extremely important to set the best example for our kids because life will devour our legacy if we allow it.

The enemy will keep his foot on our necks with these generational curses if we don't wake up and start changing the way we think, live, and understand. This curse can/ will be broken if there's a MAN in the house has a strong relationship with God. At one point we must take responsibility for our actions, analyze the pain that we caused and do our best to change the directions of our families.

The enemy wants to replace the father in the jail cell with his son, and if that cycle repeats itself, we'll continue to get these improperly trained men placed amongst us that deals with their problems with their emotions instead of their minds. This letter spoke volumes to me. It shows how a Man can lose it all because of the lifestyle He chooses to live. He loses His Love, His life, and His Legacy!

I'm redirecting my thoughts and the way I look at life. I wouldn't be able to forgive myself if my son becomes a product of my adolescent mistakes. No matter what it takes I'm going to be a positive example/father to my child, I will get my life together.

<u>**Dear Daddy**</u>

An innocent child lost her youth and her mother said where's the proof,

So, she grows up cold waiting to fold, because no one believed her truth.
Do you know how much it hurts to never come first, and you are the only child?
From the time daddy left she has not slept; cause mommy's hormones are really running wild.
She calls on dad confused and sad, why can't my daddy come home?

The voice screams in her head, you should've been dead, it's sad she has to fight this alone. A pedophiles punishment should be death, cause his sickness has no cure, Cause he'll never understand the things of a man, and the pain his victims endure.

Dear Daddy

Hey dad, I miss you and I think about you every day, I miss your smile, your laugh and going out on dates with you. I know I don't write a lot and I'm never here when you call, but don't think I don't miss you. Daddy I have something to tell you, when you left us the money got really low and things got rough. The money you left only lasted a year and we had to start pawning things, my camera, my laptop, my earrings you bought me,

Daddy it's rough. Mom met this guy named slim and after a couple of months he moved in with us, things got better financially, and I was able to get the things we pawned back. I just wanted the earrings, but mommy bought me a new camera and laptop. Everything was going good until one night after mommy left for work, slim knocked on my bedroom door. When I opened it, he asked for the cordless phone.

As I turned my back, he grabbed me around my waist and started to grab my breast, I tried to stop him daddy, but he was to strong, I screamed from the top of my lungs hoping someone would hear me, but no one came.

I tried to stop him, daddy, please believe me. I fought and fought just like you told me too but, I couldn't stop him dad, DADDY HE RAPED ME!! I cried, I screamed, begging him to stop but he just laughed and continued to violate me. I told mommy but she didn't believe me. She told me that I was lying, and I probably wanted him to have sex with me.

Daddy I didn't want that man nowhere near me. I'm 13 and I didn't want to have sex until I was married, I didn't want him touching me daddy, please believe me. I'm sorry I wasn't strong enough to keep him off me. I know I have to get stronger so I can protect myself until you come home, I really miss you, daddy, and if you were here, I know this wouldn't have happened. Everyone feared you and they loved me and gave me everything I wanted.

Daddy, I want you to come home, I don't have anyone to protect me and I'm afraid he'll do it again. I hate him and I hate mommy for letting him stay here after he did that to me. Why did this happen Daddy? What did I do to deserve this? I want to tell someone but, I'm scared they'll think it was my fault, like mommy. I didn't want to lose my virginity at 13, I wanted to be married before I gave the best part of me away. I wanted it to be special yet, he destroyed that, and he destroyed me.

I hate Men and I will never trust no one else but you daddy, please hurry home, I don't think I can survive without you. Please don't tell mommy, she said she'll put me out if I told someone what happened.

When I read this letter, I cried for hours like it was my daughter. Milly was from Baltimore and he was 2 years in on a 9-year sentence. He was Hell on the basketball court and that's how we made a connection. He was my cell mate and we had gotten so close; we were like brothers. He could read but he gets frustrated when he has to read in front of someone or if the letters were long. He asked me to read the letter for him and I wish I would've said no.

At the end of the letter I looked up and he was sobbing with the pillow covering his mouth, so no one could hear him crying. All I could do was hug him and tell him that everything was going to be ok, he pushed me off him, Before walking away, he yelled," How can you say that"?

My little girl has been violated and I can't help or protect her, so how is everything going to be okay?

Milly was right, how can I tell him it was going to be okay? I was trying to find the right words but what do you say to this? I couldn't imagine reading a letter like this from my child, I would lose it. Milly got on the phone and made some calls. I tried to tell him not to speak about it on the phone, but he wasn't hearing me, he didn't want to hear me. He called one of his guys on the street and told him what happened, and he needed to go handle that, not caring about the phone conversations being recorded and listened to later.

By the end of the week he got a visit from Baltimore Homicide and the FBI, they questioned him about the phone conversation and informed him that Slim had been shot 10 times and left for dead in an alley in West Baltimore. He admitted to being upset and telling his cousin to go check on his daughter, but he didn't say anything about killing him.

The FBI don't play. When they come to see you, they already know what they are going to do. They went back and listened to his phone conversations and those conversations got Millyconvicted on his case as they matched the verbiage. GO HANDLE THAT was an order given and that became the statement they built a Conspiracy to commit murder charge on Milly. When they came to get him, I never saw or heard from him again.

Milly's situation made me look at life a lot different, 90% of the inmates in the prison system have kids and we don't think about the consequences of our actions until it's too late. We don't think about how it affects them, or the dangers that we won't be able to protect them from, but most of all, the LOVE they won't receive that only you can give. I've prayed and asked God to keep my son safe and not to allow him to experience the things that I have. I have to get back out there to my son. Lord please, protect my child until I'm able.

GET IT TOGETHER SON

Hello Ma, it's me, your son you long to hold,
The one who probably grew up to fast, never did the things that he's told,
The one who cried every time he's caught, and spoke from behind the glass,
As you prayed to God saying help me, I need him, he's my last.
I talk to him but it's useless, I just do the things that I can,
But until you start to listen to me, you'll never become a man,

I am a man, YOU'RE NOT! Don't sit here
and tell that lie,
If you're a man, man up to your faults and wipe
those tears from your eyes,
Ma I'm sorry I promise you, and I won't do
these things anymore,
That's another lie because I've heard that, a
million times before,
For real Ma, this is it, because I'm really tired of
running,
I hope so because I'm tired, and look at who you're
becoming,
Straighten up son, I'm serious, just listen to the words
of your mother,
Stop selling those drugs it's killing you, and doing the
same to your brothers,
Just look at yall, keep fighting, over money
that's made in the streets,
My kids physically fighting, who slept under
the same sheets,
Well I'm tired now, and I'm getting old, and
I always said that I'm changing,
But you're my baby, and I love you, but don't let
me leave you hanging,
Just help me Ma, please, this is the last, once and
for all,
Son I'm just so scared for you, I
don't want to get that call,
What call, from jail, for me to say,
Ma come get me?
She said no that call in the middle of the night,
that says you're no longer with me.

THE PLACE WHERE MOMMA PREACHED!

GET IT TOGETHER SON

This poem represents the power of a mother's cries to a child she loves, yet it seems like her cries are unheard. This is one of the conversations that mothers all over the world are having with their sons every day. This piece is personal to me because I used to get into trouble all the time, and no matter what my mom would say to me, I would already have my mind made up about what I was going to do, once I got out of the situation. I remember one particular incident that opened my eyes to how tired my mom was of my foolishness.

It was a Sunday morning and I was coming from my apartment on Homer Ave, heading to my house. It was a long night and I was extremely tired. I sat in my crack house selling drugs for 3 days straight not coming out at all. A crack house is an apartment you rent out to cut, mix, and sell cocaine out of. The purpose of having an apartment is to hide you from being exposed to the police every day.

As I turned on St. Barnabas Rd heading to my apartment on Brinkley Rd, I got a call from my friend. He told me that he was taking a road trip with his family and he had stopped to clean the car out and discovered that he had a little over $1,000 worth of drugs in his book bag. He asked could I meet him on Central Ave at the McDonalds to take the drugs to his house, without hesitation I was on my way. One of my biggest flaws, no matter what the situation was, if my assistance was needed, I'm there!

Pulling up to the McDonalds I really didn't see any traffic, so it would be smooth sailing going home on the beltway. I saw my friend and we exchanged book bags and I was on my way, I hated riding with drugs in my car. I always purchased fast cars just in case I had to make a quick getaway from the police. My 1994 Black Impala SS did the job when needed, I pulled out of the McDonalds making a right then a U-turn to get on the beltway.

For some reason traffic started picking up, which made it hard to make the turn. Getting impatient I kept straight deciding to take the backstreets to my house, which is dangerous because you are exposed to so many police when you are riding through the neighborhoods.

Doing about 35 Mph, being cautious of my speed not trying to draw any attention, I looked in the rearview mirror spotting a grey 1990 Caprice Classic. It was a local drug dealer I did business with every now and then, he would always try to race every time he saw me. Today was not the day so I sped up a little to make sure that he wouldn't catch up and make a scene.

The speed limit was 40 Mph and I was well over 55 when I spotted a police cruiser sitting in the drive way of the liquor store. He spotted me and pulled out to get behind me. The street was wet, so his cruiser fishtailed almost turning the opposite direction. Watching the grey Caprice ride by, I pulled in the turning lane and put my signal on heading towards Addison Rd.

The police got behind me and turned on the flashers." DAMN"!!, I said to myself as I started grabbing for the bookbag so I could take the drugs out and put it in my shoes.

As the Policeman got out of the car, I had just put the drugs in my boot and smashed them under my foot. I remembered he could check my shoes if he decided to search my vehicle. As I pulled the crushed bags out of my shoe placing them in my pocket, I knew that I had to decide, if he asked me to step out of the vehicle I was going to run. I watched the officer get out of his car while planning an escape route. As he approached the driver side with his hand on his gun, I rolled down the window. "License and registration". The officer said, with a serious look on his face. I didn't say anything while handing him my credentials.

Do you know why I pulled
you over?" Looking stupid
I said, "NO SIR!"
"Well you were doing 60 in a 40 Mph zone"
"I apologize officer! I'm really late picking my mom up from church." Great lie… or so I thought!

As the officer returned to his cruiser to run my name, I called my mom and asked her to come get the car. She panicked asking me, "what's wrong?" As I filled her in on my plan the officer came back to the window, "Please step out of the car sir!" He said, with a more puzzled but serious look on his face.

I looked him in the eyes sizing him up by weight and height in case my next move is to push him and run. And judging his physical appearance, I knew I had a chance. I stepped out of the vehicle and turned on my pivot foot and took off across Central Ave. He was in a state of shock that I ran providing me with a good head start before he got himself together. Running and dodging my way through traffic I made it up the hill to the subway station. As I looked back to check his distance, I noticed him struggling to get over the fence, When I turned back around a cab pulled up, I jumped over the newspaper stand gathered myself to slow my breathing down without passing out.

I walked up to the cab casually and got in. Before he could say a word, I said, 2317 Lewis Ave. The cab driver looked at me and he drove off. From his actions I could tell the sirens, flashing lights, and speeding police cars scared him a little. I just laid down in the backseat and he continued to drive. The police begin to stop cars. The last car that they let through before setting up the roadblock was the cab I was in.

Pulling up in my neighborhood I got out, paid the driver and ran upstairs to my apartment. I called my mom and she cursed me out as she tried her best to keep it together. I remember the conversation like it was yesterday, "GET IT TOGETHER SON!" These conversations meant nothing at the time because I was mentally trapped in the drug game.
After I got locked up these conversations were replayed in my mind.

When my mother would come into the visiting room, I could feel her anger through the glass. I knew she was angry because here we were again, momma having to clean up her GROWN BABY's mess. I just would not listen to her and the result of me not listening is the reason why I was in this position. Mom would be hurting, seeing her son behind that glass, waiting to see what the judge was going to do.

Furious as she looked at my face not seeing that intelligent young man that she once knew and raised. My mother knew I had the potential to be great, but I chose to be hardheaded. I used to feel bad putting my mom in this situation, causing so much pain and heartache. I used to cry because my plan had failed again. I'd always come up with a different plan that landed me in the same position.

Every time I told my mom this time would be the last, it would destroy me inside because I knew I was lying. Our conversations would always bring her to tears, because she knew that I was lying as well. I remember the conversations they were real heart to heart. I heard every word she said, I just would not listen.

My mother used to curse me out for hours, and I would feel so bad because I knew that I was going to make the same decision that might lead me right back to prison. She used to say some things to me that would shatter my little boy ego. I couldn't take some of the things that came out of her mouth, but all I could do was listen. To her, I was the biggest dummy in the world.

She would always say, "Boy you have all this talent, you are smart but, you won't use any of those things to be a better man! You choose to just be a DAMN DUMMY!" It used to hurt to hear the truth, but, honestly, I knew that the truth would be the only thing that would set me free from these negative situations in my life.

I could always see the outcome of a situation but, I would continue to walk in the same direction. Guess you can say I was a BIG DUMMY! I remember one conversation my mother and I had, she told me that she didn't want to answer her own phone at a certain time because she was scared that someone would be calling to tell her to come identify my body. That conversation tore a hole in my heart. Right then and there is when I knew that I was being selfish, and I was putting the small things before the things that count.

In my mind I was only hurting myself, but in reality, there were more people hurting because of my actions. My mother would always say, "Son, I see where you are going, and you are throwing your whole life away. You are doing the same thing that your brother did."

There were times that she would ask me where she went wrong but, I could never allow her to take the blame for the way I turned out. A parent can only do their part, they can only guide you through life, they can't make the decisions for you. Parents can only teach you what they know, they can only be a listening ear when you have problems and try to help guide your decision making. You must make the right choices in life and be sure you are able to stand up to the decisions you make.

I remember one day my brother deceived me at a time when his mental state was not at its best. We ended up fighting, and no matter what he did to me, it hurt more to fight my brother then it did to lose anything in the world. The look on my mother's face when she saw her two sons fighting, her two babies that came out of the same womb. She was devastated when she saw what the drug game had done to her kids. Mom never raised us to try to hurt each other, she always made sure we knew what family meant.

She always said, "WE ARE ALL WE GOT!" Fighting my brother, really hurt me. The moment my brother and I chose to go out in the streets and participate in the unknown, was the moment that we chose to chase the dream that would never come true. The street game gave me a distorted vision of life. I thought my decisions were right, but little did I know I was not in control of my decision making, the enemy was controlling me and doing a good job at it.

Ma used to say, "you are grown, and you make your own decisions, but you must be prepared to deal with the consequences of your actions". Trust me nothing good has come from this behavior. "NOTHING"!

I remember trying to give her money during the conversation to try and get her to focus on something else. It would never work; she would give me the tongue lashing and make sure that I heard everything that she said. Sometimes she used to repeat the same thing three times, she used to make me feel so bad by just telling me the truth.

When you read the words of this poem, it should hit the hearts of those mothers who have children in the streets going through the same thing my brother and I went through. There are people who walk by their own relatives every day that are consumed by the streets and they just shake their heads yet; they never give them the encouragement that's needed.

It's crazy that we don't realize how much pain we cause others by doing the exact opposite of what they said. I recognized the damage that had been done and I am going to do my best to make the decisions to make sure that we never have to feel that pain again. Just looking at the picture that we took in the visiting room brings a sadness over me.

Mainly because my mother is smiling but, I know that she is forcing herself to smile. I know that she doesn't want to come to a building to see her son. I know that she feels as though she failed at being a mom because of where I am at this time.

I made a vow to myself and God, that I was going to do my best to put a smile on her face. Her favorite saying was, "I'M GETTING OLD, and I'M CHANGING!" When she said that, we knew she was mad and when she got mad somebody had to get it!

To the knuckleheads out there, you have to listen to your mothers, they speak from love, experience, and pain. Don't think that your mother doesn't know what they are talking about because they do. Either you listen to her as a free man or be a victim of not listening inside of a jail cell, or a hospital bed.

I want to give special thanks to the mothers that have stood by their children's side, hand and foot. It's mothers like you that need to be recognized, you deserve a badge of honor. As men we must wake up and do our best to put a smile on the faces of those who really love us. Wake up men, and let's do what's right, so Momma can sleep well at night.
GET IT TOGETHER!

WAKE UP

Some think life on the corner, is the life that we're supposed to live,
When we spend time with our associates, and not much time with our kids.
Those moments that are promised, but they never get fulfilled,
Times when we say if he was with us, he wouldn't have gotten killed.
Moments in those streets, when we constantly handled drugs,
Those streets transform momma's boys, into gun slinging thugs.
These corners substitute love, and put hate and deceit in their hearts,
A street race, that you have already lost before even thought to start.
Those kind people who spoke to you, and warned you of your actions,
But your ears are closed, and you're confused,

and the enemy's constantly laughing.
You denied these words and kept pushing, like the words never left their lips,
For some strange reason you still can't see, that life is really a gift.
Tomorrow's never promised, so don't think it will be the same,
I don't want to read the paper and happen to see your name.
Prison is never promised, so don't think it's a sure way out,
The graveyard is always closer, so don't let that be your route.
I know you think that you're smart, and probably you might be clever,
Well I'm telling you champ if you don't wake up, you'll probably SLEEP FOREVER.

WAKE UP

I was one of those guys who thought that the street life was the best life to live. I used to spend countless hours chasing a dream that would never come true. My focus was never on the time that I spent in the streets or who my actions were affecting. All I thought about was, selling drugs, chasing women, chasing a compliment, and keeping my name in the lights.

I rarely thought about the pain that I caused my mother, nor how my son would be affected by my absence. I never paid attention to the scars that were left from the thousands of broken promises that was attached to my name. (GOOCHIE). I spent so much time in the streets with my so-called homies and neglected my home. Then when I needed someone to get me out of a jam, my mother was the only one who would come through consistently!

When I sat down in that prison cell a lot of truth was revealed about myself, about others but, most of all, the streets were revealed. I realized that the streets and the people of the streets will only love their own. I realized a lot of relationships and friendships were only in place because of the drug game. A lot of the females I've dealt with never loved me; they loved the attention that came with my name.

They loved the treatment they got when they were around me, they loved the intimate encounters we had, which only existed because my name was ringing for one reason or another. I discovered that no one that you accumulate in the drug game is meant to stay in your life. The bible says that Dishonest Gains Will Diminish (Proverbs 13:11).

Everything that you gain in the drug game is not meant for you to have. The people, the possessions, and most of all, the friendships. Things are rarely genuine as most friendships are established from business deals, as soon as the business stops the friendship does too.

With the females, most just see money, it becomes the life of the relationship and when the money is gone the soul is stripped from the friendship. The most important thing I learned about my homies was, no matter how much they said with a drunken tongue, "I love you!", in most cases it was a lie. How can you love someone you don't know? You can never love a person in the drug game because they'll never show you their true self. You will always get the mask of a man, that face he puts on every day in order to survive.

I Thank God for his Grace and Mercy, if someone was trying to bring any harm to me, I made it easy for them. It was the same masked routine every day. I woke up to the same routine daily! I ate the same thing, drank the same thing, I even traveled the same way in order to get to my neighborhood.

Thinking about the conversations my homies and I used to have out there on the block, we spoke about going to jail, we always said and thought, "That's why I am stacking my money, so I can pay my lawyer if I get jammed up". We came to grips with the fact that the lifestyle had no promise. The craziest part about it though, was thinking that the worst part of this game was going to prison. We never spoke about getting killed, we never spoke about the other possibilities.

NEWSFLASH… PRISON IS NEVER PROMISED! The graveyard has an abundance of drug dealers who thought they couldn't be touched. Never be that ahead of yourself in the game to think it can't happen to you being in those streets.

When I speak about not wanting to read the newspaper and happen to see your friend's name, I say that with a heavy heart. For those that know me personally, you knew who I ran the streets with. I found out that my friend had lost his battle with the streets through the newspaper.

I got into a fight with a guy and it landed me in solitary confinement for 30 days. Solitary confinement is a small prison cell that you spend 23 hours of your day, only coming out to walk for 1 hour in a cage.

The day I came out of solitary confinement one of my buddies greeted me with a newspaper and walked off fast. When I looked at the newspaper, it was the obituary section. I yelled out to him, "What's this", He replied without looking back, "Just read it!"

The cover was filled with pictures of old people, but as I flipped to the inside, I saw the picture of my friend. I couldn't believe my eyes. A part of my heart dropped onto the pavement when I read his name.

All I could think about was the history that we had together, he was like a little brother that always got into trouble. I thought about all the late-night conversations we had about what we wanted out of life: marriage, kids, and getting out of the game.

Yet God had a different plan for his life. I knew that my friend was wild but, I could never see this day for him. This situation told me that the streets will devour any and every one that chooses to participate in the street game.

I saw younger guys come into the streets labeled as a good guy, only to see them turn into something terrible in the matter of months.
A lot of us come into the streets with our heart totally separated from the life that we choose to live. I was in the streets, but my heart wasn't.

A lot of us come into the streets with our heart totally separated from the life that we choose to live. I was in the streets but, my heart wasn't. I also realized that the ones who suffer the most are the ones who didn't have to be out there. The streets will change a saint into a sinner, a good girl into something her parents could not even recognize, and a momma's boy into a cold-blooded killer!

Pay attention, when GOD has a plan for your life, he'll do his best to get your attention. It's up to you to accept his plan or perish in the streets. I accepted God's plan for my life and that's the reason why you are reading this story.

To my younger generation, if you are reading this book and you are being tricked by the enemy in the streets. Hopefully by the end of this book you will see the truth about the lies that the enemy wants you to believe. The street life is an illusion, the only people who choose to believe those lies are people who are scared to believe the truth.

You can make the right choice that will help you achieve GREAT THINGS! Don't lose your chance at being the King/Queen that God has called you to be.

THE DRUG DEALER, WOMANIZER AND MASTER MANIPULATOR!

IN MY TIME

As I walk through the valley
of the shadow of death,
How long will I live, how long
will I have left?
When I die will I be pleased with the life that I've lived?
Am I a person who always took, when I knew I'm supposed to give?
Will I see it when it's coming, or will it catch me by surprise?
Will I smile, or will I frown, when it's flashed before my eyes?
Is it a man or a woman, or could it possibly be a friend?
Can I escape the grips of death, does this life have to end?
Will I go out in a rage, or will the moment be filled with fear?
Or will my pain set in, and take me away
from here?
When I die, will I go to hell, or sit in heaven
and watch them cry?
If it happens, I want rejoicing, I've lived now
it's time to die,
I had fun in the school of life, now it's my time to be dismissed,
Don't panic when your turn comes, you'll soon have thoughts like this.

IN MY TIME

This poem is a powerful piece. It represents the subconscious mind state of a man that knows the ending of the road that he is traveling but, he still pursues a negative ending.

Within my travels in the drug game I used to think about how I would die every day. I would have visions of someone running up to my car and taking my life. There would be countless days of having a feeling that something bad was going to happen. Can you imagine living and worrying about how and when you are going to die?

The scariest parts of this mindset were the dreams seemed so real. I would wake up in a cold sweat grab my Glock 40 and take a drink of Remy. I was fooling myself thinking a weapon and a drink could save me from the wrath of the enemy. I soon realized these dreams and visions were all signs from God. He was telling me these situations exist in the lifestyle that I was living. He was telling me all along to make a choice to .LIVE or DIE!

Writing this book about my process is my acknowledgement of making the right choice, to live for Him and not die because of me. It was crazy how I could lose friends to the violence of the streets, grieve with the family, go to the funeral, sit around and talk about the memories shared with the deceased. Then get right back up and continue to live the same life that just claimed my friend.

I always wondered how I was going to get out of the streets. I never thought that it would be a lengthy prison sentence, I thought I would grow old in the drug game. Some days I would hear that voice that would say, “If you don’t get out, you’re going to die!” So many lives are lost to the streets, and I realized the only one that could save me from the streets.... is ME!

Take a second to think about all the people who you’ve lost to the streets. How many times did you warn them to get out? How much did you benefit from their lifestyle? How did you feel when you got the call that said he/she was gone?

I realized when I made the decision to the live the street life. I was not in control of my life anymore. There are many ways to die when you are not living right. So many people were eligible to take my life the police, friends, family, strangers and rival drug dealers. My mom always told me there are two ways out of the drug game if you choose not to get out, Death or Prison.

Until the subconscious mind and the warning signs are respected, you’ll be playing Russian Roulette every day you walk out of your house. Let’s put things in prospective, there are many of you who have children and family in the streets putting their lives in danger and often nothing is said due to the financial benefits or lifestyle that accompanies the game

Some are living with guilt and regret from losing loved ones because they didn’t put forth an effort to get them out. We know better, when we hear the voice of God, we must act on it immediately and say something. If not, be prepared to visit them in jail or the hospital or pay your respects at the funeral.

If you are living in the illusion that comes with the street life, get out and get out fast. There's no right way to do wrong. You Can't Win! It's sad to say the winners are the ones who went to prison because they still have a chance to correct their mistakes.

A lot of my friends weren't as fortunate, they were called home because they didn't listen. Life is short and can happen fast! This book may be your warning, LISTEN!

TIME TAKER

Today I wake up to another day, that I really thought was wasted,
So anxious to see my family again, MAN I could almost taste it.
Yearning for strength in the word that I read, from the powers that rest up above,
Wondering when God will bless me and reach out and spread his love.
Sitting in my cell confided, but peaceful most of my day,
Fighting back those tears of pain but finding strength when I pray.
Prison is a place of regrets, broken promises and never-ending lies,
With non-believers cursing the God's, who rest upon the skies.

Wondering why you're sad, and you're scared, but you're not alone,
Wanting to be loved and encouraged, but you can't this place is your home.
Wondering who's this vicious thief who stole my joy from behind,
Knowing that the most hated thief, is the thief that we call TIME.

TIME TAKER

This poem was written in the early hours of the morning when those last thoughts are still running through your head. I thought of my family constantly. I wanted to be around them to laugh and hold them. I wanted to be home! There were a lot of things I wish I would've taken advantage of when I was in the streets, and spending time with my family was one of them. I missed birthdays, graduations, cookouts and family functions, chasing a dream that would never come true.

Seeing my son grow up through pictures and losing important family members and not be there to bury them, placed me at a crossroads with the man that I am, and the man that I knew I was supposed to be.

I had a choice of two decisions, choose to put my trust in what I have been told about God and follow him, or blame Him for my condition and turn away. It's crazy how I would get into a jam and blame everyone else for the things that's happening in my life instead of looking in the mirror first.

Reflecting on all the signs I ignored, and people who tried to encourage the direction of my life brought me to a place where I must salvage what was left of that wisdom. That's what God does, bring to your remembrance everything that he said through other people. He wanted me to see how hardheaded I was, and how my toughest times in life were caused by my disobedience.

I had to look myself in the mirror and admit that I have made mistakes, betrayed people and hurt my family but, I can't change or take back what I've done. I must move on while doing my best to make sure that my decisions don't lead me right back to that mirror.

One of the hardest things I had to do in all of this was to forgive myself, once I realized the damage that I had done. God sent me a message that said, "If He forgave me, I had to forgive myself." It's very important that we don't continue to beat ourselves up for what we have done to ourselves and others.

You don't have time to hold on to your faults and refuse to move forward. Time is the most VICIOUS THIEF in the world. I lost a lot during my prison sentence but, I have also gained a lot as well.

I've seen brothers lose their whole family while being locked away for so many years. This makes it difficult to return to life outside of prison because there's no place to call home when everyone has passed on. TIME TOOK THEM!

I've met brothers who have been stuck in time, who will never be in the 20th century. So much has happened to them in the 80s or 90s so, that's all that they remember. Time took their future. It's sad to see the joy on a brother's face when he speaks about something that he did in the 80s while in prison, he remembers it like it happen two minutes ago.

Our people are getting destroyed behind these prison walls and time plays a big part in this destructive force. It's not only for the people in jail but it's for people who are in the streets as well. If you don't use

your time wisely doing something positive while in those streets; you will either be a victim of your unproductive thoughts, or you will be in here with me watching the calendar flip year after year. Take advantage of the time that you have left before you're put in a place where time doesn't even matter. Make the right choice with your lives people, because the clock is ticking.

YOU

It was you who I betrayed, and left out in the cold,
It was you who stood through the toughest times,
and never did you fold.
It was you who I could trust, and keep your womb to
me,
But it was me that was blinded, when I knew
where I should be.
Even though you were my woman, so loyal,
gracious, and rare,
I ran through the streets reckless, I'm sorry that
you had to share.
You knew about the things I've done, but still you
stayed with me,
You saw the things that you wanted, and not
what you're supposed to see.

You deserved better I KNEW THAT, and soon your blessings will show,
I loved you in spite of what you saw, that's something that you should know.

YOU

This is a poem that described my actions when I came out of a relationship that crushed my ego. Somethings happened in my previous relationship that made me never want to trust a woman again so, caught up in myself I couldn't see what was happening to me. I walked out of a relationship with scars on my ego that were hard to heal. It was the first time I was cheated on AND THE LAST!!! The pains made me want to hurt others in return, I didn't know who but, someone had to pay for it!

I became numb to love, whenever I started to feel anything that resembled me falling in love with another woman, I would do something to make the feeling go away. I was not going to put myself in another situation that would have me at risk of being betrayed.

I met a good woman after that relationship, she was cute, had a nice shape, and she was shy. Every day she'd walk by on the way home from school, I'd be sitting on my car on Lewis Avenue trying to make a few dollars. I'd always say or do something funny to try to get her to smile. After several attempts she finally stopped to converse with me. Her name was Cynthia. She was 16 and moved from Landover to the area and lived with her mom. She didn't have a boyfriend at the time. I told her that my name was Mike. I gave her an alias because I just wanted to play the field, I didn't have plans to be faithful.

She laughed saying, "That's not your real name, and I met your cousins and they told me your name is GOOCHIE!" We both laughed it off and I walked her home. When we got to her door, I gave her my number and told her to call me.

After a couple of months of seeing each other every day and talking on the phone we finally decided to explore the sexual part of the relationship.

Cynthia was young, but no rookie to the sex game! I liked the way she handled herself, I adored her maturity. I decided this cutie would be my project; I was going to stick with her to make sure she would be something special. Cynthia didn't have a father figure in her life and listened when I spoke, like really appreciating my advice.

I was so popular and immature; I couldn't resist the temptation of a female. I ran into this girl named Marianne; she was the best friend of a girl Lee was dating. We had a class together in high school. Marianne got on my nerves every day, she had a smart mouth and all her jeans stopped above her ankles. I never liked her but, she was built like a grown woman in the 10th grade.

A few years had passed before I saw Marianne again. I guess people can change because the next time we saw each other I didn't despise her as much.

On my way to an Isley Brothers concert, Lee and I stopped by the salon on Silver Hill Rd in Suitland Md, to grab his date and an additional ticket. Marianne came out with her best friend Mellissa. Immediately I knew who she was, yet I still wasn't interested.

The extra ticket was for my son's mom, but of course she did something stupid and messed that up as usual. I was talking on the phone as she approached the car, tapping on the window she showed me the ticket as I rolled the window down.

"Who are you taking to the concert?" She asked with a shy look on her face. "Why?" I responded quickly. "Because it starts in an hour and you don't have your date with you." She said anxiously.

"I was supposed to take my son's mom, but she started an argument with me like I was her boyfriend or something!" I replied.

Mary looked at me and asked me to take her in my son's mom place, it was unexpected, so I paused and then said yes. I took her to her house to change clothes and to the concert we went. I was a little leery about taking her because of our past but after a few drinks and puffs of weed I was cool. On the way home after the concert, I asked Marianne, "Are staying with me?" She looked me in the eyes and said, "YES!"

It wasn't out of the norm for me because of my popularity, women rarely resist me. Meeting a girl and having sex with her on the first night was a regular night for me. We got to the apartment and she immediately asked for something to sleep in, I gave her the smallest T-shirt that I could find. She had nice juicy legs and a nice butt, I loved big butts, so she was a great candidate for my sexual appetite that came with drinking and smoking.

Minutes after she was in the shirt, I was pulling her panties off exploring her vagina. After a few flicks of my finger we were kissing and ready to devour each other. The sex was good because it was something new, I didn't think she would be the one that I would end up in a relationship with.

The next morning, I took Marianne home, she asked me to come get her from work. I told her I would, and off to Cynthia's house I went.

I fell asleep for about 6 hours to be awaken by my pager. When I checked the number, it was Marianne. I didn't call back from Cynthia's house I just went to pick her up. Marianne worked about 10 minutes away and I had to admit, I was kind of excited. She came out and got in the car, we headed to her mother's house so she could grab some clothes.

Instead, she came out with two large bags, I thought to myself, where is she going? I didn't question her when she got into the car I just drove to my place. She spent the night and we had sex multiple times and from that day on, she didn't want to go home and that's where the fling began.

I had an apartment in Forest Creek about 10 minutes or so down the road from my stomping ground on Homer and Lewis Avenue, I was selling drugs and living there at the same time. A big no, no in the drug game! My carelessness put me on the radar of a major police sting and two weeks later the police raided my house on a Friday about 6 in the morning. I just walked in the house and began to take my clothes off and BOOM! The door flew off and I heard screaming in the living room, "GET ON THE GROUND! GET ON THE GROUND!!!"

I peeped out from my room and was greeted with clouds of smoke, red beams, and men behind body shields with the letters DEA on the front. "COME OUT OF THE ROOMS!!" The officer screamed from the living room.

I crawled out of my room and the moment my right knee hit the floor, I felt two huge hands grab my arm and pull me into the living room. They searched the apartment and found a short-barrel shot gun under my bed, 23 grams of cocaine, two 9-millimeter handguns and shot-gun slugs. I knew I had 125 grams of crack in the spare room. God was on my side,

Once they found those guns it seemed like they were satisfied. They grabbed me by my arms and cuffed my hands so tight that I thought they would burst. They pulled me to my feet and walked me out to the police car, it was a little cold out and I didn't have a shirt on.

Pulling out of the apartment complex I saw the nosey neighbors peeping and whispering to each other. I just knew that this was the one that would finish me. We pulled up to the police station in Palmer Park MD. I couldn't get my thoughts together, my mind was racing, who would I call, and would I get a bond? Walking through the sally port I smelled the drunks in the dry tank, the liquor and beer was seeping out of their pores and they were dry heaving as they vomited in the toilet.

We stopped in front of a small cell and I was instructed to remove my shoestrings, that was a procedure they used to prevent someone from trying to commit suicide.

The same officer that transported me to the station came in to ask questions, like Name, Birthdate, Height, Eye and Hair Color, Shoe Size, Waist size, and Shirt size?

After all the questions, I was placed in a dark room and told that I was waiting to see the commissioner. I heard my name called from behind a door to the right of the room I was in. The door opened and the lights came on, the same transporting officer was standing there.

I struggled to get up because my hands were still cuffed, I was taking slow steps because my eyes were trying to adjust to the light after sitting in a dark room for the past 4 hours. I was escorted to a glass window, the lady behind the window had a thick neck and big eyes like she had been up for days.

She said her name was Ms. Aaron, the county commissioner. She read my charges and told me that I wasn't going to receive a bond. I knew that she would play hard ball because I had so many cases thrown out in the state court.

She asked me did I have anything to say, I said, "NO", but can I make my phone call. I called my lawyer and told him what my charges were, He said I'd be out in a week.

The officers transported me to Upper Marlboro Detention Center in Upper Marlboro Md. I hated this place, but no one could tell because I was a frequent visitor. I walked in the sally port and was placed in line to get my jumpsuit. A bright orange jumper with inmate written across the back.

They continued to walk me through, until we stopped in front of a cell block that had H-12 on the door. The door opened and I walked in the unit. There were about 50 bunkbeds in the middle of the unit and there were about 50 two-man cells, I was given a bed assignment and a bed roll.

It smelled bad in the dorm and everyone had their faces balled up trying to look mean or tough, usually those same guys were the ones that were scared to death. The officer's desk was off to the left facing the bunk beds, a female officer was working the unit and the men were crowded around the desk.

H-12 was the intake unit so you had all types of criminals in there trying to coexist, junkies, drug dealers, rapist, and murderers. We were all squeezed in this unit waiting to be sorted out. I approached the officer's desk and she asked me my name, I gave her my card and she looked through a book and assigned my cell, I loved the cell's instead of the open area bunk beds because you could get some sleep inside the cell, you'd be up all night on the bunks.

The junkies would try their best to steal every chance they got, so you'd have to watch your belongings and I couldn't/won't do time like that. This wasn't my first time here. I was familiar with the procedure, so I went to my cell and made my bunk and took a nap.

This would be my residence until my lawyer came through on his promise. The week went by fast. Before I knew it my named was called and I was informed that my bond had been reduced and paid. My lawyer came through and it was time to go.

After I was released, I called my mom asking her to come to get me. She pulled up in 15 minutes and we drove back to my apartment. I gathered everything that I could and went to my mother's house. I called my lawyer and he informed me that I was fighting too many charges and we would have to take a plea deal.

Six months went by and it was time to go to court. I had 3 charges pending. My lawyer went for the best deal I could get, 20 years all suspended but 3, with a recommendation to boot camp. I agreed to the plea and within months I was on my way to Eastern Correctional institute to serve my 3-year sentence. While I was away the streets started talking, which is when Cynthia found out about Mary.

Mary was the female that bruised my ego, we moved in together right before I went to prison. I wish I would've never met this woman, she was broken, toxic, and sneaky. When I went to jail Marianne cheated on me with a guy I never thought she would be interested in. "KARMA"!

I was released 366 days later and discovered Marianne's infidelity after I moved out of the townhouse, we were living in. I couldn't understand why Mary would stoop so low and do something like that to me, but the Bible says, "Do not be deceived: God cannot be mocked

A man reaps what he sows" (Galatians 6:7). What I did to Cynthia came right back on me.

I left Mary and I went to see Cynthia. She welcomed me with open arms. My heart was confused, my ego was bruised, and my pride was getting the best of me. Although she was there for me, I planned to never fall in love again! I knew I was going to hurt her; I didn't know that it was going to be to the extent that I did.

In the beginning of our new relationship things were just fine, we were laughing, loving on each other, and having sex, A lot! I wasn't making much money at that time, because I was focused on not selling drugs anymore. Her apartment was right in the middle of the strip that was responsible for sending me to jail;

I was over her house a lot and that's where the devil wanted me to be. The temptation was heavy, seeing the money and not being the one making it was getting a little tough.

I found myself being approached by customers by the dozens, the quantity of drugs they wanted equated to my pay check for a month. When you are around a drug strip constantly, there is a great chance you will sell drugs again.

I was struggling with the decision to get back in the game, she'd encourage me to go to work and be patient. That was God speaking through her, yet I wasn't paying attention to the MESSAGE but the MESSENGER. I appreciated her for that, she was building me back up and it felt like I was falling in love again. She was inside my heart but, I knew there wouldn't be any loyalty on my end, so why did I allow myself to love again? I guess you can say that sometimes your circumstances dictate when and who you fall in love with.

She was everything that I needed at the time, even though I walked into the relationship with being tough on my mind, the way she cared for me made me break that promise to myself. It got to the point where I was over there so much, I finally moved in THE DEVIL'S PLAN the whole time.

It didn't take long for me to decide I was getting back in the drug game. We started to spend a lot time together and now that I was back in the game. I was able to give Cynthia things she never had before money, clothes, jewelry, shoes, I helped her mom pay the bills, and helped pay for her schooling.

Still not mature enough to realize what I had; I was cheating 100 miles a minute with almost every girl that took a shot at me. I was intimate with a lot of women during that time. I had no regard for my life and none for no one else's either. I used to stay out all night with other women, not even thinking about the consequences of my actions. I didn't care if Cynthia would be mad, I didn't care if she left me because I knew that she wouldn't!

It wasn't until God showed up and uncovered the wound from my past relationship, which allowed me to see why I was treating Cynthia like this. I was carrying an old wound into a new situation. He showed me that I was hurting and would continue to hurt any and every woman that I met if I didn't deal with this gaping hole in my heart. I took God's advice and forgave the woman that was responsible for this feeling that controlled my heart and I moved on.

We must realize, when you are hurt, and you don't know the severity of the damage you in turn hurt other people. A great woman told me one day (R.I.P. MS. ROBIN), "HURT PEOPLE, HURT PEOPLE!"

That was a very true statement. I was hurting and doing things that would hurt Cynthia in the process. I would be out with another female and she'd call me. I would look at my phone and have no feeling and continue to entertain who was in my presence and didn't think twice about it. I did this the entire relationship because in my eyes why should I stop? I tried to be faithful, it didn't work so why try it again. I was thinking I could do this forever!

Then God showed up and taught me a little about pain, betrayal, and unforgiveness. He allowed me to feel the pain that I caused others and that's what made me say, "Lord change me!" He softened my heart and gave me a better way to look at things. I had to forgive in order to be forgiven. He told me that I was making people feel my pain because I was too selfish to forgive and move forward. God said, 'Those people that I was hurting were crying out to Him about my actions. I must admit, listening to God about this really touched the person that was inside of me.

The best thing we all can learn is, when things happen, we have to give it to GOD and LET IT GO! If not, you will damage a lot of people because of your pain. Everyone does not deserve to be hurt because you are hurting. We must deal with the pain of being hurt in order to be able to love again. Life doesn't stop with the pains of your past, if you want a new beginning you have to let it go!

THAT WOMAN

Who's that beautiful lady, that I love to
come home to,
That wonderful lady who loves me, no
matter what I do.
That woman when I was sad, she
encourages with a song,
She never breaks down SHE'S FIRM and corrects
me when I am wrong.
That woman who never left me, despite my blinded
eyes,
My beautiful angel, A BLESSING, that's set from
beyond the skies.
Oh how do I love her, the world may never know,
She'll never take my energy; she only makes it grow.
The only lady I've always loved, there could
never be any doubts,
Whenever I'm hurt or in trouble, she would
always be in route.
She even loves my siblings, she treats them
just the same,
Do you wonder who she is? Are you curious
to know her name?
It's fine that she's a lady, they'll never be one

**above her,
Maybe because she BORN ME, and that lady is who I call, MY MOTHER!**

THAT WOMAN

"That Woman" is a special poem that I wrote to my mom and to the mothers out there who have held on to their kids no matter what we do.

I put my mother through a lot by being hardheaded and immature. It's crazy how I claimed to be grown but, still call on momma as soon as I would get in trouble. No matter how old I got MOMMA will always be there at the drop of a dime. I have done some crazy things in my life; a regular mom would have given up on their son. I have seen it happen 1,000 times. There are guys in here with me that call home and their mothers would answer the phone and say, "Don't call here no more!!" TOUGH LOVE!

My mom is something special. She is a true blessing from God. Until I get a woman that I can call my wife, momma will be the only woman I can trust.

This was a poem just to let my mother know I noticed her sacrifices for my life, while acknowledging the things we've been through since I've been gone.

I remember the first time that I got arrested for possession of a controlled substance (CRACK), it was a very small amount but enough to send me to jail. I was so mad at myself because I knew I was supposed to give my last customer everything I had but, he lied to me saying that he had $50 but he only had $30. I chipped what I thought was worth

$20 off the block of crack and put it in my jacket pocket, got back in my car and pulled off.

When I got back to my neighborhood. I saw two policemen and proceeded to walk towards them forgetting the drugs were in my pocket. One of the officers looked me up and down and said, "Get against the car!!" A typical day on Homer Avenue. I got against the car; he went right to the pocket I had the drugs in. It hit me as he pulled it out saying, "JACKPOT!!!"

I hung my head and immediately started thinking about my mother, and how disappointed she was going to be when she found out her baby was a drug dealer.

This would be my first charge and the situation that changes my life, how will I tell my mother I'm not the person she thought I was? How will she take it knowing I've betrayed her trust? Will she turn her back on me and how will my betrayal affect our relationship/friendship? These were the thoughts that crossed my mind as soon as the cuffs were placed on my wrist.

I thought about the choices I had, allow this situation to teach me a lesson or take this as a stepping stone to becoming a smarter criminal? I didn't want to be a product of my environment, I wanted to get my life together but, how will I do it and is it really what I want?

It was obvious that prison temporarily changed my outlook on life. As soon as I got out, I ran right back to the streets, only to lose again and again. It seemed like nothing was going right. I was arrested 3 times in a two-month period. My mother was devastated. Every time I got out of trouble; I would tell her this was the last time. The look on her face said she knew I was lying every time. Momma knew me like the back of her hand. Even though she knew that I was lying, she still would be there as soon as the collect call would go through.

At the time I wrote this poem I've been locked up for 4 and a half years. No woman to write to, talk to, or come to visit. Momma was the only woman who was CONSISTENT with loving me. There were times that I felt like giving up. The road just seemed to be too long,

Momma would come swooping in like a super hero giving me the energy to fight another day. I felt like she had a sixth sense, because every time I slipped into that train of thought she would either write or visit.

That visit or letter would be the one that would always put me right back where I needed to be. She would give me hope in hopeless times, strength when I felt weak, say the right things that gave me that boost that I needed. No matter what I said, Momma would always see through my ego and pride, and tell me the truth!

I give thanks to God every day for my mother; she is truly a blessing. To all the mothers who don't get recognized enough for your loyalty, I salute you today.

TOUGH TIMES

What do we do when tough times appear?
Do we stand tall through it all, or beak
down and shed tears?
If we break down and shed tears, NOTHING

will be our gain,
I know the truth hurts sometimes but, Love will ease our pain.
I know it's hard dealing with, losing your special guy,
But we'll survive this terrible storm, if we laugh as much as we cry.
Please sweetheart, please don't cry, please don't shed one tear,
I'll be there for you with encouraging words, that's something that you need to hear.
I've traveled through this journey in life, with faith as a spiritual man,
It will be hard, I know that but, the Lord will lend me a hand.
Every morning I wake I'll Love you, even though I'm stuck in this place,
If they cut me open in search of my heart, a cloud will resemble your face.

TOUGH TIMES

"Tough Times" was one of the first poems that I wrote when I was still in love with my ex, Cynthia. I was trying to give her and the other women out there some words of encouragement. It's not easy for a woman to hold on to their faith while their man is locked away. Prison relationships are really stressful especially if your man didn't do right by you when he had the chance. It's always going to be a struggle between letting go and holding on when you find out all the dirt he has done while he was in the streets.

It never fails, as soon as we get locked up all the hidden secrets come out at one time, their suspicions are confirmed, Luke 8:17 NIV “For there is nothing hidden that will not be disclosed and nothing concealed that will not be known or brought out in the open”.

I remember when I was in the county jail, Charles County Correctional facility. I was still communicating with a few females that I entertained in the streets. The county jail was about 45 minutes from home, so a few friends would come see me every now and then. entertained in the streets.

The county jail was about 45 minutes from home, so a few friends would come see me every now and then. I had my plan down to a science, visiting days were on Tuesday and Thursday nights, as well as Saturday and Sunday mornings. Cynthia would come on Thursday or Saturday, anyone else would come on a Tuesday or Sunday. So, Cynthia wouldn’t bump heads with the other women.

I called Cynthia on Tuesday morning asking her plans for the day. She said she was going shopping with her mother and then out with her girlfriends. That’s what I needed to hear, I called Mikki and asked her to come to see me.

Now Mikki was a Monster. She was about 5”6 150 pounds of pure chocolate, the only woman who challenged me, making me wait 8 months before we had sex. Cynthia heard I was dealing with Mikki but, never had any solid evidence. I was so careless that I didn’t care if she did. Whenever she would question me about

Mikki, I would always fake an attitude and try my best flip it on her. It worked every time.

Well today, Cynthia was going to get the confirmation she needed. Visiting hours started at 6:00 pm on Tuesdays, Mikki was always the first one there when she came. There was a procedure all visitors had to go through before they could enter the visitation room. The guard opens the door electronically and the C.O on duty comes in with the card calling names "Bell, Jackson, Smith and Dupont, you all have visitation!"

The four of us already knew we had visits from conversing with our family on the phone. When our names were called, we were already on deck. We filed out of the unit one by one. "Y'all' know the drill!" the C.O said. The drill is term for the routine, we all face the wall and place our hands flat against it.

You spread your legs so the C.O can check to see if you have any weapons or contraband on you. Once the guard finished searching you, we walk in a straight line to the visiting room. The hallways are narrow with two-way traffic, so it was stressed that we walk in a straight line.

We stopped by other units to pick up other inmates, state and federal. The visiting room is 10 chairs and booths with a stool on the outside of the fiberglass window that divides

the inmate from the visitor. The inmate walks down the hallway until they see their visitor and takes a seat.

I walked in spotting Mikki at the first booth, she

smiled ear to ear when she saw me. That really brightened up my day, being as though I am in a situation facing 15 years and having to just sit and think about that all day. I pulled a spare sock out of my shirt pocket and placed it over the phone before I put it on my ear. This is for sanitation purposes; you never know what these guys do when the C.O walks away.

Mikki picked up the phone with a baby wipe and cleaned the receiver, we both started laughing when she looked at my hair slicked back like James Brown.
"What's going on with your hair?" she inquired.
"I'm freestyling and making a fashion statement; you know I stay fly!" I said jokingly.

Mikki almost fell off the stool as soon as the words left my mouth. That was one of the things that kept me around Mikki, she had a great sense of humor and I love a woman who can make me laugh. You don't get the privilege of getting a haircut every week and I didn't trust just anyone with clippers behind my head, so I let my hair grow out into a 70's bush.

Mikki stopped laughing and got serious, "What type of time are they talking about G?" with a look of concern on her face, that was her nickname for me." My lawyer said 5 years max" I said calmly. She stopped smiling and looked at the desk. I tapped on the glass and said, "Hold your head up, everything will be just fine"! She looked at me and said, "G, I hope you don't get that much time, it's been hard without you these last couple of months, I don't know what I'll do for 5 years!" She looked at me with pain in her eyes.

Trying to encourage her I said "You'll be fine Mikki, you're a survivor and if I happen to get the 5 years it will go by quick. I just ask that you write back when I write, come see me twice a year, and answer the phone when I call.

The look on Mikki's face said that she was offended by what I said, she didn't say anything, but I knew Mikki. She looked up with tears in her eyes, "I am mad that I fell in love with you and now you are going to be gone for a long time, what am I supposed to do?", she said.

Those words cut like a knife. You never plan for people to love you, and you never plan to go to jail, so when it happens it's like a double burden. You have to deal with the pressure of the prison sentence and the pain your absence leaves with your people.

I tried to skip the subject because I didn't have an answer to Mikki's question, so I flipped the conversation to our memories. That always made us smile. We laughed for the entire visit reminiscing about our sexual experiences to the times when we would break up and go back together the same day as little kids.

The C.O tapped on the window and said, "5 minutes!" Mikki said that she would go now because the process is too long getting out and she wanted to beat the crowd. I told her that I would call her when I got back to the unit to make sure she got out safely. "I LOVE YOU" she said, with a look of defeat in her eyes. "I LOVE YOU TOO" I said as she got up and walked away.

I loved getting visits but, I hated to see them walk away. I placed my head in my hands as I thought about what was about to happen to me. As soon as I got deep in thought the C.O tapped on the glass and said "Bell, you have another visit". I was confused because I only allowed certain people to come to see me and I stressed no pop up's out of respect for my mother and Cynthia. We were only allowed 8 visiting points a month, I rationed them out between my Mom, Cynthia, and Mikki.

My mind was racing like crazy and the door opened, and Cynthia and My cousin Whitey, walked in. The look on Cynthia's face said that she saw Mikki. I had to get my best lie together because this was going to get ugly. You can't afford to lose no one when you are about to do time. Whitey sat down at the table and picked up the phone, Cynthia stayed at the entrance of the door leaning up against the wall.

"Man, you are in some deep shit", Whitey said as I looked up at Cynthia. "What happened?" I said puzzled. "Cynthia called and said that she couldn't make it this weekend on her normal day, so she wanted to surprise you, so I said, cool and I rode with her. "When we got here and gave the guard your name, the C.O said you already had a visitor and we would have to wait.

We both thought it was your mom until Mikki came out and spoke to me. I looked at Cynthia, she didn't even look my way. I told Greg to tell her to come to the phone as I changed my facial expression, so it could look like I was mad.

Cynthia walked over, grabbed the phone and looked me in the eyes, "That's the girl everyone's been telling me about huh? You better not lie to me either" Cynthia said with a look of disgust on her face.
I didn't expect her to come off like she did, so I had to

change my entire comeback.

"Yes, that's her but, I didn't tell her to come up here. She just popped up on her own!" I said hoping to sway her. "She must be on the visiting list in order to get in, so explain how she got on your visiting list Goochie!?" she furiously replied.

"If you come from out of town, they'll let you in", I said, hoping she'd believe it but, I knew better. Cynthia looked in the air shaking her head. "Are you going to man up and tell the truth for once in your life? If you want me to be here, you better tell me the truth!" she demanded. Even though I was caught, I stuck to my story. "I looked at the visitation log when I signed my name, she's been up here every week. Cynthia said." I didn't think of that, she had me red handed, before I could say anything, she got up holding the phone.

"Since you still can't respect me on the streets or in prison I don't need to be here. Tell them other broads to come see you." Cynthia dropped the phone and walked out. I felt like trash because I should've come clean. I couldn't imagine how hurt Cynthia was from all the lies that I told her when she knew the truth.

I realized that a lie can really ruin someone, especially someone who's loyal and genuine. I wondered how much pain I was responsible for.

This memory really opened my eyes to who I was and the damage that I was doing to women. I wasn't a man worth waiting for in the beginning so, I was expecting her to leave. However, my selfish adolescent mindset was hoping because, "IT'S ME "she'd be there. Yet in my heart of hearts I knew I'd done too much, and she would really leave.

This was my last attempt to at least make Cynthia feel comfortable with just being there for me as a friend. This poem started to reveal the person that I was on the inside. When you are out there in the streets you don't have time to deal with the real you, you can't expect someone to be able to accept the real you.

I really never showed her the REAL ME. She saw the parts of me that I allowed her to see. I made a vow to never show a woman everything, you give her too many ways to hurt you. When Cynthia saw the poems and the love letters, she couldn't believe that the words were mine. She used to say, "THAT'S JAIL TALK!"

People don't understand, prison either changes you, helps you come to grips with who you really are, or helps you hide. Prison brought out the truth in me, the one stripped of the Pride, and Ego!

Cynthia couldn't take the real me, the Lover who loves to express his feelings on paper, the one that sends love letters almost every day, the one who recognizes what he neglected while he was in the streets.

I felt a little love for a few women while I was in the streets. Due to the pain from a past relationship. I would always pull back when things got a little heavy. When I felt like I was falling in love I used to make it my business to go out and cheat, just trying to make myself feel like I was still in control of my feelings. To make myself feel like my heart was still in that shell that I would never allow anyone near again.

When you are in the streets, you're not able to really focus on what you have at home, mainly because you don't spend enough time with that person to appreciate her. When you read this poem ladies, know that it is possible for a man to change, or should I say, it is possible for a man to be comfortable showing you the real person that he is.

Now don't get me wrong, there are some dudes who are good at manipulating on a professional level. They're the ones who really don't want to change but want their lady to believe they've have changed. Ladies you know your man better than anyone else, so it's all up to you and your judgement.

I just encourage you to pray for your man. If you really want to be with him, ask God to remove his fraudulent ways and cleanse him of that adolescent mindset. If you really Love Him, ask God to make him the best man for you, or for someone else (THAT'S BIG)!

I ask every woman that reads this chapter and relates, get on your knees and pray for cleansing of your unforgiving heart, so when you receive the man, he's raised up for you, you won't allow

YOU to be the reason you two don't make it. Some of your past relationships have come with so much pain, that your next relationship is over before it even begins. I ask that you go before the Father and ask Him to strengthen your spiritual discernment to identify those who are untrue.

I speak for every man inside these walls when I say, it's hard to function when we don't have the love from who we love and need. The strength and love of a woman is needed to function in this world. I don't care what these dudes say, when you are inside these walls, it's "YOU" that keeps us going, it's you that we think of every day, it's you that makes us want to change our lives for the better.

That's also the reason why God keeps you away from us, we have poisoned and scarred so many of you, which makes it hard for some of you to hold your head up. He doesn't want us to continue to break our women down, so he keeps us away from you until we can get it right.

This chapter just points out the things that goes through our heads, and the things that we know you go through. I speak for those Men who sit in this cell getting their lives right with God working to be the man they promised you.

There are some good guys in here that is worth waiting for and will be exactly what you need him to be. I encourage you before you walk away make sure your conscious is clear and you are absolutely sure about your decision. You don't want to walk away from a man that is destined to be a King, or a commitment God is telling you to hold on to.

Think about it like this, if you have done 5 or 10 years with a man while he has been inside of those walls, and you choose to walk away. Then he comes home and turns out to be that guy you always wanted him to be, how are you going to feel when you know that you have invested in this man, and then you have given your blessing to someone else?

I am just saying, some of you are walking away from a good thing, you see the potential that he possesses, and you know that when his head is on straight, he is more than enough man for you. Why walk away? I will leave you with this, God is raising up kings within these walls and a couple of you women are going to get a great guy when he is released.

I know that I have been called to be a blessing, and I will be just that. Ladies really reevaluate your decision before you make it, you don't want to give your King to another Queen. Stand through the TOUGH TIMES!

WHY

Why is my mind clogged why is my journey long? Why is my strength weak and my heart without a song?
Why is my life flawed in a race I no longer win?
Why am I in a race where you lose before you begin?
Why are my thoughts wrong and my faith

filled with fear?
Why am I so anxious to be taken
away from here?
Why is my spirit the focal point of a
tarnished and untrue life?
Why is there so much unbelief when my
faith is so much in Christ?
Why am I out of place why am I back in
line?
Why is it time for a change and a change only comes
with TIME!

WHY

This is a poem of questions I asked myself after God uncovered my eyes to the truths about my habits and lifestyle. I had so many questions about myself, things I wanted to know and understand! Often my mood would change in a split second it could be a thought, something someone said, or the way a person looked at me and BAM!

The fire was lit and, in some cases, it caused a scene or a fight. I couldn't differentiate between good and bad feelings, I knew how to react but, I always made the wrong decision.

I couldn't prosper in the drug game like I wanted to, I couldn't be loyal to my beliefs, I couldn't love one woman and be happy; I cheated, lied and deceived every chance I got. For the life of me, I could not understand why! My mind was filled with crazy thoughts ALL THE TIME! Now that I'm face to face with myself

and who I was destined to be, I wanted to know Why am I like this?
The answers!

My foolishness led me to my knees in prayer, and that's where I found my answers. My first question was why was I so easily manipulated by my own thoughts?

They controlled me because I lacked self-control, I had no power to resist that voice that told me to do something wrong. It cost me so many precious moments and years of my life.

God came into my life and changed the way I looked at things. He became my voice of reason. When I was placed in a negative situation and my reaction would be set to do something stupid, the voice would say, "calm down and think first".

He told me what I needed to hear, and not what I wanted to hear. My new relationship with the Lord is the reason why I can make smarter decision when part of me wants to do wrong.

Question #2,

Why couldn't I recognize the difference between good and bad feelings? The main reason was because the enemy tricked my mind into thinking doing wrong made me feel good. I knew there was something wrong with my lifestyle but, I overlooked it because it felt good at times.

It got to the point where I would have a positive thought, (DON'T FIGHT, WALK AWAY) and then get upset because I didn't agree with the outcome. I was totally confused.

When doing right feels bad something's wrong. Jesus took the wheel and explained the benefits of making smart decisions, even when it feels wrong. First, I had to make it my lifestyle. It became the key to having a second chance at living a good life with purpose.

God told me, "The devil will always try to make you think that there is a right way to do wrong, and He is good with manipulation and distractions that often come in disguises. Therefore, it is very important you hear my voice and trust me to avoid being tricked by what looks good but isn't good for you!

Question #3

Why couldn't I prosper in the DRUG GAME?

Every time I thought I was getting ahead, something would happen, and I would be right back to square one. God is not the author of confusion but, of peace... (1 Corinthians 14:33 KJV). He did not create me to live a life that ultimately destroys his people. He created me to live good and praise HIM with my lifestyle. He would never condone or allow me to prosper living an unrighteous lifestyle.

Question #4,

Why couldn't I be loyal to what I believed in? The streets teach you to only be loyal to tradition, it will never teach you to be loyal to what's RIGHT. God said, "You must understand who I am first, which will give you some insight on what loyalty means. You don't know what loyalty is until you are taught. When you start to

walk this journey, I will teach you to respect the laws of God and the principles that I give you to live by. You will remain loyal to me, and not to man."
Question #5,

Why did I lie, cheat, and manipulate?
God told me that the way a child grows up almost, always decides who they are going to be if they don't know Jesus. Most things are from learned behavior. We mimic what we see not always what we are told.

Often, we become victims of GENERATIONAL CURSES. Our guardians and/or authority figures have been unconsciously instilling things in us that were instilled in them passing down negative and unhealthy traits and habits. This explained my reasoning for manipulation. My mother taught me all about that, it was how she survived. My environment taught me the rest.

I couldn't understand what faith I was never opened a bible until I came to prison. I fell into a spiritual circle which gave me a desire to want to see what they saw. I always believed in God because it was what I was taught. However, I never knew His story or the sacrifices that He made for my life.

It was crazy how I could get on my knees and pray to a man that I knew nothing about! Now I know who Jesus is, I know about the sacrifices that were made for my life and if I don't follow him, I will perish in these streets. I know that prayers will be answered as long as there is faith that follows my words.

I wondered how I got to the point where there was nobody around but God. I asked myself, why I was out of place, which questioned why I in the drug game at all was. God said because you love the attention. The enemy tricked you into thinking that you were helping your mom, using the drug game to destroy you because he knew how strong you are.

I got tired of a life that was filled with false promises. No matter what you tell yourself you wake up every day knowing that you are going to fail. There is no light in a life that starts out dim. You can't possibly believe that God will bless a lifestyle that is meant to destroy you.

I changed because I got tired of letting people down. I got tired of looking in the mirror and seeing so much talent and watch it go down the drain. I had to put a stop to the foolishness and make a winner out of a man that the world said would lose.

As you read this story ask yourself, why do you do the things you know is not right? Why do you accept a lifestyle that is not compatible with who you want to be? Why do you look in the mirror every day and say, I AM GOING TO CHANGE, and then try your best to be the same? Why do you lie down at night and get direction from God but still run the opposite way?

Why do you pray and then forget what you prayed for? Why do you have so much faith in God only when you get into trouble? My last question to you is, what are you going to do with that feeling that you have in your gut as you read this story? Will you make the decision to live a life where these questions don't EXIST? If not, then……." WHY"?

DEALING WITH IT

As I wake up to these prison walls,

I sit and listen to these PRISON HALLS

Thinking about the sad stories that will soon somehow be told

Some guys come in as kids, and leave out when they're a little old Constantly not in a corrective mind state,
Only listening to those that could somehow relate,
Flooding my pillow with tears of pain, along with the pressure and stress,
Crying out these lonely tears at night, until there's nothing left.
Trying to tame that vicious beast, that's hidden inside of me,
Containing those vicious thoughts of mine, versus setting that killer free,
Knowing the cause of releasing him, will be detrimental to my life,
Constantly dealing with deceiving snakes, through the struggles, and all the strife.

DEALING WITH IT

This poem represents the mind state of a man that allows the environment that he is in, to dictate every move.

Most of the things I experienced were due to me allowing someone to control my actions or their opinion of me. I listened to everything people had to say about me, and it drove me crazy.

The smallest incident would enrage me, and my response would be explosive. For example, a guy would bump me sincerely on accident, and my thoughts would be, he tried to disrespect you, go tell him about himself, if he reacts wrong punch, him in the face.

All my life I wondered where these thoughts came from and why did they continue to haunt me. The person that I allowed people to see would never give the impression that this was inside of me. It wasn't anger, it was more like rage but, it was more of a conscious rage that just blows up at the drop of a dime. I had no control over when and why I got mad. I hurt a lot of people with my hands just reacting to the first thought that would cross my mind.

A lot of busted lips, broken hands, broken jaws, sprained wrist, and dislocated fingers were the results of my rage. One day while in the county jail, me and some guys were having a conversation about sports. I love the Washington Redskins. You couldn't speak bad about my team in any type of way.

This young guy from Miami loved to push my buttons on Sunday when it came to my team. The Redskins were doing okay that season! It was the same year starting safety, Sean Taylor #21 was murdered.

However, we made it to the playoffs and

unfortunately, we lost the first game! The young guy came in, said the wrong thing at the wrong time, I got so upset and the voice said, "PUNCH HIM!" I knocked him out cold. That was my specialty, ONE HITTER QUITTER! People would say, really homes over a game?"

Subsequently I'd feel terrible but never in the moment. I had a reputation to live up to. People in the streets knew better, and those who didn't I showed them. Honestly, those guys in jail knew about me upon my arrival, yet they'd test me by calling me names behind my back or saying something slick and those were the results!

In the streets I had thoughts of shooting people and I can't say I "never" pulled the trigger; however, I'd often think about how I felt attending one of my friend's funeral due to senseless street feuds.

Therefore, I'd do my best to avoid having to act on those thoughts. Besides, I'm not one of those dudes that would sit around and lie about how I used to shoot or shoot at people. I'm a guy that LOVED to fight, if I said anything else it would be a lie!

When I speak about setting the killer free, it's from my encounters with some. Watching them fight those thoughts of evil and repeating over and over to themselves that they didn't want to do it! But in a split-second thing would get bad so fast, and someone would end up getting hurt bad. Just seeing these people in action would always put me in the realm of thinking, could I live with this on my conscious?

Some things are addictive once you start you can't stop, you become submerged in the rush of the after effects. I have a friend doing double life plus 60 years for multiple homicides. I asked him, "why didn't you stop?"

His response, "I entertained that thought one time and felt like that was the only way to handle any situation that made me upset, and I couldn't stop!" I live with a lot of terrible things on my conscious every day I open my eyes, I'm just glad murder isn't one of them.

However, the vicious mindset was similar in a sense to me loving to fight! Once I got my first knockout and I saw how my opponent was on the ground snoring and biting his tongue, I feigned for my next one.

I went on a rampage trying to get that feeling, it was like I was chasing a high. I loved the sight of broken noses and seeing the dudes afterwards with their jaw wired shut. The feeling was crazy and often hard to explain to someone whose never been addicted to anything.

I knew that if I killed and got away with it, it would be over. The little control I had over myself would've diminished. Although I can recall many situations that warranted that action, I didn't act upon them. I can honestly say that no life has been taken by my hands. The Spirit of God was very loud in those moments and I listened! Back then I was calling the Spirit of God, "My Conscious"! God had a plan for me the whole time, His voice kept me out of a lot of bad situations.

He would allow certain people to cross my path when I was faced with having to make this decision. The person he used the most was my son, Chaz Malik Seegars. Thoughts of him would always calm me down, especially after I realized that he was the only responsibility that God gave me at the time.

I was faced with a decision and I resisted the thought the first time, but the enemy would not let up, he kept sending people at me trying to get me to set an example. A guy disrespected me on the basketball court, we were competing in the championship game and the referee was really cheating when it came to calling the fouls for my squad.

My team and I were still holding the lead despite the referee making consistent bad calls. Late in the 4th quarter I was fouled so hard that I fell and skinned my knee on the blacktop. The referee didn't call the foul and that was the last straw.

I sprang up off the ground and proceeded to curse him out, He looked me in my eye and called me a BITCH! Now in the prison system you can't call a man out of his name and not be prepared to deal with the repercussions.

When I finally realized what he said, I looked around the rec yard 500 men were looking at me waiting to see what my reaction would be.
I turned and charged him but, it was too late. Everyone that I called a friend, or an associate was on the court trying to talk me out of retaliating in

front of the Correctional Officers. When men get into an altercation, we try our best to fight, stab, and get away with it. Sometimes things happen so fast that violence erupts wherever the argument started.

I couldn't believe that I was just disrespected in front of the whole prison population, I was furious, but I had to be strategic with my retaliation I made up my mind, I couldn't retaliate right then and there, but no matter what he was going to get what he had coming to him.

When I got to my cell a good friend came to speak to me about the situation, I told him that I had made up my mind that I was going to stab him in his face until he was unrecognizable. Jalil (MY FRIEND) told me that the referee sent over his apologies and asked for my forgiveness.

I didn't want to hear it because he should've thought about that before he opened his mouth with the disrespect. I conversed with Jalil for about 3 hours, he kept reminding me of my release date and my family. After the last hour of our conversation I finally calmed down and made the decision to let the situation go.

One day I was approached and questioned about why I let the dude get away with what he did and then informed that he was bragging and boasting saying, "I carried that sucka, he isn't a man!" I was getting tired of being strong doing the right thing, so I decided that I was going to kill this guy. That voice said, "If you don't do this, you will not be respected anymore." The DEVIL IS A LIE!

After work I entered my cell to grab my knife, a 6” concrete nail with duct tape wrapped around the handle to give it a little grip. I waited for the guard to open the door. You could always count on the door opening at 4:30 sharp but, for some reason on this day the door was still locked, and the guard was nowhere around. I was heated, I decided he had to go but, I couldn’t get to him and I didn’t like not getting my way, which made me even madder!

It’s was now 5:30, a whole hour had gone past, still no guard. Then a friend of mine told me that I had mail. I’d been in prison for 5 years at this point everyone had stopped writing. I was curious and my conscious was screaming, GO READ THE MAIL!!! Steaming with fury, I backed down and went to read my mail. I picked the mail up from my bed, it was 5 letters from my son.

The letters were written in crayon and consisting of seven words, “I MISS YOU DADDY, PLEASE COME HOME.” The other letters were stick figures of him, his mom and I. After reading his letter and taking in the pictures, I realized how selfish my mind set was

Here I am focused on protecting my image to the point I didn’t care about the repercussion or how that one decision would affect my future. It was in that very moment that I told myself, my son meant more to me then my image.

It was time to decide, CHANGE or STAY THE SAME. I gave my knife away, I was really getting tired of the fights, arguments and the consequences that came from my impulsive actions. The concrete was hard and cold, but I didn't care, I got on my knees looked up at the ceiling only to see molded paint and broken light fixtures; I looked right past the sight of things and started to talk to God.

I told Him I was tired and no longer wanted to live the life that I was living. There was no more interest in being the person that everyone looked to for foolishness. "Please Lord, take my life and do whatever you want with it, I am sorry for my actions in my past and I am praying and pleading for your forgiveness.

Whatever your will for my life Lord, LET IT BE DONE! were the words I cried to Him.

See men and women, God is all wise, He will send the right ingredients to make life taste good. He knows what spices to add, and He knows when life doesn't need any seasoning. In this case, God knew these letters would pierce the invisible armor around my heart and break me down!

He knew how much I loved my son because he placed the love that I had for him in my heart. He used those letters to help me make a better decision, a WE DECISION, not a ME DECISION.

I realized negative thoughts will starve if you don't feed them. When you are dealing with any thoughts that is not compatible you have to resist, deny yourself and submit to Him. We have all been blessed with the power to control, our minds. You must use the power that he supplies and make the right decision. The keys to a peaceful life are already inside of you, you just have to do one simple thing, TURN THE KEY!

I'M TIRED

Man, it's crazy how I keep messing up, making these selfish decisions,
I know that you're wondering, how and why, I keep getting trouble in Prison!
I remember stressing miles away, wanting to be closer to home,
Because I know it would be better for us, and I could have more room to roam,

Now my roaming is over, and I'm placed in a solitude cell,
All I could hear is you cursing me out saying boy, WHAT THE HELL,
I'm sorry Auntie for real this time, I know that I told you before,
But this time I made a Vow to God, that I will change inside this door.
I'm tired of fighting a losing battle, when I know that my kids need me,
I've changed this time just read my letters, I'm not who I used to be,
It's confirmation that I need to change, I see that life is not a joke,
I sat and focused on my past mistakes, and thought about the words that he spoke,
I thought about the way I've tried, it's been what, 30 plus years,
I just can't win I'm through with that, and it's time that I try HIS!

-

I'M TIRED

This poem was written for one of my associates. We were both in solitary confinement for doing something stupid. We asked ourselves at the same time, "How are we in jail WHILE WE ARE IN JAIL?"

We always found a way to get into some trouble, in his case he was guilty by association. In prison, all you have to do is be in the area of a crime and you are guilty.

The officers don't want to hear it, you can explain until you are blue in the face but, it won't matter you will have to fight your case from solitary confinement. In my case, I have a good heart and that caused me to often be in other people's business, which lead to me getting in trouble.

There was a Jamaican guy from Northwest Washington, D.C. that use to cook for a lot of inmates for money, we called him, Dred. He was known for his cooking and preying on younger guys that came into this prison system without a support system at home.

He was a homosexual and I didn't like him! Not because of his sexual preference, but because the young men were his target. He'd lure them in by feeding them, it was like a Mr. Rogers story but, it is so real.

I watched him push up on young guys like a vulture every time a new kid would come in the door. He would speak to me every time he saw me and I spoke back but, he knew I didn't like him. I made that obvious! I hated dudes that preyed on the weak, so I was just waiting for him to step out of line in any way so I could crush him, and he gave me my opportunity.

I was sitting in the T.V room watching sports. One of the younger guys that I fed every night walked in the door, his name was Baby-face, we called him that because he had a grown man body and a kid face. He was 19 and he had a ten-year sentence for carjacking, with no support coming from the outside, which made it hard for a young man coming into the prison system

I was fortunate to have my support system, so I made it my business to help out who I could. “What’s up BIG GOOCH”, he said as he walked in the door. I laughed and spoke back. He then turned to Julio and said, “Dread sent me down here to see if I could borrow your big bowl?” Julio was from Northwest D.C as well and he knew what Dread was doing with these young guys but, he just did his time and minded his business Immediately I got upset when I heard the conversation.

I asked Baby Face was he benefiting from running errands for Dread? He looked at me and said, “He gives me a bowl sometimes! “That enhanced my anger because the youngster was at my cell almost every night saying that he was hungry. I started adding food to my shopping list when I went to the commissary just for him but, I never asked him to do anything but stay out of trouble and go to school.

I hated the fact that these younger guys came in the system like this, no support and ignorant to a lot of things. I got up out of my seat and walked upstairs to Dreads cell. When I got inside the hallway to walk up the stairs you could smell his cooking seeping through the doors.

I must admit, he could cook, and everyone loved

it but, not me, I would never eat it. I walked through the doors upstairs and he was standing at the microwave with his back to me listening to his headphones. A lot of people were crowded around him because they wanted to see what he was cooking next and they were hoping to get a sampler.

My intentions were to pull him to the side and encourage him to at least feed Baby Face if he is going to run errands for him, give him a hustle. I tapped him on his shoulder he, turned around and was startled because it was me. He pulled his headphones off and said, "What's up Big Guy?" He said with a smile on his face.

I asked him to step aside from the crowd so I could speak to him.

Rule #1 When having a conversation with someone that has potential to go sour, try to limit the amount of people you speak in front of.

For some reason men always feel like they must prove something when they're in front of people, you never get the real person you always get an image of who they want to be seen as. He said, "No I'm cooking!" and turned his back towards me.

I hated to hear that because I knew he liked to show off in front of crowds. I leaned in and said, "At least feed the youngster if you're having him run errands every day!"

A couple of guys were being nosey, and they turned around to see the show. The look on Dreads face said that he didn't like my recommendation, so I knew that this was about to get ugly. His first words were loud, "MIND YOUR BUSINESS!"

That stopped all traffic in the hallway and now we were the center of attention. I stepped back and said, "Don't make a scene, if you don't like what I said let's go in one of these cells and get it off your chest!"

He got even louder screaming words that I didn't understand, I knew that was a tactic to alert the police because he was scared but, he had to put on a front for the people and hope for the best results.

"You don't want any trouble you just want to make a scene", I said and started to walk away. I loved to fight but, I loved to get away with it as well, so arguing with him in this hallway would limit my chances of doing so.

. He took his headphones off and placed them on the microwave and started walking towards me, he was really putting on a show.

. He was screaming and pointing his finger at me as he was speaking in a language I couldn't understand. I turned my back on him as a sign of total disrespect, that shows I didn't see him as a threat. As he got a little closer, I spun around, and he was closer than I thought. I didn't wait on his next word I just crushed him with a short right hook.

Dreads body went limp like someone shot him. He was snoring before he hit the ground. When I stood over him, he was sleep with his eyes open and a smile on his face. Everyone was shocked, nobody moved it was like someone hit the pause button. I turned around and went back. downstairs.

I waited a minute to see if he would get his self together and come back for more. About 30 minutes later, I went to the gym to work out. I didn't know what to expect when I came back to the unit but, this is what happens in prison, if you put your hands on someone there are no rules when it comes to retaliation.

I got back to the unit and Julio was standing at the door, "He has a knife and He's waiting on you in the stairwell" Julio said, and he stepped back from the door. "Thanks," I said, as I stepped towards the door.

I peeped my head in the door before I walked in, the stairwell was dark, but you could see in the blind spot when you opened the door. He wasn't standing in the stairwell like Julio said so I walked to my room and grabbed my knife out of the pole on my bed. I put my sweatshirt on to try to conceal my weapon, I walked down the hallway with a million eyes on me.

Everyone was quiet and as soon as I walked passed someone, they followed me upstairs, everyone wanted to see the show. I opened the door and saw Dread leaning on the microwave, he stood up when I came through the door and said, "You have to fight me again!" He had a scared look on his face but, he had to defend his ego.

. "SURE!" I said, as I slid the knife down the sleeve of my shirt resting the point of it on my finger tip so I could just slide it out in case he pulled his knife. He lifted his shirt exposing his waistline and said, "I don't have a weapon!" I was still cautious because Jamaicans like to put razor blades in their mouths and cut you across your face. I said, "ok" as I pulled my sweatshirt off and passing the knife to Julio.

I walked up on him so confident without having my hands up. "Let's go in this bathroom so no one can see us" I said to him. With a very confident approach, Dread agreed. As I turned my head, I felt a pop on my chin and everything went dark.

I was sleep on my feet, I didn't know what happened I just heard someone say, "Snap out of it champ". I regained consciousness and Dread was standing there in shock, I think I am the first person he's ever put to sleep. He made a huge mistake by not finishing me off, he should've kept swinging until it was over.

My mouth was hurting, and I felt blood seeping into it, he pushed my tooth through my lip when he hit me, I grabbed my mouth and "said, good shot but, you should've finished me!" I lost all control,

I attacked him with multiple combinations head shot, body shot, he didn't have enough arms to block my attack. He grabbed me and begged me to stop hitting him, I pushed him back and beat him to his body, I wanted to punish him for not finishing me off and hurting my pride.

"The police coming!" someone shouted.

I snapped out of attack mode and hurried to get out of the room My lip had a gaping hole in it so, I had to duck the officer if I wanted to get away. The police do a head count at 4:00 pm every day so I had to think fast. I went to the gym and acted like I was playing basketball and got elbowed in the lip.

I grabbed a random guy and he agreed to say that he was the guy who delivered the elbow, the officer went for it and sent me to medical to get stitches. I got to medical and they put 4 stitches in my mouth, I thought I got away until I heard my name come across the loud speaker," Inmate John Bell 37278-037 report to the Lieutenants office NOW!"

I knew I was in trouble when I walked in the office when I saw Dread. His face was swollen. I mean really bad, like Martin on the episode when he fought Tommy Hearn's. The Lieutenant said, "LOCK THEM UP!" So off to Solitary confinement I went, all because I didn't mind my business.

In life, this happens a lot with males, our ego's make us Super Hero's at times. We entertain indirect comments like they're said to us and put our two cents in every conversation just because. I can honestly say most of my fights could've been avoided in my life if I would've just minded my own business. My pride and ego kept me into a lot of situations that had nothing to do with me, mix that with having a good heart and you'll get a bomb of frustration.

I grabbed indirect comments and entertained them like they were said to me. I would see someone getting bullied or taken advantage of and voice my opinion. I had so much respect because of my aggressiveness and being fair. that I felt my opinion held weight in any situation but, it always kept me in trouble.

I remember when I called my mother and told her that I was in solitary confinement, she was upset, but more concerned with why. When I finally told her why I was there she said, "You have been so hardheaded that God had to sit you down so the two of you could talk. You have been in prison 4 years and your mindset is still the same. Look at it as a blessing in disguise.

This is an opportunity for you to come to grips with who you really are, no more masks." My mother dropped a bomb on me. Inside that cell, God started to speak to me and that's when I knew that I had to make a change for the better.

God was about to move in my life, and He needed me to be in a place where I could hear Him, He had to clean me up so I could be the man He was calling me to be. There are so many people out there waiting on the message that has been placed inside of me, and these people will remain lost until I deliver this message.

Men inside these prison walls, let go of that mindset that hinders you from getting to what you have waiting on you outside of these gates. Whatever addiction you have, release it today! Drugs, Alcohol, Smoking, Gambling, Sports, leave it all alone because it will cause you hindrance on your transformation.

> Sometimes we have to let things go that don't count in order to gain the things that do. When it comes to entertaining violence, the best way to look at it, is that person or the comment made more important than what you have waiting on you on the other side of that gate? Is that T.V. on that wall that belongs to the government worth the flat screen in the living room at home?

Is the washing machine worth watching your wife wash your clothes in your favorite outfit? Just being real, is that basketball or sporting activity worth being able to watch your son or daughter play sports at home? We must do a better job at recognizing our flaws and doing our best to get rid of them.

You will not be able to submit or hear what GOD is saying as long as you allow those character flaws to exist. I hindered my blessing by playing basketball, God had given me the word to stop. He was trying to tell me something but, instead of me being in the place where I could hear Him, I was always on that basketball court, arguing, fussing, and ready to fight.

I didn't know that God was working then. When He was finished working on that area of my life, I knew that it was time to stop but, I didn't, and that's when I got hurt again.

That's when I knew it and I told myself that it was time to work on something else. He was telling me to release what I like in order to gain what I Love. I finally put the basketball down and immediately, I started to write my book. That small sacrifice allowed me to be in a place where I could hear from God and that's when his voice became clear to me.

You are reading everything that he told me to say. I encourage anyone who is reading this chapter, let go of those temporary things to grab a hold of something permanent.

Prison is for losers and it's time to get traded to a winning team. It's time to be champions.

Remember, small things can create BIG PROBLEMS and hold you back from BIG BLESSINGS.

HELLO LADY

When I called you the other day, I believe our convo was nice,
But with all the things that you told me, I wanted to give some advice.
You told me that you were happy, but your voice says it all,
Because you have no help in your household and you're scared that you're about to fall.
I've guided you pretty well I see, or should I say I installed some knowledge,
Now you see why I forced you to work and paid for classes to college.
At times you thought I was being rough, but I was being more than a friend.
Because now I'm gone and you're good, now you're placed in a position to win,
Unfortunately, you chose a child to love, I believe he's older than you.
He says he's a man, as you provide for him, while he sits around looking confused,
Out of all the lessons you've learned from me, I was surprised at who you picked.

Now you're stuck, with bad habits I see, those one's that's hard to kick.

You say that you're cool, but it's no way, I can hear the pain in your voice,

My time is coming to be released again,
soon you'll have to make a choice.
I'm a better man, for your ears to hear and your eyes will definitely see,
Keep playing with him, and live life
behind, because you know where
you're supposed to be.

HELLO LADY

This poem was written out of a little envy, I was still trying to hold on to someone that God told me to let go.

I remember when I first heard about my ex-girlfriend moving on with her life, the letters came flying in from family and friends about whom she had chosen. He's nothing like you, he's this or he's that filled the lines of the letters from a few people. It fed my ego!

When I really started to think about it he was better than me in a sense, he could be a lot of things to Cynthia that I couldn't. He could be there if she needed to talk or cry on his shoulder, he was in a better position for her because he was a FREE MAN!

The part that she was really missing in me that he did not have was the money. The money in the relationship can be the reason why the relationship lasts or the reason why it falls apart; if the relationship is built off of money it will never survive. I was hating a little bit because he had what used to be mine.

I thought I could come home and show Cynthia a man

can be a man without having to base his every thought around money or ways to get money the wrong way! When we met, she was young, honestly, we both were I just had a lot more experience and began to take care of her. When I went away, I encouraged her to do the best she could for herself and not depend on any man to help her.

To me this was sound advice, because when I left, she was in a bad position financially, I didn't want that to happen to her again. I was her sole provider, and just like that it was gone when I got locked up.

I knew without my guidance and protection the streets would have eaten her alive. Cynthia was a good girl, she smoked weed every now and then but she really wasn't the party drug type, which kept her in her league. I exposed her to the finer things in life without overdoing it, she never wanted for anything and her taste wasn't high priced.

After speaking to a few guys, I discovered her new man was broke! I guess her replacement of me was someone who would come home at night over money.

I remember calling her one day, she was giving him the blues, I laughed at the things that she said to him. She was always feisty, if you didn't hold up your end, she will let you know.

I was fighting with the fact that I had done her so wrong, she did not deserve any of it. I felt like I owed her a better me and I wanted to give her the first shot at the new man I had become. Eventually, God revealed to me that she was not the one for me and I had to come to grips with us just being friends.

Every now and then I'd call to check on her, she'd try to hide her unhappiness, but I could hear it in her voice, when you really know a person you

know when something isn't right. I wished her the best and told her, "never hold herself back from who you had been called to
be. Also, remember all the things I taught you, keep the good, but the bad, never accept them from anyone again.

Honestly, this was the best thing for us both. If I wouldn't have been taken away from Cynthia, I would've remained the man I was. I would have destroyed her mentally and wouldn't have been able to live with myself. She now knows to never depend on a man, and to always have your own. I am proud of the woman that she has become, and I thank God that she recovered from the mess that I brought into her
life. GOD IS GOOD!

MY BROTHER

My brother, my brother, you're so gifted, in many

more ways than one,
You've been blessed with these talents in life,
talents that you could teach your son.
When you slipped and fell within your
trials in life, I'm sorry that I couldn't help,
I was constantly running from my problems in
life and put yours deep on the shelf.
I'm sorry my brother, never again, will I think my
worries come first,
I have to be strong when you can't, I promise
we'll break this curse.
We were born a team that the streets divided,
and we had no strength to see,

Now look at what has been done to you and look at what's been done to me.
We may be down but we're not out, there's a second half to this life,
Now it's your turn to bounce back this time, and do those things, that are right.

Even though that I'm stuck inside this wall and the enemy has you stuck in the streets,
You'll have strength to stand if you resist his will and become who you're supposed to be.
Your life is so precious, the small voice says, you were made to do much more,
But you knew that, and it's been times that you've heard that voice before,
He also told you that whatever you did, he'll forgive you when you ask,
All those things are behind you now, that's why it's called, your PAST.
We are brothers through the struggles in life, but you have a friend in the making,
You're out of your storm with scars to bear, when you submit to the enemy of SATAN.

MY BROTHER

"My Brother" was a poem that I wrote describing the relationship that I had with my brother. Someone who will always be loved and never will I let anything come between us again. This poem represents how one brother is caught in the game one way, and the other is caught up in another.

I've always looked up to my brother because he

was and still is a strong dude. It's just that God hasn't sat him down long enough to talk to him yet. He has a gift that a man would love to have, he is extremely talented with his hands and he knows it. Yet he only chooses to apply it when he gets ready.

I use to look at my brother like a father figure, unfortunately he led a life that inspired me to jump head first into the game.

We both have taken falls in life, but we both got up every time we fell. It was like we were getting divided more and more, every time we fell. It was like he was blaming me for his faults. I tried to be there for him as much as I could financially but, that never enough, my presence was the only thing that could.

During these times, he was still struggling to make ends meet and the enemy kept sending trials and tribulations his way to make sure that he stayed jammed up in his web. When I was home, I couldn't stop the trials from coming his way but, I could always contain how hard the storm hit.

When I was taken away, he felt like he lost a part of himself, sometimes I feel like a part of me was missing as well. Every time we talked on the phone; I could hear how sidetracked he was by the venom in his voice. I knew that the streets had him and bad too. It was nothing that he couldn't deal with but, the things that he knew would kill him, He couldn't resist.

My brother would tell me all the time he was good, and life was getting better. The very next time we would talk, he would just go crazy on the phone. Cursing me out, telling me to mind my business, He was totally a different person every time that I talked to him. Our phone calls would turn into arguments, and then things would get worse.

As I am writing this letter, I haven't spoken to him in about 5 months. I hear that he asks about me, but he never reaches out." I just wanted you to know that I would never turn my back on you, no matter what and I will always be there for you.

I'm absent from your life for a reason, there is a God in heaven that does not like for his children to depend on man, before they depend on him. I was taken out of your life because God wants to be the one who leads your decisions. As long as I am there you will always lean on me for help, and you will never lean on God.

I know you pray but, I don't know if you fully trust God. My advice to you comes from the Holy Spirit, the strength I have to forgive and forget things, comes from Jesus. I just want to encourage you to lean on his faith more than anything or anyone in this world, as God is the best source for your success. He's the greatest provider and the best I can offer you!

When you choose to submit to that small voice things will start to change. Champ give it up and give it to God! I want you to always know your son is the most important thing in life. Children are the best blessings a man can have, and we have to pay attention to our blessings and continue to build them up."

I want to encourage everyone that has gone through a struggle in life to teach your children to be better than you. Do your best to make sure that your they don't make the decisions that you made. If you have a sibling out there that is caught in the Jaws of Life don't ever lose track of their life or lifestyle show them, you care no matter what.

You never know what your words or presence will do. Some will tell you to mind your business and some might get mad. "SO, WHAT", they are your business and who cares if they get mad. Tend to your family, and never turn your back on them.

WHAT IS A FRIEND

A friend is someone who's there for you,
when you need a helping hand,
A friend is someone who listens to you, and
truthfully understands.
A friend is someone you connect with, and
you call yourselves a team,
A friend is someone who tells you the truth,
and never sells you dreams.
A friend is someone who walks with you, hand
in hand through the storms,
A friend is someone who knows the cold
and struggles to keep you warm.
Who are you, MY friend? To confide in when I'm
hurt?
Are you that friend when danger is near,
you manage to be alert?
Who are you, My Friend? Can you make
these words come true?
If you're that friend that I am looking for,
I promise to be your friend too.

WHAT IS A FRIEND

This poem is one of my special pieces mainly because it describes the first time that God gave me a short description of what a friend is.

I remember writing this poem in 2003, and it was for any new friends that tried to come into my life. However, I sent this to who I considered a friend only to discover I only had one true friend. A lot of people came and went, and I thanked them for that time when they came into my life. They filled a void in my life at the time, so I considered them SEASONAL PEOPLE.

This poem describes the friend that I have become since I have come into the knowledge of Christ. For the people that are out there who don't know what a friend really is, read this poem and ask them, does this poem describe you?

If it doesn't but they want to be better friends, this is a small instruction manual to those who are looking to be better friends. I realized that the men trapped inside of this wall depend on the world to be their friend. We look for the world to send us a good woman, someone who will be there for you no matter what, that friend you need to get over the hump.

It feels like you hit the lottery when you get that one woman who just comes to see you whenever you ask, does whatever you need her to, and gives you the emotional support that you need every day. When you call, she answers the phone every time, the sweet sound of her voice just brightens up your day.

Her name was Dee Dee, we've known each other for a long time. I think I was eleven when we met and became boyfriend and girlfriend. She would come over my house and we would rub on each other and kiss for hours, you couldn't tell us that we weren't doing the nasty.

Life happened and we got separated. In 2006 we reconnected, and I have to say that she came at the right time. I made up my mind to never allow a woman to get close to my heart again, I just couldn't take another heart ache.

I was surprised that I received a letter from her, yet I was super excited. Usually you have to reach **out to people in order to get a response, it seems like once you get to prison you become a memory.**

A few months went by and she and I were reminiscing and falling for each other at the same time. I couldn't believe that a woman who never benefited off my lifestyle would be the one standing by my side beating the doors of the prison down to see me. My heart was incased in a shell that could not be penetrated, yet God sent her to break through the layers of my heart with nothing but LOVE.

God will send someone into your life that will help you get through the toughest times, they will fill that role of a friend, family, loved one and a confidant. You really can't describe the importance of a friend while inside these prison walls.

To everyone that I sent this poem to, it doesn't mean that you ae not a good friend because we don't communicate anymore, it just means that sometimes good friendships are meant for better circumstances. Be good, and thank you for being a friend, even if it was just for a season. The friend that I have now is the best friend in the world. "Jesus Christ", He is Overqualified for the job.

I'LL BE THERE

I'll love you to the end, until the air leaves my chest,
I promise to be there for you, I promise to be at my best.
It will get rough for us sometimes, what is life without the storms?
I'll never plan to leave your side; I promise to keep you warm,
My heart has been yours COMPLETELY, for about 13 years.
We've fought through all adversity, and we've smiled through all the tears.
You've blessed me with three seeds in life 3 seeds that we call, "OURS"!
I promise to be a father to them, I promise to stick to our vows,
I've always felt your pain, you're not the only one who's sad.
Soon the storm will be over, and your rain will turn to sun,
Then we'll be together a family again, and our hearts will be as one.

I'LL BE THERE

"I'll Be There" was written for a friend of mine, he and his wife were going through a little storm that all couples go through when they are trying to hold on to their relationship through these prison bars. Prison relationship are a lot of work you make a commitment that is impossible to keep, you can't possibly think that just because you made a promise that it will be easy to keep.

There are too many things that come along with a prison relationship, distance, time apart, phone bills, commissary money, lonely nights, lonely days, and lonely holidays. It seems like every prison relationship is filled with arguments are about these topics, come with some pain.

Also, it depends on the terms of the promise, When I received my sentence, I asked my girlfriend to write back when I write, answer the phone when I call, and a visit every other month (depending on the location). I knew this task would be tough for her to keep but I asked anyway, whether she decided to hold up her end or not, I would be good. A lot of women make this promise to a man and don't know the stress that comes with the commitment. This poem is for every woman out there trying their best to keep their family together in spite of their situation.

Life does not have to stop because your man is incarcerated, in some cases women try their best to stop living in order to keep their marriage or relationship. It will not work; you have to keep living and enjoying your life until you get your other half back.

The more you put your life on hold, the more that you will resent him for his decisions. There will be arguments, you a argue when you're together so don't think that because he is gone the arguments will stop.

Relationships come with a lot of work, and God puts two people together in imperfect situations to see if they will survive the transition to perfection! No relationship will be perfect in the beginning sometimes it takes years to figure your partner out, makes the relationship perfect is the process.

From the courting stages, deciding is this person worth the risk, saying I like you, to figuring out if you have the same interest in life, and then working towards a common goal. Yet all of these plans get sidetracked when a man's lifestyle sends him to prison, that's when the real challenge takes place.

Some women lose their identity when the man is home, he takes care of everything, he makes all the decisions within the household. Some women don't even know how to function when the man is not there. I want to encourage each and every one of you, find yourself in the midst of this storm. Sometimes God will take away the things you think make you, so he can help you focus on who made you. This will probably be the most stressful time of your life, there will not be an easy day, but in your heart, you know if he's worthy of this sacrifice.

If you are waiting on the right man, this whole situation should make the relationship stronger so when he comes home it should be easier for you to love on each other and move forward. He will have a new respect for you because you did the unthinkable, you stood strong despite the circumstances. When a man goes to prison, eventually he'll start to see and respect the people and things that he neglected, some men take this time to reflect on the things that he has done wrong and does his best to correct his mindset.

When a man goes to prison, eventually he'll start to see and respect the people and things that he neglected, some men take this time to reflect on the things that he has done wrong and does his best to correct his mindset.

God has a unique way of speaking to and changing a man when he's in a space where there are minimal distractions. If he accepts God's correction and puts in the proper work, he'll become the man that he's called to be. The man that's ready to lead the household, one who the family can count on to make the right decisions.

I am proud of the women who stood beside their man while he is/was away, it's not an easy task but, you did it. I am also proud of the women who walked away when they felt as though it was too much to hold on to.

Some of you commit to a situation that you know will not work. When it's time to walk away keep it moving. Stop trying to hold on to something that you were supposed to let go while he was in the streets. Find YOU during this time apart from him and never lose yourself again.

A MESSAGE TO A WOMAN

Oh how do I love her, I know I do, Lord let me count the ways,
I know I caused her life some pain, from the loneliness of my days.

A gift to man, indeed she was, while my actions didn't back my words,
She loved me despite of all my flaws, and against the things that she heard.
If I called she'd come, "A LOYAL HEART," if I needed her love, SHE'S THERE,
Those women in my vision meant nothing to her, they could never compare.
She praised her king, her man, her life, there was no one else in her eyes,
But her king was a fool, less of a man, because he acted from his pain inside.
He's carried a burden from his pass relations and unfortunately, it fell back on her,
She didn't deserve it there's no excuse, because her love in her heart was pure.
By now he must be lonely, and in life he starts over again,
The guilt, the lies has killed his courage, and her heart he wishes to win.
Now she's grown her heart is hard, to forgive him is not in her plan,
A child when he left, confused and scared, but now she'll see a New Man.
He learned from mistakes he made in his life, your experiences will definitely teach,
Changed in his mind, changed in his heart, with a spirit that allows him to Preach.
He could have any woman, because he's a Rare Breed, and he really is one of the chosen,
When you're ready to be loved like the queen you are, remember my doors are OPEN.

A MESSAGE TO A WOMAN

This poem represents how a man can be remorseful for all that he has done to a woman. How he can sit back and remember all the good qualities a woman had regardless of her motive. This also shows that when you give your life to God, He will allow the feelings and the emotions that you hid for that person to come back.

He allows this to happen so you could feel the pain of what you've done and feel the pain of her departure all over again. She left me in 2004 and no matter what, I still tried to hold on to her, I wrote this poem in 2008, the relationship that

I was in at the time was not serious yet. We both were still going through doubt, and life was still taking her through storms that was tearing her apart.

The Lord allowed me to revisit the pain I felt and the memories of the good times we shared. I picked up the phone and called her and really apologized for the pain I caused. I lied to her about everything, when she asked if I had cheated on her. I would always tell her NO!

There was something inside of me that was telling me that she already knew. When I called to confess and asked for her forgiveness, she told me she knew I was cheating when I was home, then she said something that I never heard before. “I knew that you had other women, they were getting half of you; I wasn't going to leave and give them ALL OF YOU”. That conversation blew my mind, it also showed me that money will make you overlook things you know you're supposed to pay attention too.

As the conversation went on, we spoke about life and our plans for the future. She said things would never be the same between us and the only thing I could do was accept it. Part of me thought she was just saying that to hurt me but, as time went on our communication slowed down until it faded away.

The guilts of doing something wrong to someone will really eat you up inside, I found out after a long conversation with God, you have to forgive yourself when you really hurt someone. After you have called that person and confessed to your sins and you really are apologetic for what you have done; you have to forgive yourself and let it go. I thought about the things that I had done to Cynthia in the streets, I knew I was stronger than what I was showing myself. There was only one problem, I didn't want to be strong at that point. I didn't want to make the right decisions, all I wanted to do was accept the temptation that was in front of me.

One day I was sitting in my car and I got a phone call from Chrissy. We had a short fling when I was in school, because she wasn't moving fast enough for me. I was a very horny teenager and I got bored quick when things didn't go my way.

We ran into each other at Club U in Northwest D.C and swapped numbers, every time we got together it felt like we were in high school again, we would be smiling and laughing like kids. "Hey big head" she said, hey lady what's up? I responded.

"Nothing come get me, I need to see you".

Chrissy said happily Cynthia had already left for work and she wouldn't be home until 9 that night. "I am on my way", I said as I pulled of Homer Ave onto Suitland Rd. Traffic was light that day,

Tuesdays are always quiet in the Suitland area and the police don't come out until later. Business was slow and the chance of getting locked up on a Tuesday or Thursday were pretty high, because these two days were Jump-out days. The police chose these days of the week to surprise drug dealers by jumping out of service vehicles in packs trying to get an arrest. I was happy that Chrissy called because it gave me something to do, she lived in Arbor View on Brinkley Rd in Ft Washington. It took me about 15 minutes to get to her after stopping to get Remy and condoms.

When you get that call saying, I NEED TO SEE YOU, you better be prepared for the night. I pulled up and Chrissy was sitting on the porch in a summer dress, it was summertime but, it felt like spring outside, about 75 degrees with a little breeze going.

She smiled when she saw me and walked to the car, we haven't had sex yet but that will change today I thought to myself. Chrissy opened the door and got in the car, I smelled her perfume and it made me just want to skip the small talk and get right to the point.

She must have felt my energy because the first thing she said was, where are the drinks and let's go to your house.

I pointed to the back seat as she spotted the bag and made drinks as we navigated to my apartment, I lived in Naylor Gardens on Naylor Rd in Southeast D.C at the time so it would only take 15 minutes to get there.

I tried to slow down so I could get a few drinks in me before we got to the apartment, I wanted to have a buzz before we got there, the ride was long and silent, we listened to Frankie Beverley on the way there. Frankie always calmed the mood, the look on her face let me know that she meant business and I would be prepared for it. I managed to get three drinks down before we got to the apartment, I was feeling good and ready for war.

opened the door and got in the car, I smelled her perfume and it made me just want to skip the small talk and get right to the point. She must have felt my energy because the first thing she said was, where are the drinks and let's go to your house.

I pointed to the back seat as she spotted the bag and made drinks as we navigated to my apartment. I lived in Naylor Gardens on Naylor Rd in Southeast D.C at the time so it would only take 15 minutes to get there. I tried to slow down so I could get a few drinks in me before we got to the apartment.

I wanted to have a buzz before we got there, the ride was long and silent, we listened to Frankie Beverley. Frankie always calmed the mood, the look on her face let me know that she meant business and I would be prepared for it. I managed to get three drinks down before we got to the apartment, I was feeling good and ready for war.

We got out of the car and walked in the apartment; Chrissy had on heels, so I helped her down the three steps that lead to the building. As I walked behind her the scent of her perfume got me aroused. She didn't know what she was about to get into. I unlocked the door and we stepped in the apartment.

It was laid out, black leather sofa and love seat, oriental area rug, black dining room set, with the flat-screen T. V's. I shared a two-bedroom apartment with a buddy of mine, so I had to make sure he wasn't home, if he was it wouldn't have made a difference anyway it was on.

Chrissy was standing behind me as I walked through the apartment calling Lee's name. When I re-entered the room Chrissy was naked, she caught me off guard but, she would never know it. I stared her in the eye never breaking my gaze as I got undressed. As my clothing hit the floor, Chrissy was moving closer, my excitement grew with every step she took. I loved the sound of her heels clicking on the hardwood floors, she looked at me and said, "Sit in the chair" with a look of lust in her eyes.

The dining room set had chairs with strong legs, so I did exactly what she said, I loved when women took control. She flicked the condom on my leg and told me to hurry up. I laughed but her gaze remained the same. As I slid the condom on, she was circling the chair running her French manicured nails across my back driving me crazy. She stopped in front of me as she seen that my mission was complete.

The air condition was on full blast but, I felt the temperature rise in the room. I reached out to grab her legs so I could pull her closer to me, she grabbed my hand and placed them on her breast. This is the only four play that I need she said as she straddled me, she grabbed my penis and guided it into her sweet spot, I only touched her breast for a hot second, and she was soaking wet.

As Chrissy slowly sat down on my manhood, she arched her back with every inch that entered her. Her skin was extremely soft, and she smelled amazing. As Chrissy sat on the last inch of me, she paused for a second and dug her nails into my chest while her eyes were closed. I grabbed her butt with one hand and her waist with the other. I always did this just in case my partner didn't know what they were doing, I could show them.

Chrissy opened her eyes and started grinding her hips in a forward motion. She had a pretty good stride so I let my guards down. I grabbed her breast and she leaned her head back as she rolled her hips. The Remy started to kick in and I felt myself swell up inside of her.

She sped up as I grabbed her throat, not 10 minutes into it she climaxed and got up said "Thank you" and went to the bathroom.

I was in my feelings but, I had to keep my cool. She was a control freak and she loved to play mind games. I walked in the bathroom to get in the shower. She passed me on my way in the bathroom and didn't say a word. As I turned the water on, Chrissy came back in the bathroom with my phone.

It was ringing and the screen said CYNTHIA. Immediately I tensed up. Chrissy walked back into the living room, so I closed the door and answered the phone," Hey baby" I said feeling like a piece of trash. "Where are you"?

Chrissy asked. "

At the apartment" I said, "Good I need you to come get me right now, I came on my cycle and I don't have any clothes". Cynthia worked at the Grocery store on Alabama Ave in S.E, about 4 minutes from the apartment so I had to decide quick, I'll be there I said without even having a plan.

I thought that I could leave Chrissy in the apartment and go drop Cynthia off. I jumped in the shower to get Chrissy's scent off me, when I got out of the shower and entered the living room Chrissy was fully dressed sipping Remy. Look I have to pick up some money at the

Safeway around the corner, I will be right back. Chrissy looked at me and said, "I am not staying here, whatever business you have to take care of I am going with you, your roommate is crazy, and I don't trust him". A lot of women said that about Lee but, that was another story. I'm not going to be but five minutes, I don't care I'm not staying here. My phone rang again, and it was Cynthia. I answered the phone and said, "I am on my way", and hung up.

I had to think quick because I was getting frustrated not knowing how things were going to work out. I said, "Look I'm picking up the female that cleans the money don't say nothing to her because you're not supposed to be with me". "Okay" Chrissy said as we pulled off, I made a right on to Naylor Rd and sped up the street. I don't know what made me think this would work but I felt like it would. I made a right in the shopping center on Alabama Ave and pulled in front of the Grocery store and got out.

I walked in the store as Cynthia was closing out her register, I walked up to her and asked her if she was okay, she said she was good, but she had bad cramps. "I got Lee's friend in the car they were fighting, and I am dropping her off, don't say anything to her because if she responds wrong, I know that you are going to fight".

I was lying good. "I don't feel good just get me home." She said in a low painful voice. We walked out of the Safeway and headed towards the car; Chrissy was sitting in the front seat as Cynthia stood at the front door waiting for Chrissy to get in the back. Before I got a chance to say anything Cynthia just got in the back without saying a word.

I sped down Alabama Ave until I hit Suitland Rd, the light was green as I crossed Southern Ave flying past the high rises and the cemetery, I was going as fast as I could trying to get Cynthia out of the car.

I passed the car wash and the liquor store and caught the light at the shell gas station. I made a left at the Laundry mat on to Homer Ave, then a right on to Lewis Ave and a right in Cynthia's Court, all the fellas were outside.

They looked at me crazy as I pulled up because they knew I was dealing with Chrissy and I lived with Cynthia. I pulled in front of the house and Cynthia got out, I walked her upstairs and opened the door.

I went straight to the bathroom and ran her some hot water," Do you need anything before I come back in?" I'll call you, she said. I kissed her on the forehead and walked out the door.

It's crazy because every time that I would cheat on her; I would come home feeling like trash. It was hard to even come in the parking lot of my house because the guilt would be eating me up. The women I was cheating on her with were not worth losing what we had, I can honestly say that.

I knew most of them were there for the money, or the person I'd shown them. Regardless of the fact they were not loyal people, they knew I was in a relationship and they would still pursue me, and they would be perfectly fine with being number two. I realized people will only deal with you because of your availability, if you make yourself available, they will take advantage of you.

At the end of this poem I spoke about my doors being open. At the time I wrote this poem I would've accepted her back in a heartbeat but, God stepped in and told me to move on.

God had placed another woman in my life, so I had to focus on her and what the Lord was trying to show me within this season. Men, we miss out on a lot of blessings by not being able to see what's in front of us. When God puts a good woman in your presence, even if it's just for a second, take advantage of that season and see what He is trying to teach you about her, or about yourself.

We have to acknowledge when God is trying to tell us something, whether it's through people, places, or things, we must put our pride aside and really focus on who He puts into our lives. It's all up to us, you have to ask yourself certain questions. Do you have a woman in your presence right now that you are not being faithful to?

Is she worth your time and efforts? Is she bending over backwards to be with you and dealing with your inconsistencies as a man? I ask you to reevaluate your position, decision making, and most of all, your understanding of what a Man is supposed to be. I hope you men recognize when God has placed a Good Woman in your life. It's not promised you'll get a second chance to love a good woman.
Don't miss out!

YOUR TURN

Why can't you stop drinking? Is it possible for you to care?
It's crazy how it controls you, and you get mad when you have to share.
I remember when you hit your son, to the point where his legs went limp,
That drinking controlled your thoughts, because you never took care of him.
I remember when he was small, he used to look up to you,
But that drinking took all your time, saying I'll be there but never come through.
You gave your son to the streets, put all the weight on his MOM,
Your desires had you sleep, when you woke up it was time for prom.
That's how much you missed his life, YOUR SON, the neighborhood star,

Remember you said you'd come to the game,
but instead you went to the BAR.
Now your son is in prison, and you can't see
where you went wrong,
Now you sit confused with life, as you listen
to them old sad songs.
How could you take credit, for a man that
the streets have built?
That's why you cry at the sound of his voice,
because you heart is so filled with guilt,
God is the reason why he's a man, in spite of
the life he was living,
He sends his love through letters and cards,
that tells you that, You're Forgiven.
Be there for him when he comes home, regardless of
his age,
Because it's never too late to be a FATHER, it's time
that you step on the STAGE.

THE FAMILY!
JOHN E BELL SR, MOMMA, AND CHAZ!
(MY CHILD)

YOUR TURN

This is a poem I wrote to my father; these were some of the feelings I had as a child. If I was old enough to tell him how I felt about the way he was treating me, these words would have filled the conversation. I just wanted to let my father know that no matter what we have been through I will always love him. Our past will not control how I love him today. God has a very special way of making you understand/accept the word FORGIVENESS!

I remember back in the day when my cousin lied on me, my father was calling my name but, I did not hear him. My cousin told my father that I said shut up, my father was drunk at the time so when he heard that, he slapped me so hard I saw stars. I thought my head was about to come off my shoulders.

Whenever my father was drunk, he would have no control over his anger and I hated it, just seeing him in such a weak position in his life. I looked at my father as a tough guy, a strong man but, when he was drunk, he didn't have the same effect on me. He would look so helpless and it would make me weak. I remember sitting in the yard at grandma's house and my father and his siblings would be arguing over 1,000 things.

Sometimes it would be over who drank the liquor, who bought this, and who bought that. Liquor was the main reason why they used to argue, fuss and fight, saying and doing things to each other that they wouldn't say or do sober. I used to cry sometimes when my father used to get drunk, he couldn't even understand what people were saying to him. He couldn't even see at times, didn't even know who you were. I used to hate the fact that drinking was that important to him. One moment

he would be emotional saying" I LOVE YOU BOY", and the next minute he was ready to kill someone.

I never knew drinking could make you forget everything you did the day before; it wasn't until I experienced it for myself. I was the neighborhood star, basketball and football; I was the best in the family (ARGUABLY) I used to show out on the basketball court and the football field.

The guys in the neighborhood used to come to my games and cheer me on, they were my support system. I would look to the sideline and hope I would see my father at the game, only to be disappointed because he was not there. I was hurt every time I would ask him to come and he didn't.

The field was only 10 minutes away from his house, but for some reason he would never show. He used to gloat over the praises people would give him because I was his son, "John Bell your son is tough on that court, he is so fast and physical on that football field". None of those comments were good enough to get him to that field and it crushed me.

I remember when he came to one game, I was so excited to see his van pull up. I told myself I was going to get 5 touchdowns and 10 sacks. I was going to Show Out for my dad, and I did exactly what I said. I ran around that field with so much energy and passion yearning for my dad's approval and attention. I would've tried to hurt myself on that field just to make my dad come to another game.

If he was not at work, he sat in that yard and drank All Day. At times I felt like drinking was more important than me, if it wasn't it sure felt like it. From little league to high school my father came to about 5 games, I don't know if I am exactly accurate but, I know it's extremely close. It used to crush me to see all the fathers at the games and not see mine, parents used to ask me where is your father? I used to always lie and say, AT WORK!

My sports support system came from other parents, my mom was a single parent, running her own business with no help, with three kids and a grandchild, so she could not be there. Man, I can't describe how hurt I was to be so good but, still be unrecognized by the people I thought should be paying attention, I just wanted the family to come to see me play.

I remember getting ready for prom, my mother took me to see my father and he was smiling from ear- to – ear. The first thing he said was, "I'M PROUD OF YOU SON". I didn't care what he did, every time he would say something like that all my anger and pain would go away for that moment. I loved this man with all of my heart but, I always wrestled with that one question, why doesn't he love me the same?

My father bought me a gold chain with a cross on it for prom and a car for graduation. I was so happy; you couldn't tell me he wasn't the best dad of them all. Even though my mom had to force him to buy the gifts, I still appreciated it. I really didn't understand the whole situation, and still today a lot of us won't understand. My relationship with God provided the understanding I needed. It was revealed to me that when your father is never shown how to be a father,

it will be hard for him to be one as well. You never know the damage

that's done to a child that doesn't have a relationship with his father, the pain of your childhood can really affect your future. I realized that when I repeated some of the acts that I was disgusted with, I made some decisions that trumped what my father had done to me.

I was taken out of my son's life when he was 5 years old, I knew that if everything went right, I wouldn't return into his life until he was 18. I missed the opportunity to take him to little league, moments he'll never get back. He did not have his father there to take him to practice or encourage him to play.

I deprived him of that opportunity, he never had a chance to succeed or fail at playing sports, all because I wasn't there. I tried my best to make sure I would always be able to provide for my son and be there for him. My diligence to make sure that happened, led me to make some decisions that put me in a place where I couldn't be there for him at all. This was a poem from a man that failed to be the father he wanted his father to be to him.

WHO IS HE

I'm a KILL him he did it again, this time he hurt my heart,
I've tried to help him with all his faults but, I don't
know where to start,
He lies too much he hurt my son, and he's a
terrible curse to my mother,

He sees her cry but, he never stops, and then he
says that he Loves her.

He's even killed the family name, being a victim of
those drugs,
A momma's boy a loser's game, acting like he's a thug.
He went to jail, came home early, and now he thinks he's
a star,
He thinks the meaning of making it is having money,
clothes and cars.
When he's caught, he calls my mom and hopes she
can save the day,
I used to get mad at the look on his face, as the squad
car rolled away.
He thought he was smart had all the answers, but
really, he's dumb as a brick,
Out of all the pieces in the puzzle of life, where could
this possibly fit?
I want to give up but he's my man, and I love this
dude to death,
He's killing his self, I have to stop him before
there is nothing left.
I went to see him we had a talk, and my point he
still doesn't see,
All this time I looked in the mirror, and who he
was, IS ME!

WHO IS HE

Why do we always point out someone else's problems and never see our own, for those that know my brother and I, they know our story. The entire time that we were in the streets it was like we were battling each other, when all I really wanted was for us to be on the same page. There were times when my brother didn't make the right decisions and at times I didn't either.

I realized a wrong decision is a wrong decision, my flaws were just as worse as his. I just made a conscious effort to expose his sins so I could hide my own. I caused my mother the same amount of pain he did, I was no better than him in the eyes of God.

I should have seen the pain my brother had caused my mom and chose a different route. I added to her pain instead of doing my best to take it away. Every time he did something wrong, people would run and tell me about what he had done; I would just sit there and speak badly of the situation like I was squeaky clean.

A lot of the criticizing was needed but, I had to get my life together before I could judge his. I had to apologize to him for not being a better brother and encouraging him to do better but, I could only do that when I was doing better. I had to learn to stop putting the spotlight on someone else's problems and start to focus on my own.

When people read this poem, they will think that I am talking about someone else but in the end, they'll see that I was talking about myself! When you look at someone else's mistakes and be judgmental, you fail to see that you are only looking in the mirror. We have to realize that if you are in the same lifestyle, that persons mistakes can easily be one of your own.

The best thing we can do as a people, is get our lives together so we can put ourselves in position to be a positive influence to those who are not living right, we have to realize that we are no better than the person that we are encouraging.

A lot of times we overcome our situations and speak about someone else because we think we are stronger for some reason. We have to use that same power or encouragement it took to help us get over the hump and help someone else.

Tap back into the feelings you had when you wanted someone to encourage you, then use that to encourage someone else. It's time for us as a people to wake up and see our own faults instead of always broadcasting someone else's. It's time to help those who need it, remember you are one slip away from needing help.

CHANGE ME

I once traveled a road in life, where I accepted death as my friend,
With fear in my heart "I STILL RAN" in a game that I couldn't win.
I thought that I could survive in life, with the promises of the streets,
But later I find that soon my life, would not belong to me.
It took a couple of trails I'd say, but fortunately I survived the most,
Now I know that I had to change, and refrain from chasing a ghost.

What will they say when they see the things, that
God has done to me?
One thing they'll say upon my return, is WOW he's
finally free.
Free from the stressful times in life, that had
me really confused,
God gave me a talent for good, so I know that
I'll have to choose.
Choose his road where the future is bright, where I
know I'll see my light shine,
I'll stand on His word and resist the test, I'm a leaf
on a positive vine.
I've been a soldier for Satan living wrong, while ill
things start to look good,
I've lied, I've cheated, I've betrayed the best, I've
even sold drugs in my hood.
But now it's over no more of that life, I'm a soldier in
the fight for Christ,
My eyes are open I'm focused now, and on this
side, things look nice.
The work is hard but it's for the best, and I
know the outcome is great,
I'm glad I'm woke, IT'S MY TIME NOW, I
changed before it's too late.
Prepare for me I'm on my way, this doesn't
even feel strange,
Remember friend it could be your turn,
and I thank him for MY CHANGE.

CHANGE ME

This poem represents how a man thinks he could survive the test of the streets or the broken promises the street life presents to you. Sometimes I sit back and think about the things I've been through while in the street game. I remember sitting on my bed and saying, I have to go out here and try to survive another day.

I really meant try to SURVIVE because in that lifestyle you never know who is next up to try to take your life. I realized when you are in that lifestyle, your life does not belong to you, any tragic event can claim your life, any upset competitor can pull the trigger. Your life does not belong to the person that is living it, and you never pay attention until it's too late!

One day I was sitting in the apartment counting the profit from the day before, $7,500 was a good profit for 8 hours. I had the busiest drug house in the area at the time, I had the place set up like a real business. There was a camera in the window so I could see who's coming in before they got inside the door. You had to be buzzed into building and then my door man would let you into the apartment.

I didn't have to get out of my seat to do business with you, walk in, tell me what you want, count the money in my face, get your product and leave. You could only come in one way, the back of the building was gated off and I chose this building because of that reason, mainly to limit the options the police had when they came to raid the apartment. I had acid inside a bucket in the closet, so I could dispose of any evidence when they came.

Business was good I had a new connect and the product

was amazing, everyone wanted what I had but, I wouldn't sell it to any of the Hustlers. I broke 36 ounces down into $20, $50, and $100 pieces.

My door man and I were the only ones in the apartment at the time, his name was Rue, he was from Negril Jamaica. He moved to the states 3 years ago to help take care of his mom, who was battling Cancer and she needed some assistance.

He lucked up and got a job at the post office making good money, which made things a little easier to assist his mom. He was single, wasn't the best-looking guy and he spoke bad English, so the dating scene wasn't for him.

He and his mom lived in a house about 10 minutes from the apartment on Homer, he was a working man that took a wrong turn. He paid for a prostitute one night and she introduced him to Crack and the rest was history. Now he's a full-time door man in one of the busiest drug houses in the area.

I had my head down at the time, so I didn't see the two dudes walk up on the porch. The buzzer rang and I picked up the phone and asked who it is, I didn't recognize the faces on the camera. It was My cousin's baby's father Bo, and his buddy from Seat Pleasant Md. I saw him a couple of days ago at Cedar Hill liquor store on Suitland rd.

He told me he had just come home from doing 20 years for murder and he needed some help. I told him to come to the apartment and I would take care of him, so here he was walking in the door as I was putting the last rubber band around the money.

His eyes lit up as he walked into the apartment, I had two pistols on the table beside the money, a black Glock 40, and a Silver 44 Bull Dog revolver with a black rubber pistol grip handle. I didn't know if his eyes lit up because of the guns or the money, it didn't matter I thought to myself, HE WAS FAMILY!

"What's up lil cuz/" Bo said as he snapped out of his gaze,

"What's up champ" sit down, I said.

"This is my man Duck we did time together and his lil brother Scale moves work around here as well". Bo said. I looked at Duck and automatically I didn't like him, it was something about his eyes and body language that made me keep my eyes on his every move.

"So what's up" I said, "I was at a crap game yesterday in Seat Pleasant and your name came up". My name always came up in conversation because of the product I had and wouldn't sell to no one that didn't smoke it, that's how you limit competition. "Some dudes were talking about robbing you" Bo said.

I looked up and asked "WHO"? He said some youngsters around my neighborhood you want to go around there Bo said, yeah let's go let me tighten up here first meet me outside I said. They both got up and walked out the door into the parking lot, I was mad as hell as I thought to myself these suckas talking about robbing me they got the wrong one. I grabbed my Glock 40 and the extended clip, it held 21 bullets, but I took another clip just in case.

"I'll be right back Rue don't open the door;" I said.

I gave Rue a $20 piece of crack to smoke to hold

him until I got back. I walked out the door into the parking lot and they were sitting in a blue caravan, Bo was driving, and Duck was in the back seat.

My conscience told me to get in the back, so I told Duck to sit up front, I climbed in the back of the caravan and closed the door, one of the most important rules in the game, never sit in front of someone you don't trust.

The caravan smelled like liquor and weed, and the cloth seats were stained up pretty bad, the windows were tinted really dark so you couldn't see inside. We made a Left on Homer and sped down the street, Bo was a horrible driver, so I just hoped he got us there in one piece.

We crossed over Porter Ave and Duck looked in the rear-view mirror, he was moving around too much and that made me question him more. I had the Glock in my pocket aimed at his back seat just in case he tried anything. We rode in silence all the way there until we got close to Bo's neighborhood.

"So, who are these dudes" I said.

"Black and Tye, they always running schemes and robbing people" Bo said.

"What's the plan when we get around here, we don't have any guns on us," Duck said.

"I do and seeing their faces will give me a head up so if they pop up around the spots I frequently visit, I will be a step ahead of them".

"You have your pistol on you Gooch?" Bo said,

"Yes, sir I don't leave home without it", they both tensed up.

We approached a convenient store with a big sign saying open 24 hours on it, there wasn't anyone out there when we passed.

"This is where they hang Bo" I asked.

"All day everyday" Bo said,

"Okay, well let me make a call. I responded. I called Mac, he was from Glenarden Apartments in Landover Md, but he knew everyone and what they were doing in the area.

"What's up champ" Mac said as he answered the phone,

"Homie you know a Black and Tye that hang down at the 24-hour store in Seat Pleasant?" I asked.

"Nah homie, I serve all the dudes down there and there isn't a guy name Tye or Black that hangs down there," Mac said.

"You sure" I asked?

"Soldier you know this is my side and no one moves or makes a dime without my knowledge, so yes, I'm sure" Mac said. "Ok because I am with Bo and Duck we rode through here because

"I was told these dudes are supposed to be robbing me," I explained. Mac went silent for a second then he said who are you with again?

"Bo and Duck," I said,

"Homie those two dudes are robbers champ they pull moves all the time; you got your pistol on you" Mac said. "Yep all the time" I said.,

"Homie get away from them dudes as soon as possible and don't let them dudes know anything about you, them jokers are Cut throat" Mac said.

When I said their names, Bo and Duck looked at each other, they knew that Mac knew who they were and was filling me in on their hustle and what they're known for. I watched them as we drove down the street,

"Take me back around Homer Bo"! I said with a little aggression.

He looked at me in the rearview mirror the whole ride back, Duck looked around nervous and constantly picking at his hands.

Bo was driving fast, and I really didn't care, these dudes couldn't be trusted, and I needed to get out of their presence.

When we got back around Homer it was live, all my men were outside which made Bo and Duck a little more uncomfortable. They dropped me off in my court and sped off, my phone rang, and it was Mac, "What's up champ" I said?

Homie them dudes were trying to rob you; don't let them dudes get close to you again. It never crossed my mind that they were trying to rob me, at times your ego blinds you to things that you need to see, but God was protecting me the whole time.

When God brings these moments back to my memory it just makes me praise him even more, because he was protecting me in the midst of my madness. I am just grateful that I have survived what I have been through, and able to share my testimony with those who need to hear it.

I always run into some of the people from my past and sometimes we sit back and go down memory lane a little. It gets uncomfortable sometimes because it can be easily mistaken that you are glorifying the lifestyle that you once lived.

It's easy to slip back into the memories of your past if you speak about them enough. I know that the comments will be plentiful when people find out who I have become, NEGATIVE and POSITIVE.

It won't matter, mainly because the negative comments will always be from people who are stuck in the same position that they were in before I left.

They will be the same people that will be coming to you asking you how you did it, and how can they do it! It never fails, people will talk about someone who is doing something positive or different.
Until they see that different is working, and then they'll want to be a part of the difference you're making.

You'll have some that can't forget what you've done or who you were in your past, you just have to see them; and look right past them! Your testimony is the only thing that they need to hear about, the lies that you told, the deceitful behavior, the pain, the bitterness.

You'll have some that can't forget what you've done or who you were in your past, you just have to see them; and look right past them!

Your testimony is the only thing that they need to hear about, the lies that you told, the deceitful behavior, the pain, the bitterness. Those things that you had to endure in order to get to the place where you are now, is all that you need to be speaking about. Some people will even think that you are telling a lie, but it's not up to you to make them believe you, you just have to speak your peace, and keep it moving.

I am at peace with who I have become, I

don't have to look over my shoulder anymore, and I don't have to worry about the police taking anything from me. I am very comfortable with the new lifestyle that I have been given. See in all actuality this is the life that all street guys want, we are out there doing what we are doing, yet we just want PEACE we want to be able to have a good life; we want to be able to enjoy our families.

No one wants to wake up every day and know that there is a great possibility that you might not come home. No one wants to live like that, if you are in the streets, I know you are tired of looking over your shoulder, you are tired of having to question people that you call your friends

You are tired of being scared or paranoid, every time that you walk out of the house. YOU ARE TIRED! I am challenging you today, get out of that lifestyle and let God give you the life that you deserve, the life that you want. Come on over to the other side and live in PEACE, I'll be waiting for you! GOD BLESS!

HELLO SIS

Hello sis I miss you, and I still haven't gotten a letter,
Are things still going wrong out there,
hopefully they have gotten a little better.
No little' brother I'm good, and you have
your own problems in there,
I'm always concerned for real; you know
how much I care.
I'm going through things in my marriage, and
the kids are stressing me out,
I knew there was something about him,

but I married with all of my doubts.
You rushed into that marriage sis, without really thinking first,
I thought that things would get better, but things have just gotten worse.
All I'll tell you is pray on it, I know that it sounds strange,
But that's the only advice I have, it's the only way that it'll change.
I've prayed a lot for years, and nothing seems to work,
You've tried it your way so switch it, how can it possibly hurt.
I love him but I'm not in love, I can't live life unsure,
I want a marriage filled with love, something that's special and pure.
I'll ask you sis to listen to me, what I'm about to say is true,
I'm going to point you the right way and tell you what to do.
Take a minute and get on your knees, and form relations with the Lord,
It will be times that you'll be confused, and also lonely and bored.
The outcome will be so beautiful, something you'll never compare,
It's the way to a good relationship, something that you can share.
Brother...you're behind that wall, all holy and talking really crazy,
I'm tired of running from who I am, I'm tired of being so lazy.

**I'm telling you sis if you trust in God, He'll wipe those tears from your eyes,
Until you submit to change in your life, you'll never receive that PRIZE.**

HELLO SIS

"Hello Sis" was a poem that I wrote to my older sister. This chapter is about how I was trying to protect her from a bad relationship. I used to be so overprotective of my sister that I would try my best to make her friends uncomfortable when I came around.

I tell you, she used to be so mad at me, her famous line would be "YOU ARE NOT MY FATHER!" I would laugh it off and continue to act like a fool. I looked at it like this, if you were not tough enough to protect my sister and my nephews, then you could not be around her.

My test would be to just come around when I knew she had company. If the guy would act scared or nervous when I walked in, he had to go. You had to be a strong to be able to deal with my sister, she has a smart mouth, very bossy and she can really get on your last nerve. I always said that she has the mindset of a man the way she always gets smart out of her mouth, with women or even men.

When I went to prison, I couldn't do my little test on the guys that my sister would get involved with, so I kind of felt bad when I spoke to the dude that she was planning to marry.

The minute he and I engaged in a conversation I knew he was not the one. He made to many promises to me and he didn't even know me, it was all a front to try to get my approval. When a man really loves a woman, he doesn't worry about impressing the family, he doesn't worry about making them like him. He just concentrates on making her happy and that should make them happy.

I asked her to come to the prison to see me and when she came, I just asked her two questions," DO YOU LOVE HIM", and "ARE YOU HAPPY?" She couldn't look me in my eyes when she answered both questions. Right there and then I knew that something was wrong, and she was marrying him hoping that marriage would make things better. It's a shame that a lot of us get into relationships after we see the flaws that we don't agree with, hoping that things will change.

These things have to be acknowledged and addressed before we move forward, and before we say, "I DO". We go through a thousand arguments and fights before we're able to say, THAT'S IT, I can't do this anymore.

You have to look at how much time you've wasted, trying to figure out something that you already knew. Sometimes you have to go through somethings in order to see the real person, everyone has a representative (the person that they want you to see) then once you get comfortable, they show who they really are.

I feel that if a woman really wants a man to love her, she has to love herself first, she has to know what love is, and she definitely has to Love God. In life and relationships, we tend to focus on the Creation and not the Creator, I believe that He is the only person that knows the truth about both parties, and I believe that He is the only one who knows what each person needs.

When you are getting into a relationship, you have to go to God first, and ask for his approval, and his direction. Once he sends you the message, you have to believe that it's from him, and listen the first time. When your girlfriends say, GIRL HE ISN'T THE ONE, and then one of the family members says, he isn't the one. Don't be blinded by love and look over the warnings, trust your gut and get out.

This is a warning to those who are in a situation like this as we speak, don't wait until the bank account in empty, don't wait until you are sick from stressing too much, don't wait until he starts to hit you or starts disrespecting you.

Don't wait until you have destroyed your relationships with your family because of the relationship that you have with this guy. Do yourself a favor and listen to the voice of God, no matter who it comes from get out, it's very important that you listen, your life depends on it.

MY FAMILY

I remember back in the days, when we kept a smile on our face,
We could be found at 2224, or DEFINITELY at 2228.
These were the places of sacred land, where our family would always meet,
I miss those days and we all can agree, there was

nothing like Houston Street.
When hard times would come, we'd pull together, and weather the toughest storms,
If the power was off in one house, we'd bring heaters to keep them warm.
Through a series of tragic events in our lives, our family has split apart,
These events have stolen a lot from us but can NEVER possess our hearts.
That's the true place where the love is, away from the Ego and Pride,
Where we show interest in our associates, and the love for our family, WE HIDE.
As I look at our family from the outside, some cool, some still in the streets,
Some spend money on frivolous things, and some struggle to make ends meet.
Well I'm tired of it all I'll need your help; we all know that things must change,
If we do it together, we can conquer it all, and get that flag off our names.
I'm home, now my thoughts are clear, and all my decisions are wise,
You'll have the real me, no more illusions, I've come out from behind the disguise.
I know we'll prosper if we come together, our strength can conquer a city,
I've been strong for years I can't do it alone, I'll need my whole family, WITH ME.

MY FAMILY

"My Family" is a poem I wrote, which is inspired by

the memories that I had left of the family that I knew. I sat on my bed every day and remembered the good times we had in our past, I call home only to hear that after my Grandmother died, (MARY ESTELE HALL) our family has just taken a turn for the worse.

See, my family is just like any other family, we argue, fuss, fight, talk about each other but, one thing I do know, our family would always pull together when it was time. If one of our family members were in trouble, WE WERE THERE, if someone needed advice, THEY GOT IT.

It was just certain things our family did not tolerate; we were like a big gang and you couldn't mess with one and not see the others. We had a meeting spot back in the day, you could always find someone at Grandma's, or my Aunt Jennie's house.

Those were the two places you could always find a cousin, uncle, or an auntie, but most important you could find GRANDMA, the backbone of our family. Arguments could be about to happen, and grandma would step out the house and the arguments used to stop. You could be sitting on the wall in front of the house and grandma would come out, you knew that you had to move.

There was no cursing around grandma, it was her presence that used to change a lot of things, when grandma died things just started falling apart. I remember when I got the news, I was in solitary confinement and I called home to find out that my grandmother had passed on.

I knew that she was sick, but you never think that when a family member goes to the hospital, they won't come back. I didn't think about grandma not coming back from the hospital, I just thought that she would be sick for a second, and she would be fine, but that was not God's plan for her life.

You are never prepared to lose someone that you love, it's hard to deal with but you must move on. I have learned to deal with death in a totally different way now, I understand that God has a plan for everyone's life and we're his kids.

Knowing that I can't question what he does with the people I love. I also realized a lot of people depended on my Grandmother, she was their crutch, and if she continued to live some of our family members would've never grown up.

Like God had to take a life for someone else to live their own. I got a strong revelation from God, He said," Your family members are my children, I have a plan for each one of my children so, when it's time for me to make a decision for their life," I WILL". I was just letting you borrow them until they fulfilled their purpose, then I'll call them home."

I had this revelation after I called home to check on the family after grandma's funeral, only to find out that my cousin Tonya had died. The same cousin whose daughter got shot in the neck a couple of years back and was on life support in the hospital. She knew everything and could tell you everything about someone in the family.

She was one of the other pieces that kept our family together. For those of us that was in the street life, my cousins house was the safe house, I'm really going to miss her. It seemed like every time I would call home someone was dying, it got to the point where I didn't want to call home anymore. It was hard doing that time without my family members supporting me, but it was harder calling home only to hear that some important pieces of the family had passed on and I could not be there to say goodbye.

During my incarceration both of my grandmothers passed away. I had a special relationship with them. I love my mother's mom's (Erma Lee Matthews) fried chicken and lemonade. I loved to hear her sing while she sat at the window.

I loved to hear her soft voice, and the way she used to bribe me to go to the corner store to buy things she knew she wasn't supposed to have. I loved that woman to death! I heard she was in the hospital, so I called home to speak to her and our last conversations were painful. She'd ask me questions that let me know she was about to pass on.

"Are you going to be
here before I go"?
Grandma would ask
"Yes, ma'am!"

I knew that I would not be there before she passed on. That was one of the things that still bothers me today, I didn't spend the time with my grandmothers like I was supposed to. I don't have the memories with my grandmothers that everyone else has with theirs.

I never taken them out to eat, sat with them and just loved on them, or bought them anything to put a smile on their faces. Their last memory of me when they passed on, I was in jail and I couldn't be there to say goodbye.

smile on their faces. Their last memory of me when they passed on, I was in jail and I couldn't be there to say goodbye.

That crushed me the most, see you never know how much a family member means to you until they're taken away. I call home now only to her someone talking about the other, but not doing anything to help them. Family, we have the same problems as any other family, but we possess strength that other families don't have. All hope is not lost, we have time and plenty of opportunities to get it together.

Yeah some of the family members get on each other's nerves, but that doesn't mean that they're not family. Yeah sometimes we argue and fight, might say some things that hurt, but that's what families do, nothing is done within a family that cannot be healed, you have to want to do what's necessary to heal the situation.

Most of the things that we fight about are so PETTY, how can this be? All I have left is the memories of our past, those memories allow me to keep hope in our family, those memories have me in constant prayer, hoping God can/will restore what we have left.

We must put our pride and ego aside and move on because that's where the problem lies, we must tap back into the times that we had on Houston Street, when love kept us defending one another.

I feel as though that we don't love God enough as a family, that's why we can't see past the small situations that keep us apart. Hopefully we can put a little more time into praying about a situation, instead of gossiping on the phone about it. We can allow God to do what he does best. RESTORE BROKEN SITUATIONS, but we must let him in as a family.

I am on my way home and I know that I am not going to like what I see but, I am going to do my best to get things back to the way I remember before I left. I have a strong desire to get things back to the way we used to be, when an argument was just an argument and never turned into years of not speaking.

Where a little tussle would be talked about over some ribs and a beer, where we would come together and fight for our family, instead of fighting with our family. I love every one of you and I really hope and pray that we all accept this warning from God. We have to make sure that the laws of God are preached in every household from now on.

We must make sure that we teach our kids about Christ, because we are an example of what a family goes through when their foundation is not built upon Christ. Let's teach this next generation how to Pray, how to Love, let's show them what we used to do as a family. If we don't make the decision to heal these wounds, we will allow the devil to keep pouring salt on it, and the wound will continue to infect the next generation.

I have waited a long time to get back to you, and it's going to be a couple of more years until I get there. Just know I am praying until I get there, because I know Prayer is the only thing that will hold you guys together until I get there.

Listen family, I Love you, ALL OF YOU, and just know that I don't hold any ill feelings for any of you,

I am not mad that you don't write, send money, pictures or come visit, I am more upset that you take advantage of the opportunity to love on the ones you see every day.

WOMAN OF HONOR

The woman of the world deserves more praise,
which should be easy for us to give,
If it wasn't for the women who loved us, it would be impossible for us to live.
They say we can't live with them, but how
can we live without?
They heal our wounds and protect our
hearts and erase our minds of doubt.
When the kid inside controls us, they accept
our adolescent mistakes,
They listen to us when we need them, and with
our problems they would always relate.
This is the day that we praise them, for the
sacrifices made for our lives,
A special woman deserves this, your MOM,
your Aunt, and our Wives.
This lady I call my mother, who held me when
times were sad,
Who encouraged, loved and consoled me, and
played the role, when things got bad.
I bet all my money on MOMMA, and believe she'll
know what to do,
This card is for a woman of honor, so accept the
praise that's DUE!

WOMAN OF HONOR

This poem represents the mothers of the world that don't get enough PRAISE for the things that they've done or acknowledged for the mothers that they refrained from being. Sometimes we tend to forget about a lot of things that our mothers have done for us, or we look over the sacrifices they've made.

We wonder why every time we get in to some trouble, we call on our mother for some advice, and then they end up helping out, physically or financially, we know she is going to help, that's why we call.

Some of us are 30 and 40 years old, what happened to WHEN YOU ARE GROWN, YOU ARE GROWN? So many of us say as youngsters, when Momma don't let us have our way. I CAN'T WAIT UNTIL I AM GROWN, so I can get out of your house.

Then later on in your adult life, you realize when you were at Momma's house, you had no worries. Momma's protection is the best protection, and in most cases momma's advice is the best advice, even if it is one word like, NO!

Sometimes if we just settle down and just listen, we can escape a lot of the problems that you have been experiencing. I remember every time I got into a jam. I could always call on my mother, and whatever the issue may be, Momma would find a way to get me out of it. Then I realized that my mother made a lot of mistakes growing up, while ducking them as well.

I have to tip my hat to her for not falling into the temptations her environment was presenting to her. She could have easily fell to the temptations of drugs, or prostitution, this is the temptation a young mother was facing at the time.

Some mothers fall on hard times, and the first thing they do is start to scope out the big boy drug dealers and start to have sex with them in exchange for monetary gain. That is what I call, CONTROLLED PROSTITUTION. Some mothers allow a man in their lives at a low point, and he introduces her to abuse.

I am not speaking badly about the mothers that have overcome these things or are experiencing these things as we speak. If you are one of these MOMS, or one of the women that are experiencing these things, take a stand, and step out on your faith and trust God to give you a way out. You are stronger than the addiction that binds you, you are tougher than that man who's trying to control you. The reason why he is trying to control you is because he cannot control HIMSELF, or anything else.

This poem is to just acknowledge the mothers who didn't allow the things of the world to interfere with the life that they wanted to live, and who they wanted to become. YOU MOMS ROCK! I want to thank all the moms who got it right the first time.

I want to thank all of the moms who bounced back, I also want to thank the moms who are struggling now but will get it right this time. If Momma didn't raise you, someone in your life has played that role, so let's start to acknowledge who they are, and the person they refrained from being. Sacrifices can't be overlooked anymore, you have to acknowledge who they are, and who they are not.

A MESSAGE TO THE PARENTS

My heart bleeds for these children, who are gunned down in the streets,
My soul cries for these kids, who break law to make ends meet.
It's painful to see parents give up on kids that they raised
I praise the parents who are strong, who keep their kids out of that maze,
As I look back in my past, I dreaded walking past a Hurst,
But the things that I see now, are Bad
and they're getting worse.
Alcohol, pills and weed are considered
as party drugs,
It's empty inside these households, so these things substitute the Love,
I put my hands up over my ears, when I hear the things they did,
Parents I pray that you hear me, PLEASE go and get your kids.
This message is for all the guardians, from here to across the nation,
If we don't stand up and stand out right now, be prepared to lose GENERATIONS!

A MESSAGE TO THE PARENTS

I was watching the news and I saw that some young kids had been killed again, and they were killed by some kids who were younger than them. My heart ached and my spirit was sad, I felt so bad for the kids and their parents, I went to my cell and I thought about the funerals I'd been to and the death that I had seen along the way. Which put me in a deeper state of depression. Then I thought about the guys that I used to run with and what they had to deal with inside of their household, I see that all of our households were just the same. Momma manning the ship, and Daddy living without acknowledging his responsibility.

I wondered why we all thought and act the same way to a lot of situations, then I realized it was because we all were being raised by our Mothers. Neither one of us really had our fathers in our life, our conversations would always be about MOMS and never about POPS. After doing my research, I knew why the kids I saw on the television were acting up, it's because they lacked the leadership of both parents.

That plays a big part in a kid's childhood, the love and the nurturing of the mother, and the guidance and discipline of the father. When you look around today, how many of you mothers are raising your kids without the father? How many of you have to deal with your son hanging out in the streets trying to be like one of the local guys he admires? Regardless of how many times you say, I don't need no man, or I am good, you are LYING. No parent can sit here and tell me they wouldn't appreciate the other parent stepping up and helping out.

You can be good but, its better when you can wake up and know you have the help from the person that helped you create the child. I see some mothers working two or three jobs and I used to say, that's so unfair but, moms had to do what she had to do. The way the system is set up, a single mother has to make the ends meet regardless of the circumstances, and a MOTHER will.

So, she has to work as many jobs as she can but, the result of that, the child is left to fend for himself while mom is at work. Mom can't/won't be there to see the signs of him changing, or when he needs to talk about something on his heart. Or to stop a mistake she would've caught if she would've been home to catch it. If there isn't a father figure in the household, there's a great chance he'll be attracted to the life he sees in the streets.

If she's not home and there is no guardian to help guide the child, the streets will do it for them. Parents listen to me please, if your child is one of those kids that's acting up out there in those streets, go get your child. You can make all the excuses you want but, I bet you the Judge or the Jury is not going to care about your excuses.

The prison system or the graveyard is going to claim your child. I don't want you to just sit back and watch the enemy destroy your child and strip generations from your family.

Every chance you get, LOVE ON YOUR

CHILDREN, whether it's Hugging, Listening, or just having a one on one just to see what's on their mind. There are a lot of kids out here in society that would love to have a friendship with their parents, and I feel as though it would help out a lot. Some parents work so much that their kids grow up right up under their noses and the conversations start off like this, WHEN DID YOU START DOING THAT?

I don't care how old your child gets, they will never be too old to receive the Love, you have to offer. Don't neglect them of the Love they need and have them to go out into the world and substitute the Love they need with the Love that's presented.

Drugs, gangs, crime, and teenage pregnancy are waiting for your child in those streets. I encourage you to go get what's yours. Sometimes your form of Love will be tough, but it's the Love that they need.

Sometimes it's going to be tough to love them after you hear some of the things that they have done, it's still your job to show them you care, even if they don't like it.

Ask yourself this question, do you think God gets mad at his kids? Do you think that he stops loving them? Well no matter what we do, when we get to far out there, he comes to get us, so if you think that you need to go and get your child, GO GET THEM!

A MOTHERS PRAYER

Please Lord, Protect Him, don't let Him die in those

streets,
Please Lord, Lead Him, and guide the path of His feet.
Please Lord, Father Him, show Him the things that'll cause Him harm,
Please Lord, Love Him, because He's out of the reach of my arms.
Please Lord, School Him, show Him how to love His lady,
Please Lord, Instruct Him, on the way to take care of His baby.
Lord hear me, I'm sorry, forgive me for the things I've did,
Please Lord, help me, show me how to raise my kid.
Lord Hear me, I'm pleading, I beg for His soul to be saved,
Lord please give Him mercy; I don't want to pray over His grave.
Please Lord, I'm pleading, and in my heart, you know I care,
So I beg you Lord for mercy, and I thank you for hearing my Prayer.

A MOTHER'S PRAYER

"A Mother's Prayer" was inspired by the time I sat in that cell and wondered how much pain I caused my mother, or how many times she didn't get any sleep at night, because she was up praying for me. Or how many times she was scared to answer her phone at night, because she was scared it would be a phone call about me.

I used to pay attention to the parents that

would be in the visiting room, it would always be the mothers or the grandmothers, you would rarely see the fathers or grandfathers. I just sat back and listened to conversations sometimes and I would hear the grandmothers, or the mothers say. "I AM PRAYING FOR YOU", or "I never stopped praying for you, you need to get your act together so you can come out here and take care of these kids".

I used to hear those conversations and they would always be about the prayers that were had for us. I understand the only reason why I survived out there in those streets, was because I had someone praying for me, I don't know exactly what they were saying but I'm glad they were saying something on my behalf.

I also understand that some parents are praying for themselves, some parents became responsible for another life before they were even ready. Having kids at an age where you're still trying to figure out life, will cause you to make some mistakes. Some of our mistakes are a direct result of the mistakes that our parents have made that never got fixed.

We all need forgiveness, and we all need a time to sit back and reflect on what we did as parents and children. We cause each other a lot of pain but, never accept our part in the way things are playing out. I will say this, my mom was/is the prayer warrior that kept me alive while I was in my madness.

I had to call my mother and apologize for the pain I caused, and I had to thank her for the prayers that went up for me. For the mothers that are reading this chapter, don't stop praying for your kids, you have to understand that your prayers are the only prayers that's keeping your kids safe, or in some cases. ALIVE.

I really appreciate the mothers; you are the reason why some of us got a second chance. I also understand that some of the mothers have prayed for their child and still lost them to the streets, leaving them to question God's ways. Just like I spoke about in "SHE'S HOME", your kids are God's children, you only get to borrow them until God is ready to call them home.

The only thing you get to do is love on them, pour wisdom into them, and guide them until God calls them home. You didn't fail mothers, you raised them with the knowledge you had, so let go of that burden that weighs on you. God has the last say, you must make sure you are direct in the things you ask Him to do for your children.

I LOVE YOU MOMMAS!

THE HIGH SCHOOL STAR!
THE ONE WHO MOMMA PRAYED FOR!

MRS. MARY ESTELLE HALL!
(MY DADS MOTHER!)
THE BACK BONE!

MRS. ERMA LEE MATTHEWS(GRANDMA)!
THE PRAYER WARRIOR!

SHE'S HOME

At times in life we lose, and the pain just makes us cry,
And we get on our knees and call on God, and plead with him asking him WHY,
How does a family endure, the pressure of a life being taken?
Just get on your knees, He'll put you at ease, knowing that God restores his creation.
The pressure and pain will go as it came, if we trust in our Lord and Savior,
Even though she's moved on, we'll still have a bond, as she rests in the hands of our creator.
The joys of life we had, the memories we'll always cherish,
She's smiling in her storm as her soul moves on, because a child of God can't perish.
Family I pray that you're smiling, I know how hard it can be,
If you hear God's voice, just Smile, Rejoice, she's safe, because now she's WITH ME.

SHE'S HOME

"She's Home" was inspired by the pain of losing both of my grandmothers all in a 6-month period. I remembered calling home and getting the news one after another, first my mother's mom, and right after that, my father's mom.

I had my own relationship with them, but our relationship was filled with adolescent memories as an adult. I really didn't spend a lot of time with them because I was so distracted by the streets. As I sat inside this cell, hurting by the fact that I was losing so many important pieces to my family, and not be there to say goodbye.

When they both got sick, I spoke to them and they both asked the same question, WOULD I BE HOME BEFORE THEY LEFT! I responded in tears YES, but I knew that I wouldn't be there before they passed and that was the reason for the tears.

I wrestled with the fact that the last thing that they heard from me was a lie, I knew it was the wrong answer to give, but I didn't think the truth would help their condition at the time.

Can you imagine never meeting your grandfathers? and now as I look up, I am about to lose both of my grandmothers and I never had a chance to really create any new memories with them.

The only thing that I could do was go to prayer about the situation, because it made me feel so guilty, I felt like I deprived them of a relationship, and of good memories with their grandson. I needed some relief from this pain because it was eating me up.

I called upon the Lord and He gave me an answer that I'll never forget. He told me that my grandmothers were His kids, and He allowed me to borrow His kids until He chose to take them back from me, He said that once they have completed their purpose, they had to move on.

I couldn't wrap my mind around this answer at first because this was an answer for a mature Christian, and I was just a babe at the time. It took me at least 5 years to really accept this answer from God. For 5 years I carried the guilt along with me until I was mature enough to move on.

It was crazy how we can get an answer from God and not accept it until we let go of our stubbornness. What God did was allow me to go over the memories that we shared, I realized that we had a lot of memories that could not be replaced, I had more memories with my mother's mom, then I did with my father's mom.

My mother's mom lived with us for a minute, so that explains why I had more intimate memories with her, she would sing and make lemonade and fried chicken. The best in the world, I have never tasted fried chicken like the one my grandmother cooked, her lemonade had just the right amount of sugar that made it sweet, but not too sweet.

I used to come in the house from playing outside and the first place that I would go is straight to the refrigerator. I would gulp the lemonade down right out of the jug (NASTY) but, it seemed like it tasted better when it came out of the jug.

She caught me one day, smacked me in the head, and said that I was selfish because I didn't care about the other people in the house. I will never forget the memories that we shared. I remember my father's mother was the backbone of my father's side of the family, a little woman but, she had a Strong

Will, and a Loud Voice. She would stand on the porch and scream your name and you could hear her blocks down the street. I used to hear her, and I would say, somebody is in trouble, it would always be my cousins Shawneese and Tisha. She would be on their backs like a book bag.

That was the place where we all would meet, GRANDMA'S HOUSE. We shared a lot of memoires at grandmas and I was wrestling with the fact that I would never hear her voice again. I would never taste the fried chicken and lemonade again.

I was wrestling with the fact that the memories that we shared would be the last memories that we share. I had to go to God and ask for comfort, He told me that my grandparents were sent here for a reason, and once they have completed their purpose they had to come home. I understood what God was saying, and I knew that everyone must go at one point. I was just thankful that I had a chance to share those memories with my grandparents. I guess it's better to have brief memories, then to not have any at all.

Thank you, Lord, for letting me borrow your kids, and thank you for restoring your creation. I bet my grandma is in heaven frying chicken, and my other grandma is watching the Orioles game and hollering off the porch.

Remember people, when we lose our loved ones it's not our job to get mad and question God, it's our job to enjoy them while they are here. If you are not spending time with the ones that you love, start to take advantage of the borrowed time that God is giving you. Don't end up like me, regretting the memories that you didn't make, or not taking advantage of the time that's given.

THE TRANSFORMATION

I came in this cell confused, blinded by my own sight,
I thought that I knew it all, and all my decisions were right.
I was placed in a cell with a friend, who was already deep in the works,
But he was smiling, reading, and laughing, but I thought this was supposed to hurt.
I told him that I was cool, because I knew why I was here,
No, this time it's different, there is something that you need to hear.
Forget that champ FOR REAL, I'm not trying to hear what they're talking,
He said no my son IT'S YOU, and the path that you are walking.
Who me, man I'm straight, somebody really set me up,
No my brother please listen, it's God who's holding you up.
See you're looking at the things that you lost, and not the things that you'll gain.
Just be patient you'll see; God will soon explain.
See you're sinning, living wrong, and it's cool when you can laugh,
But you're still not doing what He told you, and you're not walking your path.
A strong path was laid for you, from the womb into

the grave,
But you chose a path UNRIGHTEOUSNESS,
and you've been the enemy's slave.
WHAT, Man not me, I'll never be a slave to no one,
Just look at all you had, what was lost, and what was won.
You sat deep in thought confused, staring at the
walls in this place,
But I knew that look, I seen it before, because it
once was on my face.
Are saying that this is a message from God, is this
how this thing works?
He said he has to deal with you, but brother it's
going to hurt.
Hurt, what you mean HURT? Man, I did this before
Okay my brother relax, but you'll CHANGE when they
close that door.

THE TRANSFORMATION

This was the first poem that I wrote, which started my transformation. I dreamt I was granted a sentence reduction for immediate release, but in my heart, I knew I wasn't ready to go home. I knew I wouldn't survive the streets in the mindset that I was in, as it was only the beginning of becoming the person I was destined to be.

I asked GOD to make sure that I'm ready mentally, physically, and spiritually. When it's time to be released I want to be more than ready to fight in this war. He answered my request, shortly thereafter, I was sent to solitary confinement for an investigation for contraband. This punishment was a blessing in disguise.

As I entered the Sally Port corridor where processing for

solitary confinement takes place, I felt at peace, a calming if you will. After changing into the orange jumpsuit, I was asked, "Do you want any books from over there?" as he pointed to the cart that served as a library on wheels. "Yeah", I answered immediately. "Give me the bible!" After I asked for a bible we headed to my room. I was ready to start this journey.

At first, I thought my cell mate and I weren't going to get along, he was Hispanic. At that time our communities did not get along well, especially in confined quarters. Out of my immaturity and ignorance, I judged him walking through the door.

Regardless of what my feelings were, I used prison etiquette, I spoke and introduced myself as I entered the room. The cell door shut and immediately the temperature started to rise.

The toilet was off to the right as soon as you walked in the door, the shower was encased in between to slabs of steel with a filthy shower curtain hanging in the front to block the view.

The bunk beds sat to the left connecting to a steel desk and chair that sat under the small skinny window facing a concrete wall. The walls were pale grey and moist from the humidity in the cell, I hated this place immediately, but I was here now.

My cell buddy name was Hector, he was from Mexico City. He had 5 kids, 4 girls and a son Jackie, Irene, Miya, Rosa, and Hector Jr. Their ages were 16,15, 12,10, and 8, His mom and dad passed in a car crash while coming to see him while he was in prison. I felt sorry for him because I couldn't imagine the pain, he was going through knowing that his parents died trying to support him with a visit. I looked him in the eyes as we spoke, it was a form of respect and to also let the person you are conversing with know that you demand the same.

I saw the pain in his eyes as we spoke, tears would well up in his eyes as we got on the topic of family. He would pause a few times to gather himself, then we'd continue. All of his kids were by his wife Ana, she was from Mexico City, as well. They met when they were teenagers got married at twenty and started a family. Ana's family ran the drug cartel in Mexico City, they were responsible for a lot of the drugs that entered the U.S. Also, they were responsible for a lot of the killing that took place in Mexico City.

Hector was a hit man for the cartel. He said he was given an opportunity to make some money smuggling drugs across the border. He was making $20,000 every trip, but he had to stay in the U.S until the same person he delivered to brought back the money. Sometimes it would be 3 or 4 weeks. He missed Ana a lot so he asked the cartel could he be assigned another position, that was the question that changed his life.

There were a few tough guys the cartel did business with that were slow paying for their product after it was given to them on consignment. That was a huge mistake when you are dealing with someone's money after they have trusted you with their product expecting you to pay. They asked him to go collect the money from a local drug dealer in town. They gave him a picture, a name, and colt 45 pistol 8 shot automatic. His only instructions were, “Don’t come back without the money”!

Hector said he thought it would be an easy task, go to San ‘Angel a neighborhood inside the city, locate Ramon get the money and it would be done. Hector didn’t know that Ramon ran San ‘Angel, he was a ruthless kingpin that loved killing. Hector said as he entered the neighborhood, he felt uneasy, as he navigated the streets to the address on the paper. He was on high alert clinching the pistol in his jacket pocket.

As he bent the corner to the last street he knew this would turn out bad. The man that was in the photo stood at the end of the block, 5 more steps and they would be face-to-face.

Ramon was a huge man 6”6 300 pounds with hands the size of baseball mittens. He stood by himself smoking a cigarette holding a bookbag in his giant right hand. As he turned his eyes said that he knew who Hector was. His eyes started to squint as Ramon got closer. With sweat pouring down his back Hector clinched the pistol and approached Ramon.

Hector looked like he was about 5”9 185 pounds all muscle which looked like a midget as he looked up at Ramon, they didn’t speak they just nodded their heads as Ramon held out the bag. Ramon grabbed the bag and gave a slight nod and walked away, didn’t check the money because he felt that no one would be crazy enough to cross the cartel. As he bent the corner of the building two men jumped out with mask on, Hector was still clinching the pistol and his reflexes made him pull the trigger while the gun was still in his pocket.

The first shot hit the bigger guy in the gut as he collapsed to the ground, spinning on his heel he fired again, hitting the smaller attacker right in the head. Hector said that it happened so fast that he didn't have a chance to think. He turned to his left to find Ramon standing right next to him, grabbing the gun in his pocket ready to fire again,

Ramon put a Bulldog 44. revolver to his head and said, "Stop shooting, give me the gun and get out of here." Hector froze at first and then he did what Ramon asked and walked away.

As he broke his gaze, he continued to speak to me about the situation, I was shocked that he even shared that with me. He said that he remembered every detail because that day got him a life sentence. He has no chance of seeing his family in the free world again.

The two guys he shot were the sons of a big politician in Mexico City. Ramon gave the gun to one of the police that was on the payroll, his normal routine. The police won't find evidence that they already have. When the news got out who the two dead men were, things changed, a $500,000 reward was issued for the person who was responsible for these kid's death.

The police officer didn't make that much from being on the payroll and took advantage of the opportunity. They lived in very poor conditions, so a man's dream was to get enough money to move his family to the U.S.!

He turned the gun in, and the gun had Hectors fingerprints on it, no matter what the cartel tried it was too much heat coming down on them because of this case. It was either give Hector up or give their business up,

Hector turned himself in hoping he would get Self Defense. Mexico Cities laws were different, especially when it comes to politician's son's getting killed. The only good thing that came out of it was he got extradited to the U.S to do his time, they would've tortured him in Mexico City jails.

Hector was in prison for 8 years before he gave his life to Christ, he said that he makes it his obligation to spread the word of God to anyone he meets. Hector said he was given a Life sentence by the judge, but he doesn't serve that judge, God has the last say. It seemed like God opened the door for us to converse with each other like we had known each other for years. We talked about God and family for hours, and a lot of the questions that I had about God and spiritual things, were answered during our conversation.

When God wants your attention, He will use the strangest people to speak to you, sometimes it's better to hear the truth from someone who doesn't know you. After about 10 minutes into our conversation I knew that this was the work of God.

I knew HE allowed this to happen to me, I had to be in a place where I could really hear him. This is the place where I would reach my full potential and discover the man that I was called to be, the man he needed me to be so I could fully serve him.

While I was in this cell, I encountered several looks into the mirror, but what I really didn't know was, these looks in the mirror were really looks into MY SOUL. I saw the character flaws that needed to be corrected, all I saw was the love for self. Not listening to no one and thinking the only person opinion that mattered, was my own.

He allowed the truth about a lot of things I was hiding from to come to light, so I could face it head on. That was the only way I could be in right standards with him, confront my flaws, and deal with the lies I have been trying to hide from.

Everything that was hidden inside of me God brought full circle. I was face to face with it all! It was a constant process, test after test! I couldn't reach my full level of worship because I was holding on to a lot of bitterness and hatred. I was a hypocrite and a back biter. I always told people how much I hated my associates with these characteristics, yet I had them myself.

God ordered me to get in contact with people who I had wronged or hurt, to ask for forgiveness, but first, I had to forgive if I wanted forgiveness. Even the people who hurt me and would never acknowledge it or apologize for it! HE told me, "It's impossible to serve ME while holding on to unforgiveness!" and it wouldn't be until then that he would expose my gifts to me.

I had an amazing conversation with God about the desires of my heart! Nothing was off limits; I bared my soul. From entrepreneurship to blessing me with a talent or gift so that I could serve him and edify the people, but most of all, "FEED MY FAMILY."

After that conversation, the next night it was like

God was sitting on my shoulder whispering in my ear. I managed to write 25 powerful poems that night. I couldn't believe what I was reading, the words that were spewing out on to that paper brought me to tears. To be able to pull situations from my past into the forefront and write about them in poetic form was amazing.

God allowed me to get my hands on a book that gave me a divine understanding of the spiritual gift that he blessed me with, the gift of exhortation, which is like spiritual counseling. Poetry is my talent; exhortation is my gift. It was like my heart was fully revealed and the person that I saw when I wasn't surrounded by crowds, was who I saw inside of that cell.

I've always had a mean streak and a temper that was hard for me to control. When I sat back and measured the good and the bad things that came with this temper of mine, I knew that there had to be a change. I never wanted to hurt people but, I did it because it was expected of me. That was the image that I had to chase in order to be protected and respected in the streets. I endured the consequences that came with that image as long as I could until God said, "NO MORE".

They came and took my cell buddy away, as soon as I was left alone, the process got a little tougher. God saw that I was depending on my cell buddy for the answers that he wanted to give me. One thing about God, he is a Jealous God. Whatever you put before him or trust more than him, He will remove it, person or thing. I started to hear

His voice, it was loud and clear but, yet it came in a whisper. I had no desire to read nothing but the bible! There were so many books in my cell but I was only motivated to read the word. In the midst of digesting the scriptures so many things became clear to me.

Before this interaction with God, every time I would try to read the bible, it was like reading a blank page. This time was different, I started to get the full understanding and a revelation of what I was reading; It seemed like everything I read was pertaining to me and my experiences. I stayed in that room for a month and a half by myself.

When I was given a new cell buddy, I realized that a lot of the old me was gone! A lot of the old thoughts were not there anymore. My cell buddy tested that a lot, almost every second of the day.

At times I would be furious with some of the things he would do or say. At times, the old thoughts would come back like a raging fire but, it was always a calming that would come over me. It felt strange but, it felt like I was really accomplishing something every time I listened to the voice that said" NO" and submitted to that calming peace. I didn't know what was happening, but I know it felt good.

There were times I wanted to be ignorant or immature I would feel so bad for even entertaining that thought, later I discovered the feeling was called CONVICTION. I had to humble myself a lot, I had to hold my tongue. I never had a handle on my anger, it always controlled me and it was like when the button clicks on, it was time to perform. To avoid my former result, I started thinking before I reacted.

In my past I'd make up my mind to move and once I was there it was no turning back. Now that I'm finding my way, the off switch to me was called," JESUS"! It felt good to know that you could physically hurt someone but have will power to walk away resisting the urge to expose someone who's not physically capable of defending themselves.

It was crazy, here I am this tough guy and instead of being who people have come to know me to be, I encouraged him to be himself, and not the person that's socially excepted. I saw so much of me in him! That's when I knew that I had to go back and teach those who were just like me.

Once the spirit got into me fully, I just submitted and let it take its course. Oh, it wasn't easy submitting; in fact, it was the hardest thing I had to do. It's crazy that the hardest thing I ever had to do was BE MYSELF. Everyone used to tell me how real I was, funny thing is, I only allowed them to see what I wanted them to see.

The real me was an easy- going jokester with a good heart. Although that was often exposed, once my ego or image was challenged, I would just snap. This was the change that consisted of tears flooding my pillow at night, or just breaking down crying during the day. It wasn't hard coming out of character, but it felt good knowing that I could control my actions.

The Lord finished the first stage of my transformation, which was me letting go of the image, taking off the mask, and accepting myself. That's when God allowed me to start encouraging others in solitary confinement with me. I shared my testimony a lot while there, I found myself getting more comfortable sharing it after every encounter. It was astonishing to see brothers that knew me before my transformation come into the SHU and see me after, and hear the words spoken by the spirit. The look on their faces would say it all. I knew that I was going to be used for something way bigger than what I was seeing.

This transition in my life took nine months! It was nine months of different cell buddies, different attitudes, different religions, different understandings, but it also was nine months of discovering the Real Me. I loved what I discovered within me, or should I say, I loved who the Lord delivered from the experience. John Bell Jr. was finally here. I can truly say those nine months were the best months of my life.

Without those nine months of training with God, I would have never been able to accept who I really am. I would have never been able to listen to my inner man and the spirit of God, but most of all, I wouldn't have been able to write this book.

To those who are living behind a mask, hopefully you submit to change before you are forced to. It took me nine months in a cell 23 hours a day, to get to the next level of me. Please don't let this be the steps that God has to take with you, in order for you to see and accept who HE has called you to be.

There is an easier way but, they say the ones with the most talent is extremely hard to get to. What will it take for you to TRANSFORM?

A PURPOSE FOR PAIN

There's a purpose for pain is what they say, every time my eyes turn red,
When my souls being stretched, and my heart feels pain, as I listen to the words God said.
When there's a bump in your road, a halt in your walk, and things seem like they're wrong,
Get down on your knees and thank our God and praise him through prayer and songs.
Lift up your head and endure the pain, in this storm you'll have strength to stand,
There's knowledge to be taught, a lesson to be learned, the tools that will make you a Man.
Uncover your ears unharden your hearts, and trust in God, BELIEVE!
There's sun in your storm, have faith in Christ, and soon a blessing you'll receive.
At the end of your storm, you'll surely give thanks, for the blessings of Abraham,
The voice will say, thank you my child and I told you that, I AM!
I heard when you called for relief in your storm, and I wanted to give you a hug,
But I've healed your wounds and now you're pure, and believe it was out of my LOVE.
As I raise you up, dry your eyes and testify of all my works,
Tell my children if they choose my ways, at one point it's going to hurt.
So when the storms come and the weather gets rough, and your heart cords feel the strain,

Always know that there's a light in the night, and there's really a purpose for pain.

A PURPOSE FOR PAIN

I remember when God first showed me his POWER! I was running around reckless thinking I had all the sense: selling drugs, chasing women, fighting, and other things that didn't make sense. I was in love with a lifestyle that would eventually lead me to two places, prison or the graveyard. I remember going into prayer when I had to face a tough decision in the streets.

My moves affected more than just me, one wrong move, interaction, or connection could cause someone to lose their life or spend a lot of time in jail. Although the reasons were wrong, I knew to go to GOD to cover me.

As a little boy I was introduced to prayer so, I knew to call on God when I was faced with a tough decision. It's funny how I would run to prayer and ask God to help me make a good decision in a lifestyle that I am not supposed to live. I was asking him to make situations go away while I was living with the enemy. Wow, there I was confiding in the Savior when things went wrong but I never thought to speak to him before I made choices.

Every tough trial that you have been through in life is with great purpose. A lot of us don't know what the reason is but we know that we must go through. Often, we blame God because we don't understand, and it causes us to question Him. Understand God is so strategic that when He wants to get your attention, He'll do it in a way that you won't understand but works in your favor.

I was listening to God when I really needed him not when he was trying to lead me away from what I wanted to do. I am guilty of beneficial obedience! Only listening to His voice when it's comfortable for me. However, God will send a storm that will shake your foundation so viciously, that all you can hear is his voice.

The more you resist the harder the battle, you'll feel like your world is crumbling, and you can't breathe. The trials are a test to keep your focused and on track.

God built us; He knows how to break us! I was extremely hardheaded and created my own storm that put me in a place where I could hear Him, respect Him, and later, love Him.

My storm came in the form of prison, I started my journey January 31, 2002. I was sent to the county jail where I stayed for a year and a half. I walked in the county jail mad, bitter and confused, saying how did this happen to me, thinking that I was a good guy. How did God allow this to happen to me? Not knowing that He was giving me what I needed not what I wanted.

I sat down in my cell and I immediately started to talk to God. I asked him, "Why, and how long?" He didn't say anything verbally, or at least I didn't know that it was him at the time. I remember hearing my mother say, "This is for your own good!" I hated when she would say things like that. I wanted to hear, "I am coming to get you baby!" Those famous words I would always hear when the long arm of the law would snatch me up. As long as momma came to get me, I could listen to the verbal discipline on the way home. I would've never thought that I would be a victim of not listening.

I was faced with a decision to take a plea agreement to 5 years or go to trial, I took the 5 years and was excited about getting the time. I remember calling home to my comrades bragging about the time offered to me. "I took a plea for five years, don't worry about it- I'll be home in three and a half", Excited, they replied "Good!" I said, "We'll be popping bottles with models!"

Little did I know at sentencing a year later, my time would be tripled. The judge told me; you have a lot of priors that were dismissed. I'm under the impression that you think the judicial system is a joke!" She then said," I hope by the time you get home you would've changed your life. I sentence you to 188 months with 5 years' probation!" I couldn't believe my ears, I was devastated and mad at God, but ironically, at peace.

However, I couldn't believe it. My method didn't work this time. I used to get into a jam and make that call to the Lord with a promise that I wasn't going to keep and BAM, He'd just show up. Not this time, this time it was different. He showed up in a way that was not comfortable for me but, ultimately saved me from myself.

This time he showed up in a different way, a way

that was'nt comfortable for me. Yet the strange feeling of peace came from living a stressful life that was leading nowhere, wanting to get out, and missing every opportunity to. It was a relief for it to be all over with.

Even though I was in jail, I felt free from that lifestyle, that mask, I could finally rest! I didn't have to worry about the police banging on my door, getting robbed, money missing or coming up short, getting shot or even me shooting at someone. All there was to concentrate on at this point was "WHO I WAS GOING TO BE"

In the beginning of my storm I didn't know why I was there, I was just running around fighting, drinking and smoking weed. I was not paying attention to what this storm was supposed to be teaching me. I went with the flow of the prison system, doing the things that took my mind off being there, which hid the reason why I was there.

I was receiving all types of messages from different people and from different directions, I wasn't ready to receive any of it. I was still stuck in my madness, in sort of a weird way it helped me cope with the time given at sentencing.

Later, I received a message that really opened my eyes, God spoke to me and said, "Stop focusing on being here and start to focus on WHY YOU ARE HERE!" I heard that loud and clear. After that encounter, I started to read a little and for some strange reason everywhere that I turned, there was a bible waiting on me.

I used to pick it up every now and then but, I

couldn't understand it. Soon I realized it wasn't my time. Eventually I got to a place where I started to question myself and I needed answers! God showed up and started to give me my answers through the scriptures.

I ran around the prison yard for 5 years doing the same thing, ignoring all the warning signs. There were several attempts to try to get me into church but, I wouldn't go. I went a couple of times and it seemed like every time that I went the sermon was directed at me.

That would scare me into not going the next time someone offered. The whole time I was not allowing my storm to serve His purpose. It was like I was being allowed to run because he knew that I couldn't run for long. Then I heard that small voice that said," IT'S TIME!"

I had a feeling of fatigue after every argument, every fight, every disagreement! I didn't want to be this way anymore, with tears coming down from my eyes, I asked God to please change me! It was crazy, here I am asking for change and my storm got rough! You have to be very careful what you ask God for. He allowed a series of events to happen which lead me to a cell that isolated me for 23 hours of the day. He sent a guy who told me, "This is the place where I would be transformed!" He was right. It was then my storm began to serve its purpose.

After my cell buddy left, I was alone in my cell for 4 months before I received another, during that time I had one on one talks with God all day. I was faced with a lot of things that I kept hidden; I was forced to deal with them but in a way that I could bear the pain. After about 3 months I could hear all of the conversations that I had about my lifestyle, no matter how long ago the message was delivered to me. I remembered them word for word, like we had spoken yesterday.

I can't lie, this storm was rough because it was forcing me to deal with the truths about myself that I believed to be a lie. I had to come to grips with the fact that I really wasn't this person that I made everyone believe that I was. My cover was off in that cell and I cried for days just thinking about all the pain I caused. It's like I felt the pain of every lie, betrayal, and disappointment of every broken promise. All the pain that was caused by my actions, I felt it!

I became more transparent to people and most importantly, I became transparent to God. This was a place where I could speak without a filter, discuss my fears and accept who God wanted me to be.

He told me something that really made me feel bad. One night I spoke to Him and I said, "Lord, I Love You!".

He said, "Why do I have to allow these things to happen to you to hear those words out of your mouth? Why do I have to allow you to feel pressure or pain to hear these words? Why don't I hear these words when you are doing well, and life has no worries?" I felt so bad because I realized that the only time that I spoke to God, was when I was in trouble or about to get into trouble.

I made a vow to God. When I got out of that cell, He would hear from me every day no matter what was going on in my life. In that instant God said, "I KNOW"! This storm was the reason why I came to God with my greatest sacrifice in hand, MY LIFE! It was also the reason I begin to accept John Edward Bell Jr. instead of the GOOCH (short for my nickname, Goochie).

I allowed God to transform me into the man I am today. I accepted my role as a man of God, and let the immature ways go.

My storm served its purpose! I encourage all those that read this chapter, don't be the one that God must punish in order to get a prayer. He should not have to put you through several storms to get your attention. Always know that every tough situation you encounter in life, has a PURPOSE.

THE TOUCH

I started to release things and change things, that were once a part of my world.
The lust, the way of thinking, money, lies and girls.
God touched me with a convincing tone, He said son you must think higher,
Right now you are living a life untrue, and to me that's called a liar.
You must be true expose yourself, and reveal who's inside,
You are my child and I Love You, you really don't have to hide.
The person you are is righteous, a beautiful

blessing to others,
Don't be ashamed I did this to you, "ME" not your mother.
You will have enemies but "YOU'RE PROTECTED",
I'll provide you with survival,
Don't be scared I'll give you a sword, and your sword is called, YOUR BIBLE!

THE TOUCH

This poem represents the feeling that I got after I gave my life to the Lord, and how the spirit spoke to me through the scriptures.

The more I read the scriptures, the less things I used to glorify meant to me. The money, lies, and girls, became less important; I found happiness in them before, but the feeling would always be temporary.

When you live a temporary life, you are only allowed to get temporary satisfaction. The only thing that was there every day, was stress, anger, bitterness, and unforgiveness. These things would be permanent if I chose this life, and these things would have killed me!

I realized what ran the world: money and the desire to have it is the power, lies is what keeps the world going and the world would not exist if it wasn't for a FEMALE! These three things rule the mindset of a man that lives without Christ. He unconsciously allows the enemies tricks to distract him, which kills his chances of having a positive influence on the next generation. The only thing that can help a man resist this temptation is a touch from God!

I thought I needed those things to be prosperous in this world but, when I found Jesus, I realized that none of the happiness I received from these things could amount to the pleasures and the joys of living with Christ. He allowed me to see that my whole adult life was based upon lies and manipulation, and the women only loved the money behind the man. The lust for these things is what led me to prison and would have led me to my death.

He asked me one question, "Do I want to give up my family to pursue these things?" It's an easy decision for a man who really wants to lead his family, he will always choose FAMILY over the things of the world. I have gained more than I could ever have in the drug game: peace, knowledge, wisdom and most of all a better understanding of life because of my commitment to Christ!

Who knew that the answers to my problems were in a book that I always saw but, never chose to read? "THE BIBLE"! Take time to read the instruction manual of life. If you want to know the truth about the way you're living, Pick up that bible and prepare to be CHANGED!

THE MESSAGE

Turn from your ways RESIST HIM, he'll
never tell you the truth,
He'll always give you promises, but he'll
never show you the proof.
He'll leave you in an instant, while you're

stuck in life's confusion,
He'll promise that things will get better, while
in life you're constantly losing.
He tells you that your decisions are right,
and things will work for the best.
But every time you take his advice, you
feel that pain in your chest.
The person you hear is Devious, he's not
the one to receive,
He's your enemy, a Fraud, and his words you should
never believe.
The voice to adhere is the whisper at night,
that speaks as you lie in your bed,
Those visions and dreams that dance around,
at night in the back of your head.
Those people who come and speak to you,
that you never have seen before,
That person who told you constantly, don't do these
things anymore.
This voice is from our father, not on earth, but who
looks from the skies,
That one who found our lost souls and uncovered
our blinded eyes.
That one who held us in moments of pain, and saved
us throughout the years,
The one who loved us despite our flaws and
wiped away our tears.
The one who you called, and he saved you,
within a matter of seconds,
You don't have to receive the messenger, but
you must receive THE MESSAGE.

THE MESSAGE

How often do we walk through life doing what we know is wrong, and feeling terrible after every bad decision that we make but repeat them? How many times do we hear the warning of our peers or a friend, yet ignore the message? How many after-the-fact moments of "SOMETHING TOLD ME NOT TO DO IT," will we need to get it?

Well, this poem is one of those poems that describes my life at a time where I heard what people said but listened to what I wanted to hear.

We often listen to the wrong voice because we don't want to hear the truth. All my life I was warned of my actions; my peers would come up to me and tell me about the way that I was living, or the way that I was doing things. I can honestly say that I didn't pay attention to what they were saying for two reasons:

I've been making my own decisions for so long so the thought of listening to what someone else was "Telling me" to do even if it was the truth, it was hard to hear and second, I looked at the lifestyle that others were living and blew off their advice because they were hypocrites.

It was confusing, they were doing all the thing they advised me not to do to get my life together and their lives were filled with the same flaws. Mentally I filed their advice as junk mail.

Reading the bible, I came across a story about a man named Saul, he was crucifying Christians, and he had no intentions on stopping. God used a donkey to deliver a message to him.

He was obedient, and he's the reason why we have those 13 Powerful books in the New Testament. God rewarded Paul for his obedience, he changed his name to Paul, forgiven him of his sins and allowed him to start over.

If he would've been hardheaded like me, a lot of us would have been in trouble. Paul's wisdom saved a lot of souls! That whole story was written to show us that God can and will use anyone that he wants, to deliver a message. It's not up to us to concentrate on the messenger, it's up to us to listen to the message.

The people I thought were against me would always give me good advice. I just never paid attention to the words that was spoken to me, I thought that I had all the sense. I soon had to go through some things to realize that all that was said to me came from God!

I've noticed along my travels, when you judge a person by their outer appearance, you'll never get a chance to see who they really are. You'll always be looking for the negative in him/her distracting you from the positive message they came to deliver. This is what I call, Premature Judgement!

Just imagine if we as a people, would stop judging people by their actions or their outer appearance. Then just get to know a person before we do our final assessment on them. The world would be a better place, filled with more peace and less stress, I guess that's a lot to ask.

I realized I missed a lot of blessings by not listening to the message from people who I thought did not count. Those same people that I chose not to listen to, still encourage me today.

When you are living an unrighteous life. You can't expect a person to hear what we are saying; your message will go in one ear and out the other. If we want our families, our community, or our society to be better, we must be the example that we want to see.

Sure, God still can use you to deliver a message, but do you think that you are going to heaven because you have delivered that message? You must do your part after the message is delivered. NEWSFLASH often times the message is for you first!

You have to apply the message to your life and see if God is giving you a warning to get it right first. You can't give people a reason to point the finger at you for any wrong reason. Your walk will speak for itself, if you are living right, your message will be well received.

I can't promise you that everything you say will be received, but I can say that you have a good chance of getting through to someone when you are living right. I realized that when you are living right, people will notice, they'll start to get behind you and then they'll start to listen to you. That's the place where God wants us to be.

I noticed no one would listen to me when I was living wrong, but now that my life is being lived the right way. People are really listening. From walking one way in life, then to choose to turn and walk with God, it really amazes people. The weak and the strong will gravitate to you, you'll be in possession of a lot of lives and you won't even know it. Just touching one life could create opportunities to touch a million. That's why it's important to pay attention to the messages that have truth within them. These messages are from God and they will either turn you around and/or save your life. You never know who God will used to guide you to the right side of the tracks.

My advice to you is to keep your eyes open and never deny any wisdom or knowledge, no matter who it's coming from. When the message comes, RECEIVE IT, then do a self- check to see if the message is pertaining to you, or the way that you are living. See what you can change about yourself that would help you make a better impact on those around you.

We can't change anyone around us before we change ourselves. In the book of James, the bible tells us to be spotless to the world. Meaning, don't give the non-believers a reason to continue to not believe. Only then, will you be able to deliver a good message to someone.

So many of us possess the power to change a life but, first we have to change our own. Remember people, God can use anyone to deliver a message, it's not up to you to judge the messenger, it's your job to listen! You don't have to receive the messenger but, it's imperative that you receive the message. Take heed to the warnings because you never know if it will be your LAST.

<u>THE STORM</u>

The storm you're in is rough, because it's filled
with thunder and rain,
Things will get better I promise you, because
there's a purpose for pain.
Just be patient keep living, and soon the blessings
will show,
Whatever don't kill you makes you stronger, that's
how the story goes.
I know sometimes you wonder; I don't know is
God really there?
Put pain in one and blessings in the other and
look how to compare.
Blessings are things we've been through, all the
storms of our past,
Those times when we thought it was over, and
the storm would never pass.
All those nights of crying, and the tears would never
stop flowing,
Those times when our world was spinning, and we
wondered where we were going.
When you got on your knees and prayed to him,
indeed you went to that place,
Soon you noticed a light in your storm, and the
tears would stop on your face.
You asked the father to help you, bring me out, I'll do
what I can,
I put you through that storm out of love, and I
knew that you could stand.
But why God, why, what am I doing that's not so
right?
He said you're living for worldly things, YOUR
FLESH, and the spirit you fight.

I don't fight you; I LOVE YOU; I'm praying, can't you see?
But why did it take the pain in your storm,
to bring you back to me?
I want you to focus on me, when the smiles
and joy is here,
I want you to love me and PRAISE ME, when your face isn't filled with tears.
That's the love I want, and I refused to settle for less,
As soon as you give me this love son, I promise you'll be at your best.
MY GOD, MY GOD, please mold me into that one,
I can see that you're still blinded, because my process has already begun.

<u>THE STORM</u>

"The Storm" was inspired by the times when we go through life enjoying ourselves without a care in the world, shining with the sun without giving credit and thanks to the Son! Even as a sinner He still allows us to have a sense of joy that keeps a smile on our faces. We run to the father in prayer when times are rough and acknowledge Him as having all power and might.

Think about the time when you were about to lose your job but, didn't, the time when your marriage was about to end but, you reconciled, when the doctor said that you had a lifelong disease, only to hear the next doctor say that there is no trace of it in your system? These are situations that God is supposed to be acknowledged in. Instead we often give credit to ourselves with, “Man, if I didn’t catch that in time”, or “I’m glad that I was on point.” Your survival had nothing to do with your thought process, nothing to do with your awareness, nothing to do with you at all, it was all God, and him ALONE!

Nothing can happen that God doesn’t allow, when you see things going wrong and they don’t. It’s because God didn’t allow it, that’s it and that’s all. We must stop taking credit for something that was beyond our control. We have to start praising God for the things that we know He was responsible for.

Some of us never acknowledge God in the situations because faith isn’t socially accepted in certain circles. We hide our beliefs out of concern for what others might say or think. We can’t be considered leaders with fear in our hearts. So many of us are scared to be different. So many of us are scared to step out on your own and embrace the person that’s screaming inside of you to be released.

I remember when I was young, I used to get locked up a lot. Everything I would tell God out of fear, that if he gets me out of this situation. I will never do it again; I would promise him this! However, God knew what I was going to do before he released me, but He still released me. God knew I was only praying to Him because I was in trouble, I only believed when it was beneficial, “When I wanted something”.

I realized that if God didn’t allow certain things to happen in our lives, we probably would never pray to

Him. A lot of times we run to God because there is nowhere else to run. Sometimes we dig ourselves in a deeper hole trying to get out of the first one, trying to figure it out on our own. The bible says in Proverbs 3: 5-6, "Trust in the Lord with all your heart and lean not on your own understanding."

We are not built to have every answer to every situation, it all comes from God. He knows and sees everything! God will continue to bless us, but in return He wants and deserves His praise. He doesn't want to only hear from us when all hell is breaking loose, but when everything is just fine.

Reflecting upon my time in the streets, I was praying but still doing everything that said I didn't know of Him. I would get on my knees and pray, then get right up and sell drugs to one of His people. I saw the things that happened to those who said they didn't believe, and God wasn't real, so as someone with a little knowledge, I knew better!

Having no control over their desires, God would allow them to experience the consequences of their actions. The effects would either help them make better decisions and often times it would save them from themselves. So many of us have to experience something tragic that brings us back to God.

We must stop trusting in man, drugs, or self when we go through things. We always have to trust in Him, He wants us all the way in or all the way out, it's just that simple! Make the right choice or the desires of the world will make them for you. There are two types of people in the world, losers and winners, which one have you been, and which one do you desire to be? Remember, storms come to transform, and your blessings will not always feel good. God will bless us how He sees fit.

SUBMISSION!

My heart is hurt my mind is stressed, from running my legs are sore,
My guards are down, my arms are tired, I just can't fight no more.
My soul aches, my spirit is weak, as I search from deep within,
No options left I must submit, to the person who I know is a friend.
My head in the air as I wait for relief, from the strong emotion of rain,
Hoping my questions are answered soon, to heal these wounds from my pain.
As I fight the world year after year, my strength is removed by the layer,
My cover is off my knees won't hold, so I find myself deep inside prayer.

When I opened my mouth, my eyes start to flood, when I heard the things that I said,
Now I see that the words I heard, are the painful thoughts in my head.
I had a talk with a friend, it went on for hours, I really can't remember the length.
But suddenly, my body feels numb, and I start to feel great strength.

My friend told me He was always here, and
He saw the things that I've seen,
Ask for forgiveness have faith in me and
believe I can make you clean.
At first you were weak, but I've made you
strong, you've survived the enemy's plight,
Stand tall my child and hold your head, I'll give you
steps to the light!

SUBMISSION

"Submission" is inspired by a mindset that begin to drain my entire body, I was tired and couldn't do it anymore! We all come to that point where a certain situation or thought makes us say, "THAT'S IT!"

Submission describes a time in my life where I really wanted to change, but my ego and pride wouldn't allow it. It got to the point where I had to make a decision, hold on to what hurt or submit to change so I could get healed. I had to be incarcerated to really focus on my flaws and trust that God could help me fix them. People often build their lives upon alter egos, which becomes a masked identity.

When I submitted, my entire lifestyle changed! I submitted to changing my thoughts, my walk, and my actions. I neglected God and my family by giving into my ego. It wasn't until that day I finally opened my eyes and counted all the negative situations that my ego had gotten me in, and how tired I was of living my life based upon a perception that was not even me. I got on my knees and prayed, I asked God to release me from all the things that were unlike Him. My pride, ego, arrogance, boasting, and any other thing that were considered as a hindrance. I had to admit to myself that I was puppet to distractions, I wanted out quick.

I didn't gain anything by submitting to distractions, yet plagued by broken hands, multiple shootings, fist fights, and the glorification from people that really don't care if I lived or if I died. When I submitted to God,

I couldn't believe how many tests came my way, and they came at an alarming rate. Every time I would get pass one test; another one was waiting. It got to the point where I realized the stress of holding on to these things was just too much. I had to let go.

My eyes were open to a lot of good character traits I possessed but never got a chance to enjoy. I would refuse to submit to the person inside, THE REAL ME! There were occasions I'd be around a certain group of people and wanted to laugh or joke but, I wouldn't in fear of losing respect.

There were moments that called for the man in me to show up, but the little boy would confront the situation. I lost a lot of the good times in my life by masking the part of me that I loved.

The Lord ordered my steps to the right side of the track by letting me walk on the wrong side for a while. He knew I was going to get tired, the things He allowed me to go through really broke me down

. I had no other choice but to say, "FATHER NO MORE!" It was like Rocky getting beat by the Russian, he wanted to say no more but, in the movie, he has to win. Well in my life there were no cameras, and no Adrian to root me on from the side. I leaned on the only person that could give me a shot at a new life! That person was God.

I am writing this chapter in tears, mainly because a lot of people I know didn't make it. They didn't yield to God's voice when He said, "Come back to me!" Repeatedly they made the same mistakes, ignoring the pleading and praying of their loved ones.

Not realizing that Grandma's knees were not just hurting because of her age, but because of the countless times that she spent kneeling and praying for the protection of her grandchild.

I'm thankful that after all the mistakes and promises that I made and broke, God still gave me a chance to get it right and walk in my purpose. I am nothing without God, and I will always be grateful for the opportunity to tell my story.

I hope this chapter encourages someone to let go of the things hindering the fulfillment of their life. God will open your eyes to the life he has called you to live. There are many benefits to walking in your purpose. I just encourage you to LET GO and LET GOD!

I'LL SMILE

The sun is shining my eyes are open, and the clouds are starting to break,
My smile is back I'll laugh again, because I stand strong on my faith.
I never knew that I could be loved, by someone with my wrongs and rights,
Then I stepped aside and realized, that
it's not my battle to fight.

Now I see that all of his words are good,
so believe what he said,
Because if there wasn't a plan for me, I would have already been dead.

The storm is over my talents are shown,
because I trust in GOD to believe,
Now I sit back and laugh at Satan, because all my blessings will be received.
I lost a lot when I slipped and fell, to the test that Satan sent me,
But through it all I'll get it back, all that's supposed to be.
I have to admit I was really hooked, and I had questions for about a mile,
But now I've learned that when storms are here, I know I can sit back and smile.

I'LL SMILE

"I'll Smile" was a poem that I wrote when I felt like the storm was finally blowing over. I was still in solitary confinement but, the pressure was easing up a little. I could honestly feel my joy coming back There were certain times within the storm where I was extremely happy, but it would only last for a second.

This feeling was the joy you get when you don't know how you are going to get through it in the beginning but, you do. God solved all the problems I had within myself; all the insecurities I had in the beginning were gone.

The character flaws were not as bad as they were before, if they were even still there. I finally was content with being the man that I was expected to be, not hiding behind a mask.

See, when you know God has promised you something, STAND ON IT, and know that it is coming, in God's time. Whatever you encounter along the way is just training for the position that He has for you once your training is complete.

The King needs soldiers to fight the good fight, He doesn't need weak individuals that'll crumble at the first sign of resistance. I've seen weaker vessels be transformed into mighty men and women of God!

The reason why He chooses flawed people like me is because I possess the tools that will be needed to fight this battle. That same respect that I got in darkness, will be the same respect that I will use to get people into the kingdom.

We can't lose focus on our mission because the sun is not shining at a point in our lives. When a storm hits, remember what the Lord said, "Don't let the enemy tell you anything different". Believe in God's word and keep looking towards the sky, that's where the blessings come from.

This revelation was music to my ears. The joy you'd feel when as a kid you were able to go back outside after the storm. I remember sometimes it would rain for hours and we'd sit in the window mad because the lights went out and we couldn't watch TV.

Then the storm passed, and we could return to play. It was the joy in the freedom after being locked in the house for a few hours. If you happen to be waiting

on something from God and a storm has hit in the process. I want to encourage you to stay strong, trust the process, never stop listening, look towards the end, don't get caught up in what things look like, focus on what you believe. Get prepared for some childlike joy and
remember, it's your turn to SMILE!

DENIED

Here's my chance at a whole new life, no excuses I promise to get it right,
This lesson has taught me a lot about war, it's important I choose a different fight.
Finally, I get to just sit with my son, without an officer dictating my time,
Or to hear that voice with one wrong move, VISITS CANCELED cause your out of line.
God is so good He gave me a chance and I promise to do better this run,
I'm going to laugh if possible, pop a few bottles, yet my focus must be on my son.
Will the contents of this letter make things a little better, the excitement bought tears to my eyes?
With one small rip, in big bold letters, MR. BELL, your appeal is DENIED!

DENIED

MAIL CALL…. MAIL CALL!!

At 4:30 pm every day the mail comes in and the C.O hollers down the hallway for everyone to listen for their names so they can receive their mail. I stopped coming to mail call 3 years ago. I got tired of hearing I SENT IT and going to mail call repeatedly not hearing my name. I got tired of being disappointed, so I stopped putting myself in position to be let down.

The key to survival behind this wall is to stay focused on what's in front of you. you must be sharp and sometimes staying sharp means disconnecting yourself from the outside world. Sometimes family can be the biggest distraction, worried about their problems, who's sick, in the hospital, who's not speaking, all those things must be set aside because you can't help everyone with a 15-minute phone call. A lot of times we call home to see what's going on in our neighborhoods, who has the new car, new girl, new position, who's beefing, all those things that has nothing to do with us.

It's extremely important to know what's going on the compound because wars start between races without you knowing, and you can get killed like that. I had to really re-focus my mind behind this wall, sometimes I use to push my family in this special pocket I had reserved for them in my mind and live like I didn't have family waiting on me.

To be totally honest I was at peace whenever I mentally separated myself from the streets, I feel like it was a healthy space for me, I was able to function without any distractions. I must concentrate on bettering myself if I really wanted to get out of here and stay out of here.

"BELL, LEGAL MAIL"!

That was Music to my ears I've been waiting on a letter from my appeal lawyer for 3 months now. I filed a motion for a sentence reduction due to the new Crack

Law that congress had passed. Guys were getting immediate release every day and I was hoping that this would be the letter that set me amongst those numbers

I've been getting letters from the Courts and my lawyer saying my case looked good and I have a good chance of getting the reduction I filed for. If I win this motion I will be released immediately, as I thought about the letter, I started getting excited.

Thinking about taking my son to football practice, basketball games, things that my father never done with me, I'll be able to do them with my son. As I started walking down the crowded hallway it seemed like the air was starting to get thin, was it excitement or fear? Even though it was crowded in the hallway it seemed like it was empty, the anticipation of the contents of this letter had my stomach in knots. The hallway was short about 19 steps total, yet it felt like I was walking forever, my palms were sweating, felt like someone was pouring LAVA on my forehead.

I finally stepped in front of the C.O.'s office so I can retrieve my mail, I knocked on the door and waited for officer Bailey to wave me in. Officer bailey was light skin with pretty teeth and thin lips, big brown eyes and long hair that she kept pinned up because of her religion.

All the inmates were crazy about her, I wasn't in a place mentally to converse with her because my focus was always on going home, so I use to see her but not pay attention like everyone else did. She finally waived me in and gave me a book to sign saying that I received my legal mail.

I was in a trance it felt like my body was there, but my mind was all over the place, I only saw a silhouette of her face, I'm usually a little more cordial with her but not today,

I just wanted my mail and move on with the rest of my day. She always smelled great, her scent made you want to spark a conversation just, so you could hold her scent for a little longer, I greeted her, grabbed my letter and walked out of her office.

The walk back to my room was long and miserable, I was getting dizzy and my feet felt like I was walking in quicksand. This could be the letter that sets me free, the one that gives me my life back, this could be the one.

I turned the letter over and in big bold writing it read, THE LAW OFFICES OF JOSEPH POSEY attorney at law! I never sat face to face with this lawyer, he was assigned to me by the court system to handle my appeal case, PRO-BONO.

I opened the envelope and unfolded the letter and read the contents, Dear Mr. Bell we are writing to you in regard to your appeal case 71650-09 for modification of your sentence, we are sorry to inform you that your appeal has been denied because of your career offender status.

I was crushed, I felt the heat rising the side of my neck, my stomach was doing flips, anger, confusion, bitterness, disappointment were the words that described what was going through my mind at this point. For the last three years I've was promised I had a good shot at winning my appeal and here I am being denied after 3 whole years.

Tears started to well up in my eyes, I got to my room laid down on my bed and placed my hands behind my head. I wanted to cry in this very moment, all the lies that I've been told, all the broken promises and disappointments I thought I had tucked away in my emotional closet came back and I was about to explode. I had to go outside; I couldn't allow nobody to see me in such a weak state of mind.

LOCKDOWN, LOCKDOWN the C.O. yelled, this procedure meant that there was a stabbing, or someone was fighting, and they make everyone lock in the nearest cell or housing unit until they contain the situation. Fortunately, my cell mate was outside, so he was probably locked on the rec yard where most of the fights, stabbings and arguments happen.

When I locked the door, I felt like God knew exactly what I needed. I needed some time to get these tears out, I've been holding them in since I got sentenced and I'm overdue for a moment of cleansing.

I turned over on my bed and put my face in the pillow and cried like a baby, all the pain, letdowns, heartache, lies, and broken promises, came out on that pillow. I heard a voice during my sobbing that said… 'PRAY"!

I was confused because I've been praying, fasting and praising and this is what I got from all of that? God why did they deny me, I've been living right, I've read your word and I've changed my life, so why is my blessing being held up, WHY WON'T YOU LET ME GO HOME EARLY?

I heard him loud and clear, YOU'RE NOT READY!!!!!

I TRUST YOU

**As I stare deep inside this mirror, am I a
reflection of this place?
Will God come change my surroundings? Is it
possible to change this face?
My body is sore from the punishment, my mind
slowly adapts to the stress,
I travel with the weight of the world on my
shoulders, looking for answers to each test.
As I look at my life through new eyes, I could
suddenly see much more,
I've changed now, and I refused to move, like I did,
once before.
I've lived my life with a mask on my face, so the
world only could see my eyes,
Everyone though they knew me well, but they
only saw my disguise.
I sat and wondered how they would act, when
they're exposed to revelations of me,
But I'm still confused, and I still don't know, when it's
exposed, who will I see?
Knowing this true revelation of me, will soon turn out
to be great,
At times I thought of ending it, but the voice would
say… JUST WAIT.
Handling the frustrations with the temptations of life,
and those lies that's told in the streets,
All my sins are exposed to the world, and
my flaws are no longer discreet.
Hoping and praying for the things that's
promised, and all my dreams will come true,
Lord you know I'm scared and confused, but**

my question is, what do I do?
Father you know that my trust is in you, but believe me it truly is hard,
I depend on your strength when temptation is near,
when life starts to deal its cards.
I'll depend on the scripture in the sword of life,
and the promises I know will come true,
I'm exposed to my calling, with faith I'll move,
and Lord my trust is in you!

THE ONE WHO TRUSTS GOD!

I TRUST YOU

I trust you was inspired by the feeling I got as I submitted and agreed to let those things go that truly had me thinking that I was strong. God was speaking to me, telling me to let those things go or allow those things to destroy me. I was fighting it because the enemy was constantly telling me that if I stop being who I was, life would be over, and I would never be able to survive in this world truly exposed of who I really am.

There were some moments when I got weak and I started to listen to him and proceeded to put that mask back on that I constantly hid behind. Every time I would grab hold of an old part of me, that voice would say, put it away, no more. It was a constant battle in my subconscious mind, and day by day I was truly exhausted from the war going on inside of my head. Fighting the old thoughts and fighting the thoughts that I really needed to take heed too was being revealed every day.

I started to address situations with humility, when I would lose my temper, I would feel bad, and I would go and apologize. I didn't know what to think at the time, all I knew was if I was going to be able to live a life behind these new eyes, I was going to have to trust God as I moved on.

The more the old me faded away, the way that I thought, understood, and the way I was looking at life, all started to change, and things had started to make sense.

The sincerity of my heart started to take over my thoughts, my letters changed, my conversations started to change, I slowly started adapting to the new me, the humble part of me that I always wanted to submit to but refused to. I finally realized that humility has power, it always put out a fire before it got started. Humility showed me that a soft answer brings better results, when you attack a situation with humility, you will always get a more reasonable result.

For those brothers out there living behind that mask and thinking that you are fooling someone. It's time to take the mask off, and start to be the person that you are, when the lights are off. That person who just wants to be respected, just the way he respects others.

I lived my life following an image that would never be my own, I wore a mask for my entire life, and I was feared and respected because of it. As the process moved on, I realized that when you are feared; you create enemies that you don't even know about, and the respect that you are trying to obtain, who are you respected by?

You are trying to gain the respect of people who are just like you, people who are living behind a mask and scared to death to come out from behind it. Living behind an identity that was created by an image.

I have gained more respect and love as a righteous man then I did when I was a knucklehead. It goes to show you that living behind an image will always surround your world with the image of people who are not authentic, like a world full of mirages.

Righteous living will gain the respect of leaders, and you'll become allies with those people that really count. When you get to that point where you want to submit and trust in God, He will see you through. Lord my trust is in You, I feel stronger than I ever have, it's because of you that I'm able to stand tall in the midst of a storm. I know that you created me to do marvelous and powerful things.

See, I know that the hardest thing that a believer will ever have to do is, "Trust God" that is one of the toughest tasks that we will ever have to face as believers. Coming out from behind the mask and being who God has called you to be, is extremely hard.

You are not going to be able to do it alone, you are not going to be able to handle the reaction of your peers, and the attack from the devil without fully trusting in God. You are going to have to trust Him when you want to slap someone for talking crazy, you're going to have to trust Him when people start to act funny around you.

You are going to have to trust Him when you hear people you love are talking about you behind your back. In all situations that you encounter after you have chose to submit, you are going to have to fully trust Him!

I remember one incident that happened to me when I was in the streets, God allowed a situation to be brought back to my remembrance. One of my friends had got into it with some guys, and it was about to get ugly,

I knew right then and there that it was a great chance that violence was the only remedy to solve this problem. I got up one morning, and I had plans to go and take someone's life if I had to, a foolish act that could have sent me to prison or cost me my life. Something inside me told me to get on my knees and pray before I left the house, it felt strange, but the feeling was very strong.

I got on my knees and I told God in a Full Confession. Lord you know that this is not me, you know that I don't want to do this but, when I walk out of this door and I see the guy that is involved in this situation," I AM GOING TO KILL HIM". Lord if you don't intervene it's going to happen. I guess the Lord heard my prayer, before I left my house, I got a phone call from the guy's comrade telling me that it was a misunderstanding, and the guy wanted to meet so we could talk about it.

God showed me because he wanted me to see that I had already started trusting in him in all of my madness; so, it should not be hard to trust in him now. He then showed me that a man can walk away from a situation that is asking for violence and still be a man. In the age of broken promises, God stands to keep his word with the believers who choose to stand in humility! ....TRUST HIM!

GOD'S ANGEL

I'm sending this angel to protect you, at times
when your strength is weak,
When your eyes are focused on the test of
the world, and faith is not under your feet.
I'm sending this angel to restore your trust, when
you think your prayers aren't heard,
To renew your thoughts and cleanse your mind,
as you remember what's in God's word.
I understand you saints, your storm is
rough, because it's filled with thunder and
rain,
But this angel I sent will spread her wings
and heal your wounds from your pain.
Just believe in his promise and never look
back, in your storm there's strength to stand,
His words are pure, so trust in your heart,

because it's hard believing in man.

But this one is different, the one who sits high, but indeed He really looks low,
I've been through that storm, so I know that it's rough, I survived because I never let go.
I know it's rough storm after storm, being stuck in an emotional twist.
But I won't leave you so lean on me, because God's love REALLY EXISTS!

GOD'S ANGEL

"God's Angel" was written as an encouragement to women trying to maintain their sanity in households while waiting on a good man, or just waiting on things to change. It was inspired by a good friend of mine going through a storm that was really getting the best of her. She questioned her worth and her self-esteem was diminishing. She has so much potential but, her current situation was holding her back from fulfilling her purpose and receiving the fullness life has to offer.

The cares of the world can make you lose focus and take your eyes off God. Many women without a man think that life is on hold. Women, you don't need a man in your life at all points to survive! Don't get me wrong, every female wants a good man to complete their life, but the reality is a man really needs a WOMAN to be complete. Without you in our lives we would be lost, and that is a fact.

There are some good men out here, but far too often women's physical standards are so high that an average man doesn't stand a chance. "He's too tall or too short", his credit score isn't a 700.

Some of you get so caught up in appearance that you overlook the most important part of a man, HIS FAITH! Life has a lot of our women so focused on a man that they lose sight of the one who created man.

Women please realize a man can't make you happy, only the spirit that's within the man can make you happy. If he's not connected to God, it's a 90% chance he's not happy with himself, so that makes it impossible for him to add to your happiness.

The best advice is within the poem, don't lean on the person that you see, lean on the person that you don't see. He knows all and see's all. Every relationship that you've had, good or bad, were learning lessons.

When you get that right one, the one that God has for you, you will know how to treat that person, and how to handle the relationship.

The tricks of the world crumble a lot of people, and some women and men question God's ways. These trials and tribulations were allowed to make you stronger but, you can't rely on your outer strength. You can only rely on the spirit within. If you can't hear the spirit of God, then you will be led by your feelings or your emotions. It's been proven that when you make decisions out of your feelings or emotions, it will cost you most of the time. Mainly because that decision will be made because of a moment.

I just want to encourage the ladies that's reading this book, don't give up because it's often hard to refocus. I ask you to read this poem a thousand times if you have to, just don't give up.

Although you may want immediate answers or gratification, God works on his own time. Continue to pray and trust in Him.

You have to really dig deep and see who God has created you to be, you have to fall in love with yourself before you can fall in love with someone else. You have to really reconnect with God on a level that no one else can offer you.

Until this process is complete, you will not get the man that God has for you. When a woman receives a man before she is ready, the wrong man will really hurt her. The enemy will use that man to take her so far away from God that she will be looking at prayer as a sin.

The whole process of this single life is for God to point out the things that you have to change about yourself. Remember the scripture, "I can do all things through Christ who strengthens me" (Philippians 4:13). Those words are life, so live it!

Queens know your worth, you are of great value because you are daughters of the most high. Stop giving discounts by selling yourself short! Accepting 2nd or 3rd place in a man's life is not what you were created for. You are a gift from God, but you must know that! Adjust the crown on your head and step into your position. You were made to do wonderful things, he didn't make you to be mistreated by a man, or to live your life chasing one. Remember, you were sent to complete us!

Just because you have kids, doesn't mean you have to accept any man. God's man is going to love you and the kids. So, what gorgeous is not what they call you, what do you call yourself? Don't let the pressures of life have you living in bondage of wanting a man.

Newsflash, if you are focused on yourself, and getting closer to God, a good man is getting closer to you. You might not see him, but indeed he is being allowed to see you.

Clean house. What I mean by that is, you have to recognize any and everything that will hinder you from being a good woman. Whatever it is, LET IT GO. Have you been holding on to a man that is making your life worse?

Some of you have been holding on to character flaws that you know are hard to deal with. How many of you have been saying that you were going to get back in shape, yet you never go to the gym.

You want a man to respect you for your mind and not your body, yet you still wear clothes that overexpose your body, instead of wearing clothes that shows your shape but covers up enough to make a man curious about what lies beneath. A good man is going to be looking at that smile and wondering what's on your mind.

The last thing that he'll be thinking about is your behind. You must show a man that you love yourself with your actions, however you present yourself, that's what a man is going to respect. A man will only treat a woman how she treats herself!

THE VOICES

What is my name how can I survive,
with the cards that life has dealt me?
Who am I? What is my life? And who am I destined to be?
A question of many that's asked by
most, who walk through life confused,

The answer is there just open your eyes, and in order to see what to do.
Then a voice came, I heard it before a familiar tone I'd say,
A gentle sound, a comforting tone sometimes it helps my days,
Sometimes the voice tells me things, according to the way that I walk,
At times the voice condemns me, it's like it can hear my thoughts.
Sometimes I want to ad hear that voice, at times when my eyes turned red,
I finally realized when temptation is near, there are 2 that speak in my head.
One voice says yes, one voice says no, I really don't want to believe,
I need some help, some direction I guess, on which one I should receive.
Go ahead and do it, it's only one drink, man it really can't hurt,
Keep selling those drugs you're getting that money, look at those dudes who works.
Everyone loves you, just look around, you can never be put in a cell,
Look at those dudes' man they're your friends, they'll probably come up with the bail.
Then a light flashed, my mind went blank, and I dropped the drink in my hand,
Then a voice came, it was loud and clear that said, I made you a man.
A man of what? A man of mistakes, a man who constantly lies?

Don't listen to that, I am that voice, the one who rest in the skies,
There's a book on you that told me that, if I obey, you'll give me the land,
That's the answer to your questions, and believe me son, I CAN!

THE ONE WHO WOULDN'T LISTEN

THE VOICES

This is a poem describing the war that went on in my mind as I was stuck between two lifestyles. One voice told me to do right, and the other told me to do wrong. That voice was always the strongest, not sure if it was because that voice had a lot of help from flesh desires, friends, associates, significant others, ego, pride, and notoriety!

Although the voice of God is powerful and you feel a little strange when you hear it, most aren't familiar and/or too far gone that it's dismissed.

Most of us listen to the negative voice so much, we can't even hear the good one anymore. Do you remember the cartoon when the character has to make a decision, he has the devil on one shoulder, and the angel on the other?

Well that's the same way that you have to deal with the voices in your head. It's up to you to make the right choice, every time that life deals you a hand you have to know which voice to listen to. You must know which card to throw away and which one that will make your hand a winning hand.

I chose to listen to the wrong voice so much that I got tired, tired of the stress from the decisions that I was making, the heart ache, the lies. I just got tired of losing every time I listened to that voice. Hearing the voice say

EVERYTHING will be alright, just do it, then getting the exact opposite of what the voice said, instead of a smile I got a tear. I must admit, since I gave my life to God, the wrong voice still competes, but my thinking and my outlook on life is totally different now.

Now it's the good voice that really holds all the weight in my decision making. Once righteousness is what you stand for, it's what you live by. Any conversation or situation that you encounter that does not go in stride with your lifestyle or your beliefs. You don't even want to be in the presence of those people or the conversation.

No matter who the conversation is with, it could be your mom but if she is not speaking right, then you cut the conversation. I don't care who it is, if they are not speaking positive, you either get out of the conversation or you add positivity to the conversation. It's very important that you know which way that you want your life to go.

You have to make a decision and stand on it, no matter what. Stop listening to that same voice that continues to get you in bad situations.

Remember those times when you were about to do something that you knew was wrong, and that voice told you not to go, or not to do it.

Then you did it anyway, and BOOM, all hell broke loose. That is the voice of God, some might say that it was My Conscious, but your conscious is the voice of God. He has been speaking to you the whole time, you just did not know how to listen to Him; and that's why you have been experiencing trials and tribulations ALL YOUR LIFE.

He has been trying to keep you out of negative situations your whole life, please start to adhere His voice and make the right choice.

The only one that hears His voice and does not listen, is a person who wants to Fail. The Lord is trying to get you to the right side of life, He's trying to get you to understand that it's your life you're losing, every time you listen to the voice that doesn't sound like His. If you don't start to listen to the right voice, you will always make the wrong choices. I hope you received this message, because life is so much better when you are living the right way.

I'VE CHANGED

As I sit in my cell at night, with a million thoughts on my mind,
Wondering when I go to sleep, in my dreams, what will I find?
Sometimes they're pleasant, joyful, and sometimes they make me scared,
Wanting to go home so bad, but wondering am I really prepared?
Wondering why I am in this cell, to describe this feeling is strange,
Finding out through prayer this process is called, the first process of CHANGE.

THE ONE WHO WANTED TO CHANGE!

I'VE CHANGED

This poem speaks to how I felt in the beginning when I first noticed the changes God was making within me. It felt strange, maybe because I never chose to really accept who God was calling me to be.

When you accept the person inside screaming to come out, a lot of things will have to be released; a man wears different mask and holds on to different identities living behind a false image. In the streets, he may be known as a tough guy when in reality he's a teddy bear, and in the circles of the most popular women he is known as the player; truth be told he's really confused.

When I first decided to submit to God and accept His will for my life, He exposed me to myself through various situations, so I could grow. For example, my prideful selfish ways. In prison, we had a TV room it seated about 15 people with two wall mounted televisions for our entertainment.

I'd enter the room and turn both televisions to something I wanted to watch. When someone would ask, "Are you watching both T. V's?"
I would say, "YES! "Frequently my actions would lead to an argument, which would always result in me getting my way.

I did this continuously, until one day James and I had a conversation about my behavior. James was well respected in the prison system; at the time he'd been incarcerated for 20 years. We knew a lot of the same people, which is how we connected. He simply said, GOOCH you're selfish and you have pride issues. You only treat people like this because it feeds your ego, yet a man doesn't take advantage of weaker people. Gooch, remember no one respects who you're trying to be, they respect who you are!"

God used James and that situation to point out the first thing I needed to work on, PRIDE and EGO! When I sat and thought about what was said during the conversation with James, I had to accept the fact that he was right!

The worst mistake we make as believers is identifying the characteristics that we need to work on and overlook them consistently. We ask God for his best, but we don't give him our best efforts when it comes to doing the right thing.

During my transformation, there were times when I felt less than a man. Mainly because I couldn't react to situations with violence like I wanted to. I had to bite my tongue in front of crowds of people, I really felt like a chump.

The most valuable characteristic a man could have is HUMILITY, and I was being taught by the best teacher. The hardest part of humility was learning to pick and choose your battles, and often being the bigger person while appearing to be the smaller one.

It takes more strength to walk away from a situation then to entertain it with violence. Anyone can entertain and act like a fool, but it takes a strong MAN to have self-control and substance to gain respect, but more importantly respect himself!

I started to see more of myself for who I was

and the things I chose to accept, the lies, manipulation, betrayal, malicious thoughts, anger, bitterness, and unforgiveness! A lot of my decisions were influenced by these character flaws, and they all had to go!

They were a part of me for so long when I finally started working on releasing them, I felt strange. They clouded my judgement and blurred my vision for so long, that it hid the good in me and caused me to lose out on many blessings. It affected good situations, relationships, jobs, and business deals. It's true when they say, "WHAT GOD HAS FOR ME, IS FOR ME!" but it's only when you are ready for it.

However, He will reveal to you missed opportunities and blessing as a wake- up call. In my heart I know that's why He did not release me when I thought that I was going to be released, He knew that I was not ready to go, honestly, I knew it too!

In order to get the good things of God, you have to be in a good position SPIRITUALLY or they will be a burden. When I finally submitted to change, and dropped these characteristics, I felt a lot lighter than before. I realized that it hurts more to hold on, than it does to LET GO!

It was amazing, at one point in time anything would set me off but after my first encounter with God, I just didn't have that fuel anymore. No matter how mad I wanted to get, I just didn't have it in me. I felt like I was weak, I had to turn the other cheek to someone who I knew could physically dominate. That was a tough task, but that was something that I was willing to endure to get to the next level in life.

When the Lord finally finished the first part of my change, I stood confident and dealt with situations like a man. I no longer had the venom to deal with situations like a kid, it was MAN TIME! It wasn't easy, but it's much better and smarter.

The only thing that will hold you back from the things God has for you, is the desire to hold on to the life that you are living. Let Go and Let God, because CHANGE IS MANDATORY, and it's better to do it on your own free will!

PAST FEELINGS

As I look back in my past, with all the good and all the bad,

All the times that made me happy, and the times that made me sad.

What I did in my trying times, how I felt when things got rough,

The things that I chose to sacrifice, and still wonder was it enough?

As I look at all I've lost, and wonder was it worth it?
I made a lot of mistakes in life, and I know that I'm not perfect.
At times my past would haunt me, is this story at its end?
As I look towards my future, is it possible for me to win?
Everyone has given up on me, as I was

almost out for the count,
Lord I'm thirsty for help, will you pull me out of this drought?
Will I ever have some peace? Am I stuck inside this maze?
Submit to my word and believe in me, I'll multiply your days

PAST FEELINGS

This poem was influenced by the feelings I had when I used to sit in my quiet time and ask God questions about my Past and my Future. I continuously confided in everyone else for answers, instead of going to God first. I found it easier to think when I really sat down and got quiet and talked to GOD, I asked Him why was I here?

He responded by showing me a glimpse of who I would be at the end of my training, I saw myself surrounded by people and I was talking to them. It seemed like I was ministering or motivating the people and I wondered was I the right man for the job?

When I sat back and watched the visions He allowed to come back, I couldn't believe some of the things I had done. He just sat with me and explained to me, He said when I chose to follow His ways, I chose to leave this lifestyle behind. There would be no more drugs, lies, meaningless sex, unrighteous living, NO MORE!

Everything I have done when I was living in agreeance with the enemy's decisions for my life would be left behind, never to be revisited again.

I then started to entertain the feelings that caused me sadness or pain, I asked God why did everyone turn their back on me? He said you were tricked into thinking they were really in your corner, and that's the greatest illusion.

He (THE ENEMY) will have you thinking everyone loves you, they'll say things like, you are so important to me and I'll love you to the end of time. Then he makes them all walk away at a time when you think they should be there.

A lot of people don't recover from situations like that, it's hard to deal with but it gets easier when you start to listen to the voice of God, as He gives you the answers to why these things are happening. He said how could they love you when they don't even love themselves, how could they love a man they really could not see? You never showed them the man you were on the inside, you always showed them a fraud, so why would you expect them to love someone genuinely when they really don't know who you are.

I remember the day my mother said "the streets and no one in the streets love you. The streets only show love to the people who are a part of the streets, now that you are not a part of the streets anymore, your presence will be a memory. You will always be a thought that existed but will eventually fade away. You were only important to them because you made yourself available for them to use, no one loved you, they love the fact that they could use you.

My conversation with God got deep, he said they

can only love the person that you are hiding on the inside, and until that person is exposed, you'll continue to have temporary friends.

Most of your friends don't love themselves so until they choose to love self, they'll never care about anyone else. I was amazed at all the answers I got from just sitting and asking God questions, I will never stop asking or seeking the truth. I now understand why the scripture says, Ask and you will receive, seek and you shall find, knock and the door will be opened (Matthew 7:7).

When I knocked on the door and poured out my feelings, He listened to me and gave me answers no other human would ever know. He told me by trusting and confiding in him for direction, he would add years to my life. He did just that by pulling me out of a lifestyle that was leading me into an early destruction.

I thank you Lord for adding years to my life, and letting your spirit add Life to my years. Listen friends, it might be your turn to sit down with God and pour out your feelings and ask him questions. You will be amazed at the answers and the revelations you will get. Open your heart to God and watch him open LIFE to you.

THIS ANGEL

This is the angel I spoke about, to provide you strength in your storms,
This is the angel to trust in, whose wings will indeed keep you warm.
This is the angel to believe in, who reminds you of

your worth,
This is the angel who'll protect you, and confide in when your hurt,
This is the angel who CHOSE YOU, to help when life gets hard,
This is the angel who never fails, and this angel was sent from GOD.

THIS ANGEL

"This Angel" is really a follow up or a part two to GOD'S ANGEL! This poem was written to let anyone who reads this piece know that God truly is watching over you, and he will release his angels to comfort you in the midst of your storms.

I used to ask a buddy of mine to make cards for me and put GOD'S ANGEL inside of it. I would send it out to someone who needed a little encouragement, or reassurance that God will always be there. We all need reassurance sometimes; we know and trust the fact that God is going to be there. It's just that in some moments when the storm gets a little rough, we need God to say, I AM HERE!

At the time that I wrote this book, I had been following the Lord for about 2 and a half years and my faith is strong at this point. As I write these words on this paper, my strength is weak, I feel like giving up physically, but my faith is what keeps me going.

I believe that God is going to send me home soon to my family, I believe in HIS promise made to me but some days it gets a little rough. A lot of people believe in God's promise and sometimes we need to hear that he will keep it.

This angel is the poem that provides that reassurance, it doesn't matter how strong you are in Christ you are still human, and the devil will attack what you say you believe. He wants to sow seeds of doubt, he wants to make you question God's ways, His word, and his will.

God doesn't expect you to never doubt or never sway in your faith, he knows that as long as you are in your own skin you will sway and be scared at times. That's why he created guys like me to send you words of encouragement to make sure the devil doesn't win any battle you enter.

I used this poem a lot of times during my walk towards the light. It seemed like every time I would read this poem it would put a little pep in my step, I'd find a reason to fight and stand strong another day.

The bible says, "They that wait on the Lord, shall renew their strength" (Isaiah 41:30). If there is anything in the world that you can always trust in, it's the WORD of God. His word will never change, His word is what got the elders, and the prophets through while they were on their journey. His word has helped generations of people and if you 'BELIEVE', His word will help you too. Rely on God's angel, I can guarantee God's angel is stronger than your storm.

MY LIFE

Sometimes I sit back and wonder, where my life took this horrible turn,
Was I wise, or was I young, when I still had life to learn?
Sometimes it's really painful, to stare deep inside my past,
How long will these memories haunt me? Does this pain really have to last?
What is my answer to these storms of life, that constantly hang over me?
I wish I was a bird in constant flight, and in life, I could always be free,
I pray to God constantly, in hopes that my pain will subside,
He gave me plenty of answers, to love him and not to hide.
The power of life is in the tongue, so I'll watch the words I speak,
There's danger down the wrong road, so I know that I can't cheat.
My moment has come to stop the pain, by confessing to all my faults,
God sees that and hears my voice, so my blessings are out of the vault.
There's a plan for me so I know it's true, that God will forgive us all,
So stay on that road or death will come, as soon as you make that call.
It's easy to forgive but hard to forget, but who am I really to judge,
When the enemy's here I'll have great strength, my God won't allow me to budge.
When my faults are forgiven and my spirit is

strong, he'll give me the eyes to see,
That my choice was wise, new life began, the day you turned back to me.

<u>MY LIFE</u>

"Life" was written one day when I was sitting in my cell, just trying to wrap my mind around how this all started. I was just going over the details and the facts of the decisions that lead me to this time and point in my life, I remembered when and why I started to sell drugs.

One day I was sitting in my room and my mom was talking on the phone through a closed door, the walls were not that thick in my house, so I could hear the conversation. She was speaking to my aunt about bankruptcy I just listened but, as I started to tune in more, I got scared. I did what a curious teenager would do, I went and asked the wrong person the question that I should have asked my mom.

I asked one of my friends, and the first thing that they said was, your mom is going broke! Those words hit me deep in my heart, because we always had what we needed, and more then what we wanted at times. I could not see us not having, being broke was not an option, just thinking about it made me scared.

I couldn't be the one without designer outfits, I couldn't be the one with regular shoes on, I could not see myself being the one people were talking about, and cracking jokes on. NOT GOOCHIE.

I did the stupidest thing that a young man could do, PANIC! I thought to myself, I will sell weed and just put the money in my mother's drawer.

When she sees it she will never think to question me about it she will think that she misplaced some money and she found it. Then I thought about giving the money to one of my brother's friends and telling them to give it to her like they were sending my brother money in JAIL.

That thought went away quick, because she would have sent my brother the money. I went to one of my brother's friends and asked him to show me how the weed game was played. The game was so easy, I didn't have to do anything but sell the weed, the weed was already bagged up and everything.

I got the weed and I went to school with it in my socks, ready to sell to anyone who would smoke it. I was confident and I thought that I was really doing something, people were buying the bags left and right. Out of $100 of the weed that I was being fronted, I was making about $40 profit for myself.

I thought I was the man because I had my own money. It just did not seem to add up to what I saw the guys around me making, I didn't see the profit that my brother or cousins were making, there was no way that I could help my mom like this. I had to step it up, so I went to another source and allowed him to teach me the COKE GAME.

When I first got them drugs in my hand, I was scared to death, I had to hustle in a spot where my father always visited. THE LIQUOR STORE! I used to duck and hide every time his van would pull around, I didn't know my father drank that much, he used to come to the store three or four times a day. The coke game was easier than the weed game, the money was faster, and the profit was better. Little did I know that this decision would create a monster that only God could contain?

My whole plan was to make money to help my mom, but

when I got started and the money was coming in, my mind went to the things that I wanted. My thoughts started to be about the mall and the new shoe that was coming out. I was making about $300 a day at the time. I was going to school, and then going to the liquor store after basketball practice to sell drugs.

I thought my plan was full-proof, $300 a day, 7 days a week, that's $2,100 a week. I could put something aside for my mom, and I could keep the rest. That was the plan, but the plan always gets sidetracked when you see things that you like.

I stopped selling drugs at the liquor store and went around the neighborhood that I was told to stop hanging around, the neighborhood that my brother had sold drugs in, and the neighborhood that was flowing with my family. I couldn't let no one see me, they would have killed me or told my mom, and she would have killed me.

I could have told her I had cancer and I was selling drugs to get medication; she would have killed me right on the spot. I found myself prospering faster than I planned. I graduated from high school and then my mom left the apartment to me, I was finally cut loose to live how I wanted to live.

That's when the devil really took over, I didn't have to hide what was going on. I did not have to hide the money or the clothes that was being made, or brought into the house, I was free to do whatever I wanted. You could not tell me nothing, my own car, my own apartment, and my own drug money. I was the man, but really no man at all.

A lot of stupid mistakes were being made in the drug game, some I wish that I could take back, and some I wish I could have done better. The first thing that I wish that I could have done better was, get a better understanding of what I thought that I heard, instead of leaning on my own understanding.

I found out bankruptcy did not mean going broke, I found out that it meant protecting your money in a different way, By the time I found out, it was too late.

See, that's why we must talk to our kids and see what's on their mind, that's why we have to speak to them and make them comfortable with speaking with us. If I would have sat down with my mother, and asked her what that word really meant, it could have saved me from making a lot of bad decisions.

As I sit back in my cell, and pour out these words on this paper, I feel the pain that I caused others with my decision making. I see the things that I could have done better and wondered how I got so caught up in being someone else, that I no longer saw myself.

I just sat back and thanked God for the second chance that he has given me. I allowed God to reveal my flaws, and then made a vow to change them. I finally confessed my sins and went to the Lord and said, Father, "DO SOMETHING WITH THIS MESS." As soon as I started to release everything that I had done, my vision became clear.

I started to see what was, and what is. I knew that if I didn't stop allowing the lies of the world to dictate who I was going to be, I would perish inside of the lies that I chose to believe. I made a vow to God, that I was not going to live that life anymore, and in that moment, I felt the weight of the world taken of my shoulders.

God said son, "I FORGIVE YOU!" When those words settled into my mind, I fell to the floor and thanked him for loving me enough to forgive and change the man I had become. I started to speak positive, I started to feel more positive, the old man had to go. I had finally accepted a New Life, and this New life was totally free.

I knew that the only way that I could get a second chance at life, was to get back to the one who created me, my life began when I got back with God. No matter how far you have gotten off track, it doesn't matter what you have done, as long as you are sincere with your repentance, God will give you a second chance.

He will forgive what you have done, he will erase your past if you let him, he will give you an opportunity to get it right, all you have to do is, ASK HIM! New life awaits you, it's very important that you make the right choice.

COME GET YOUR NEW LIFE!

THE ONE WHO ASKED GOD QUESTIONS!

HOW

How does a man walk through life, paying
attention to the things he's heard?
How does a man be shaken, by the lies from
then enemy's word?
How does a man not stand his ground, on
the things he really believes?
How does a man spend most of his time, talking to
a man on his knees?
How can a man take a woman's love, and time after
time he betrays her?
How can a man promise protection, when he's in no
position to save her?
How can a man be understood in life, when his
speech consists of slurs?
How does a man crash in life, when direction is
within God's word?

HOW

"How" was another poem that was written in the middle of the night, the spirit was really at work and I couldn't resist letting the spirit flow. How represents the things that were running through my mind now that my run is over, and all the things I've done flashes back before my eyes.

After God transformed me into the man that He wants me to be, I asked myself why did I do these things to myself and to others? How could the man that I am today, be responsible for the things I've done in the past?

How could I have hurt so many women by telling

them I love them but show them something different? How could I spend a lot of time on my knees praying to God, then spend most of my life walking like I didn't even know him?

How could I lay with a woman and make her all these promises like, I will always be here for you and protect you, when I couldn't even make that promise to myself? These are the feelings I got after I went through the first steps of my transformation, and the answer to those questions was, because I was listening to the wrong voice, and I was playing for the wrong team.

In my past I didn't know God, and because of that I didn't care about doing the right thing, so the consequences of bad decisions were far from my thought process. I just did whatever came to mind and dealt with the consequences later. I heard the enemy loud and clear when it came to making tough decisions, I knew that was the voice of the enemy because the consequences would be bad every time, I did what the voice said.

I now know the voice of God at that time was my CONSCIOUS the voice that told me to make the unpopular decision in every situation. Tell the truth, don't lie, don't cheat, be authentic, don't go to the club, stop selling drugs, be truthful to that girl, keep praying, you don't have to fight everyone who disrespects you.

This is what God was saying to me when I was in the midst of my madness, He was trying to get me to do the right thing in every situation, but I would only listen SOMETIMES!

The Lord was telling me which way to go to not have to deal with these kinds of storms and feelings. My eyes were flooded by those things I wanted to see, instead of the things that I needed to see. That's how the enemy works, he keeps the foolish things of the world in your view so you can chase them, and never get on the path that was set for you.

See, the devil knows how strong you'll be once you find direction. He's scared of you and the damage you'll do to his kingdom once you find the light, which is already in you. Don't let those distractions of the world stop you from being the strong Man or Woman you were created to be. You were created to be GREAT, so BE GREAT!

NO LOOKING BACK

Is there anybody out there, I swear I
feel so all alone,
Down on my knees again, ask God to
bring me home,
In my mind still confused, as a tear
drops from my eye,
I haven't smiled in years, and still
can't figure out why,
Is it the death that I escaped, or the
demons of my past?
What's the meaning of this pain, and
how long will it last.
The solution lies within me, as I wait for
the light to shine,

To relieve me from these thoughts, that have been trapped inside my mind
I've been saved plenty of times, there's a purpose for my life,
Will I do the easy wrong, or submit and do things right,
There's an answer to my question, and I'll keep digging until I find
But I'll never take a step forward, if I keep living from behind.

NO LOOKING BACK

"No Looking Back" is a poem that represents the mind state of a man, that realizes he has more to offer than what he has been giving. He sees the damage that he's done and makes a vow to himself that he will never repeat those same mistakes again. This man was me, I realized what I had done, the damage that I had caused, and decided to move forward.

When I looked back on all that I've done I could not get over some of the mistakes I've made, I couldn't smile because, NOTHING WAS FUNNY! Sometimes I faked a smile during more pleasant times, because I knew the moment would only last for a second.

The only way to see past the things you've done, is to let it go. I know it's easier said than done because there are so many distractions that remind you of the things you've done, or the person you've overcame. I am a walking testimony of a man caught up in his past, but when I was given the opportunity to give my past situations to

God, I did just that.

A couple of months after I submitted, God relieved me of the pain, the regrets, and the guilt I carried for a long time. I had a special saying I quoted every day, "I am relieved of the regrets and the guilt of my past", I found myself not thinking about or dreading the past less and less as the day's went on.

I stopped talking about it and soon the people who knew of my past, didn't want to talk about it anymore either, it was just a sign from God telling me that it was time to let it go. A lot of times we are prisoners of our past because we refuse to let the memory go, it's like your holding yourself hostage in a place where pain exist.

No matter what you have done in your past don't let it hinder you from enjoying the fruits of a prosperous life. You'll never be able to see who you're supposed to become or the blessings that belong to you, by taking constant looks into life's rearview mirror. Once you have made a conscious decision to change your life and give it to God, "you are a new creation, Old things have passed away, and all things become new" (2 Corinthians 5-17).

What happened then doesn't even matter anymore! The enemy will do his best to try to make the things of your past become a part of your life today but, you must make sure your focus is stayed on what lies ahead.

There were times when people would try to remind me of who I use to be, I would ignore them because they can only remind a man that's listening. A new man does not listen to old things, it's like they are speaking another language. I encourage everyone reading this chapter today, step out on faith and let go of anything and everything that is tied to your old life or lifestyle. The future is what counts, the past is gone, so it's time to move on.

A LETTER TO MY FATHER

I'm writing this letter to you my Lord, in confession of all my sins,
I've done so many horrible things, so I don't know where to begin,
I'll start at a time as a kid I guess, where wrong things felt so right,
Running around chasing girls, and always looking to fight.
I'm older now, my sins are greater, and those flashy things start to look good,
Now I'm deep in the game a neighborhood star, envied and loved in my hood.
Running with guys, deceitful men, surrounded by thoughts that's shady,
Cruising through girls, and loving my moment, not knowing how to treat a real lady.
It's time to be punished for the decisions I've made, as the doors are shut in this cell,
Down on my knees, letting go of the GOOCH, to discover the real John Bell!

A LETTER TO MY FATHER

This was a small poem describing my thoughts, and feelings while I was living within my adolescent lifestyle, and how I gave it all up to have a second chance to do right.

I remember when I was young, chasing girls,

running around playing “Freaky Friday” and loving every minute of it. I remember fighting all the time, in my era you had to fight to be respected or you would be the punching bag. It was fun being a kid, not having any worries, no bills, and no temptation, as a kid there weren’t too many opportunities that arise that forced you to make a right or wrong decision. Life was just so simple, the only worry I had every day was if my girlfriend was going to let me get a kiss or let me rub on her butt the next day.

Then you hit that age where you start to see things and start to pay attention, make tough decisions and asking questions. At this stage you can honestly say, life has just gotten real. Negative things start to look good and an adolescent eye falls in love with the chase only to be disappointed when you have to pay the price for making a decision to pursue something that’s not good for you.

Whoever thought I would have to pay for adolescent mistakes as an adult? Who knew that the status of the neighborhood star would lead me into a life of stress, betrayal, deceit, lust, and a jail cell?
My past lifestyle was influenced by the things that I saw as an adolescent.

Temptations were everywhere and every time I gave into temptation the consequences got a little tougher. The pain that came with a bad decision was almost unbearable. I found myself down on my knees asking God to change the way I think, change the way I look at life, I don’t want to be looked at as the GOOCH anymore, I want to be John Bell Jr., the one that my mother birthed.

As a kid I was never taught how to do certain things, I didn't know how to be truthful, until the teacher (GOD) allowed me to go through a few situations where I was lied too. I would call home and ask a family member to send pictures, only to hear I am sending them today and never receive them. He was teaching me by giving me a taste of my own medicine.

I was taught how to treat a lady by keeping me away from them. At the time that I am writing this letter, I have not been with a woman in 7 and a half years. The absence of a female gave me a strong desire to treat them better, it's unique how God chooses to teach us how to be men.

Now that I was in the place where I am supposed to be, he is downloading information in me that I really needed. He's teaching me about Trust, Honesty, Loyalty, Love, Family, and the most important, He's teaching me about Christ. The information He's giving me will be very helpful when I leave this jail cell.

As I sat and listened to God, I paid less attention to things that were not righteous, maturing to a point where I needed to be around righteous people. I started to see the real motives of the guys that I was running around with, these guys who I would call my friends.

I understood why I betrayed friends and was disloyal to people, it was because I was betrayed, and people were disloyal to me. They say you become what you surround yourself with, so if you hang around negative people you will eventually become a negative person.

I never knew the real meaning of trust, until I

felt like that I could not be trusted. It's like I had to betray someone and see how it affected them, to realize that it was wrong.

I was at the Classics Night Club on Allentown Road; it was the place to be. Women spent all day finding the right outfit to get guys attention and men would try to spend all they could to be the one taking it off that night. It was in a secluded area of Morningside Maryland, tucked in the corner across the street from Andrews Air Force Base.

I would always go there to see Rare Essence, a popular Go-Go Band in our area. People would come from all over the DMV to see R.E. I loved going to see them, but I loved being seen. The atmosphere was mine for the taking, I would sit by the bar and wait for the women to acknowledge me, which fed my little boy ego.

This night in particular was different, I was mesmerized by this female, Cathy was her name. She was the girlfriend of Pete, a guy I did big business with from time to time. We had a code amongst businessmen; we don't come onto your woman, sister, the mother of your child, or side chick nor allow them to come on to us.

Cathy was so pretty with a gorgeous dark brown complexion, her body was shaped like a Greek Goddess, she stood about 5' 4" at 145 lbs., long natural hair, and eyes that made a man melt. I saw her coming and I couldn't take my eyes off her. She looked me in my eyes as she slowly glided towards me, I watched her shiny soft lips part as she spoke,

"Hi Goochie."

She spoke to me before, but it was something different about this night, it was like she was trying to seduce me with her eyes. I snapped out of my gaze and I returned her greeting,

"Hello, Cathy! "I said with lust in my eyes

She said, "Can I buy you a drink?

That was strange because I always bought the drinks. I told her I couldn't allow that.

"You are such a gentleman", she said as she gave me a long hug wrapping her arms around me and pushing her pelvis against mine.

I was already two drinks in and feeling a little freaky. Remy Martin VSOP was my go-to drink when I went to the club, it was the Drug Dealers' Viagra. I tried my best to honor the code, but she was making it hard, literally. I bought her an Apple Martini and a bottle of water.

She said, "thank you so much!" and gave me another hug. This time she held on a little tighter holding my back pulling me closer to her. I was shocked at her advances because her boyfriend was getting a lot of money, I was getting money too, but not like him.

Pete was from Glenarden Apartments in Landover Md, a popular drug strip on that side of town. He was about 4 years older than me and had been in the drug game longer. I met him when I was a youngster around Homer Ave, he was one of the guys I watched when I was growing up. We ran into each other again when I came home from my first prison sentence; we greeted each other and immediately started to speak about the Drug game, and how we could help each other. At that point, he became a business partner and that made his woman off limits.

We didn't want to mix our relationships with business, and we didn't want to go to war and mess money up over a female. So, we set rules and everyone who was committed to getting money honored the rule. Cathy knew the rules, so that made me feel awkward when she approached me the way she did. As I broke her embrace, I looked her in her eyes and told her if she needed anything I would be by the bar.

Men were staring at her with their mouths wide open, gazing at her body as she danced around swaying those full hips attached to that nice round Butt. She loved attention and she ate it up that night. Her vibe was different, she is usually more reserved and antisocial. Not this night, she was more sociable and aggressive.

Usually when a woman changes up her moods like that, her boyfriend has been caught cheating and she wants a little revenge. She stared at me the entire night, I stared right back envisioning having sex with her from the back grabbing that long pretty hair of hers. She turned around swaying her hips from side to side in a motion that held my attention, she backed up towards me almost touching me and then she would walk away. She was a master and whatever it was, it was working.

The Remy kicked in and my morals washed away

with each sip. She walked back over to me and whispered in my ear, "I am so horny, and I can tell by the print in your pants that you are too." When she pulled her head back and looked into my eyes, I was lost in her gaze, I remember saying, "YES I AM!"

"What are we going to do about it?", she said as she grabbed my hand and led me to the door. All rules and codes were broken the moment she walked in the door and approached me, can't blame it on the liquor I knew what I was doing. My car was parked in the front of the club almost at the door, she asked me to follow her and I did.

We made a right out of the parking lot onto Allentown Rd, passing the Dunkin' Donuts and McDonalds and made a right into the Holiday Inn on the corner of Suitland and Allentown Rd, about a quarter of a mile down from the club. We parked in the back and made our way to the rear entrance of the hotel. She stopped at the elevator and flashed the key letting me know she already had a room.

At this point I thought it was a setup, because the night had gone strangely smooth. I had my Glock 40 on me, but I was thinking with my penis so the thought of being setup went away.

The elevator chimed and the doors opened, she grabbed my hand and said, "We are breaking all the rules because they need to be broken." Not really caring about what she said because the Remy killed my conscious.

Cathy pushed 4 and the elevator took off, I

couldn't wait to get to the room. She lifted up her skirt and pulled her pink satin panties off, I could smell her perfume and it was driving me crazy. The elevator stopped, the doors flew open, she grabbed my hand, and we walked off.

Room 401 was the first room to the right; she pulled the key out her purse and opened the door. I stopped for a second because my conscious tried to kick in but the Remy and the anticipation of having sex with this woman killed that quick.

She reached around and pulled her hair to the side and snapped the clasp on her dress, with a slight twitch it fell to the floor exposing a work of God. She was well put together and she knew it! The view of her body from the back was incredible she had a deep arch in her back that made her butt sit up, her skin looked so soft and moist I wanted to taste her.

She turned on her heel slowly to face me, I gazed at her perky breast and freshly shaved vagina; everything on her body was so cute and well put together. I looked her in her eyes as she asked if I wanted her hair pinned up. I broke my gaze and told her no! She walked towards me slow and seductively until I could feel her breath on my neck, she flicked her tongue up a grabbed the center of my pants.

I wanted her, and I wanted her bad, I pushed her on the bed and took off my jeans like they were on fire. I went in my pocket to grab a condom, but she grabbed my hand and pulled me on top of her -REMY MARTIN allowed this to happen. I laid on top of her and she guided me inside. Guilt, Pleasure, Guilt, Pleasure, were the thoughts I was wrestling with at the time.

Her body was soft and warm; it felt like she was trying to match me, stroke for stroke, I looked in her eyes as I made sure I held my reputation of being a good lover every time I thrust my manhood inside of her.

"Deeper...Deeper", she moaned as I explored different parts of her vagina by swirling my hips from side to side, alternating deep long strokes as I elevated my body into a pushup position. This angle allowed the head of my penis to caress her clitoris with every stroke, "A MASTER"

I thought to myself as I watched her bite her bottom lip as she squirmed in ecstasy. I flipped her leg over to my right, so she could be lying comfortably on her side almost in the fetal position. This was the position I worked when I really wanted to show off my size.

I held her left hip and slid her by the waist to the end of the bed, which was leveled in height with my waist giving me good leverage. Pap, Pap, Pap, was the soundtrack of the moment as our flesh met with every aggressive stroke; I wanted her to feel me in her soul. "GOOCHIE, GOOCHIE!!" she yelled, it turned me on even more!

Another slight shift and she was lying on her stomach, arching her back to give me direct access to my favorite position. Sweat was dripping from our bodies as I straddled her with my legs on each side. “Cross your ankles”, I said as I slid back inside her.

She twitched as I grabbed her hair. I love to feel a woman’s skin against mine while we’re having sex, it gives me an adrenaline rush. As I started to grind and swirl my hips, I exited and re-entered with aggressive strokes just to watch her body shiver. I knew she was beginning to climax, so I sped my stroke up pressing my body up against her while nibbling on her ear interlocking my fingers with hers.

It was important that I executed these maneuvers because it heightened the intimacy and kept me in control. I learned how to listen to a woman’s body during sex, which made me a great lover. I knew when to slow down, speed up, change positions, grab her throat, allow her to lead, stop when she’s climaxing and/ or aggressively stroke. Also, when she wanted to be held in her moment or wanted to be dominated. I had it down to a science.

After an hour of moaning, grunting, competing, kissing and pulling, we both climaxed and collapsed on the bed. She got up and went to the bathroom, “YOU ARE A MONSTER” she said as she disappeared, I smiled and said “YOU HEARD ABOUT ME.”

We both laughed as my phone rang, I just knew that it was my girl but when I picked the phone up off the floor, the name on the screen shocked me. ‘PETE’ was the name that I saw on the screen of my phone. As she came back out of the bathroom, I showed her the phone, don't answer she said as guilt set in we both seen it on each other's face, I put the phone back down as it stopped ringing.

The phone chirped letting me know that I had a voice mail, I picked it up and hit the button to listen to it, pressing the speaker button and whipping myself with the rag she brought out Pete's voice came from the phone, he was drunk, and he was crying.

Homie I know that this call is out of order, but I always can talk to you, this isn't a business call I need some advice. You're a good dude and you always have something good to say when I'm in your presence, GUILT was killing me with every word.

Bro my girl answered my phone the other day when Lisa called, Lisa was the lady our connect used to call us when the shipment arrived at the drop. He figured a female calling talking to us about sex would always throw the police off if our phones were tapped.

She asked me who she was, and I couldn't tell her because of our code, 'Never tell your girl about the business so she will not have nothing to tell the police if you get caught'. That was the rule, she got mad at me and left the house, I haven't seen or heard from her in two days.

She is everything to me homie, I can't see life without her. I heard that she was at the club tonight and I know you are always there. Homie I just want to know that she is alright, I haven't cheated on her I don't even talk to no other women, I bought the wedding ring and I was planning to propose to her on her birthday next week. I looked at her and told her who Lisa was, she burst out crying and I felt terrible.

She started grabbing her things getting dressed, I got up and put my clothes on with my head down feeling like trash. We both were dressed in minutes and we left the room, we got to the elevator not even looking at each other, guilt was eating us up.

The elevator opened, and we stepped in, I pushed L and the door closed and we rode in silence. The elevator got to the bottom floor and opened, we stepped out and went out the back door to the parking lot. Headlights came on and I turned my head to see Pete's car pulling up. I knew that his phone call was strange,

I didn't know what would happen next, but I was prepared either way. As his car rolled up, we both stood there in shock, He got out of the car with his pistol in his hand and looked me in my eye's, I pulled my pistol and placed it by my side.

I wasn't a shooter, but this type of betrayal would cause pistols to be drawn, you can't put anything pass a man who has been betrayed by a friend, especially when it comes to his woman. In that moment my head cleared and my conscious kicked in, here I am standing in front of my comrade after sexing his woman that he was in love with.

Here I am guilty of dishonoring so many codes amongst men because I wasn't strong enough to resist temptation of a female. One wrong decision can be responsible for multiple wrong decisions and tonight I realized this wasn't a good decision.

"So, you gonna have sex with my girl and shoot me?" Out of all the dudes I thought were capable of something like this, you never crossed my mind. Nigga, you have taught me a valuable lesson today, we had multiple conversations about how much I loved my woman!", he said with rage in his eyes."

Did you really think about this before you did this? How could you possibly think I wasn't going to find out? Nigga you WEAK," Pete said as he raised his gun, Cathy screamed as I raised mine.

In this moment my mind was on overload, my family, his family, the business, prison, and death were my thoughts. The backdoor to the hotel flew open as three drunk women stumbled into the crossfire not realizing what was going on. They were so drunk they walked right pass without acknowledging us, we both put our guns down. As the door to the hotel began to close you could hear multiple voices coming our way.

"Today changes everything slim," Pete said, as he was getting in his car Cathy tried to speak. He turned towards her and said, "I'm glad this happened because I was about to give my last name to a WHORE, the right pressure produces the real person EVERYTIME!" You were waiting for an opportunity, if one unanswered question caused you to sleep with a comrade" Pete said.

Cathy started to speak, Pete raised his gun, "Shut up!" "I don't want to hear shit, you don't exist to me, I'd rather be hurt in this moment rather than wake up beside someone for the rest of my life who's waiting to be disloyal."

The backdoor opened again but this time it was hotel security, Pete tossed his gun on the seat when the security guard looked at Cathy concerned because she was crying.

Pete was a major part of my money, this would really hurt my business, he tried to hold it back, but he couldn't, he looked at Cathy and asked her why, the sound of his voice made me feel like trash. I tried to walk towards my car, but Pete cut me off, now physically I could crush Pete, but because of my betrayal I had to go with the flow.

"Why is it that every time I trust someone, they betray me, he said?" I felt like this was a perfect time to try to calm the situation while still holding my ground. I came within striking distance as he raised his head with death in his eyes and said, "Slim I promise you if you come any closer, you're going have to use that gun."

I was wrong, so I had to swallow that statement and walk away. He pulled his self together got in his car and sped out of the parking lot. Every step I took towards my car felt crazy; his words danced around in my head for hours. I couldn't believe I allowed a woman to put me in a position to kill or be killed but, most of all lose the respect of a genuine dude.

God brought this situation back to my memory, but he allowed me to feel Pete's pain. As I sat in that dark cell, I realized I've hurt so many people with acts of betrayal. I thought to myself, that's it I have to change!

It sounds funny but it's the truth. I had to feel the pain of the people I hurt, in order to want to change the character flaw within me that gave me the capabilities to be disloyal, deceitful, and ingenuine. It's like I had to be wrong first in order to be taught how to do right! I am very appreciative of the things I learned in my past;

I embraced my failures so I can move forward. I am glad God has opened my eyes to allow me to see that it's the mature mindset that people respect. Thank God for the chance that I have been given to correct an immature mindset.

STILL STANDING

I've been standing in the storm, and my eyes are filled with rain,
I wonder when the sun will shine, I hope that things will change,
As I look around, I see no friends, who spoke their love to me,
But I noticed after constant prayer, they were not who the said to be,
Even the women who laid with me, and lied in a moment of lust,
They were the first to leave I wasn't surprised, the ones that I could not trust.
My sun will shine they'll see me again, the ones who did me wrong,
They thought their absence would make me weak, but it only made me strong.
Look at me, I'm wiser now, and my mind is clear of stress,
I'll be home soon to reclaim my crown; I promise to be at my best.
I've given my life to God for good, and his work

is real demanding.
So all that left me you'll be ashamed, because you see, that I'm still standing.

STILL STANDING

God opened my eyes and allowed me to survey my support system, I looked around and saw my own reflection! This is when I realized that no matter what people say to you, their actions is what really counts.

I remember being out there in the streets thinking everyone was my friend or in my corner. I realized that the streets only love their own, no one or no friendship acquired in the street life is meant for you to keep. Nothing is based on who you are, it's only based upon what you bring to the table.

You see who's a true friend in tough times. It really hurts to find out the people you thought were really for you, "YOUR RIDE OR DIE PEOPLE" were all smoke and mirrors.

Most friendships and relationships acquired were only for business, and business alone and I learned that the hard way. I had a tight circle of money makers; you couldn't tell us nothing.
It was five of us and money circulated in 3 different ways: Powder Cocaine, Crack, and Weed.

I sold Crack; it was a lot of work turning the powder cocaine into crack, but it sold fast, and the clientele was plentiful. Powder cocaine was a quick flip, I could get 36 ounces for $17,500 and sell them for $1,100 a piece; $39,600 is a good profit. I wouldn't have to sit in a crack house or stand on the corner.

We all had different styles of hustling and every plan made a profit; we ate, shopped, and counted a lot of money together. Competition begin to set in from: watches, cars, clothes, and most of all the attention of the females. Loyalty was tested in tight spots; I saw the signs of envy and overheard a few conversations that told me what I needed to hear.

We went out one night and one of my team members got into a fight, his fault as usual. Apparently, the guy looked at him too long, so he cursed the guy out and put a cigar out in his drink. Lee was a shooter, he loved to start trouble with the biggest guy even though he was only 5"7 150 pounds.

He loved to fight and argue, but for some strange reason I would be the one who would end up settling his beefs by voice of reason or violence. After he dropped the black & mild in the guy's cup he went off, I watched the whole situation transpire in disbelief.

Here we were again about to mess up a good party because of Lee's foolish pride. I looked over and saw an old business partner of mine; he was a big dude, about 6'8" 310 lbs. with a terrible temper. He was security at a club in Upper Marlboro. I attended a party he was working one night, and he informed me that I left my lights on in my car and that's how we started conversing, I've seen his work.

Damn, I said to myself as he came across the room moving people out of his way by choice or force, he made his own path. He was the head of the crew that Lee just disrespected, I got his attention and he smiled and signaled his crew to stand down. We smiled and embraced each other with strong handshakes, I told him Lee was with me and I would buy his team a round of drinks.

We clearly out gunned them, but it was more sensible to buy a few drinks and leave it at that. I was hoping

like hell he didn't decline my offer and we could settle this without anyone getting hurt, yet I was prepared for the outcome either way.

Big dude looked down at me and said,

"Don't worry about it I got it. I just got a new connect and he doesn't tolerate any unnecessary attention, he is giving me great numbers, I am not messing that up! Tell your man he almost messed up a good thing and got a lot of people hurt."

"I'll take care of it", I assured him.

This was an ongoing thing with Lee, he felt he had to prove a point to the people who already knew that he was a fool. I pulled everyone together and we exited the club. By the time we left Lee was drunk out of his mind with two females escorting him to his car. Although I would drink, for the most part, I'd still be sober, I'd always make sure everyone got to their cars safely.

Walking to our cars I saw two guys walk up behind Lee, they couldn't see me, and they never bothered to look around. I got closer as one of the guys grabbed Lee and spun him around.

"What was that you were saying in the club, sucka?" One of the guys said. By this time, I was on his heels he never heard me creep up behind him. Lee couldn't even focus as he slurred something the guy couldn't understand. The two females grabbed the guy's arm yelling "get off him!" I slid between the girls and asked the first guy, "What was wrong?"

He looked at me and swung. He was drunk so it was in slow motion, I dodged his punch and hit him with a short right hook on his chin, I tried to crush his face with the amount of power I put behind the punch. He fell to the ground and started snoring.

The second guy took off and I grabbed Lee and rushed him to my car. As we were walking to the car shots rang out, I ducked and dodged as we scrambled to get to the car. We got to the car in one piece and pulled off. I was so mad at Lee because this is his normal routine starting fights or arguments for no reason at all.

I dropped him off at his mom's house and sped off, I would get a phone call from Lee the next day apologizing for his actions, he repeated this act so much that I didn't believe him. I decided to stop going out with him, he would call and ask about my plans for the night and I would say I'm not going out.

After a couple weeks of avoiding the club, he stopped asking., I realized he only called when it was time to go out. I was the bruiser of the bunch and he loved the fact that I wouldn't allow anyone to put their hands on him.

In this lifestyle people only use you for what you're worth to them, if they can't benefit off you it's no reason to be friends. I don't care how loyal you were to them, or how many times you stood against crazy odds together, no matter how many times you risked your life for them, or saved them, get into a financial jam, or go to jail and that's it.

Then there are the women. I don't know why I thought that these women would be right by my side during this storm. They weren't random women, these were women who looked me right in my eyes and say, "I LOVE YOU, I WILL ALWAYS BE THERE FOR YOU, I'M NOT LIKE THEM OTHER GIRLS YOU DEALT WITH."

All that was smoke and mirrors as well, it took for me to go to prison to realize that people are not who they say they are. I made a lot of mistakes in my life and those mistakes exposed their motive. They weren't there because of love, they loved the benefits of being around me?

I remember having a conversation with a female and she said, "you keep going out there messing with all those women, but who is going to be there when things hit the fan, ME!" She was the first one to leave, I thought she would be the first one to put that head gear on and take every punch, every blow, endure every storm. No matter what I went through, in my mind she was supposed to be there.

It's funny that when things happen like this, it's always the people that you wouldn't think would be there end up being your help in a time of need. The ones that you never paid attention to or disrespected every chance that you got. I did a head count the other day, and I can count on one hand who has really stood strong with me. I don't want anyone that reads this to get it confused, I am not mad at no one, I am totally cool with the fact that NO ONE is here.

I had to really sit back and go over the things that I have been taught by their betrayal, I learned that no one is obligated to be more to you then what they are. I've learned when you do something for someone, you do it because you want to. You don't do it to get something in return, that's one of the most important lessons I've learned since I have been walking in this storm. No one is obligated to you because of what you have done for them, their only obligation is to themselves!

God said, "as you step into a new life the old people and old places will be stripped from you" (2 Corinthians5:17). They still aspire to see that man that got you this 15 year. "He said when you walk out of here, you will not be that guy anymore, you will not need these people anymore."

Just be happy that they have served their purpose and move on. Always get what you can out of a relationship/friendship, as in learn as much as you can. God also revealed to me the reason why I was counting on people to be there for me, was because that's what I would have done for them. He said son, I only made ONE OF YOU, and everyone is not going to see life like you are, so get over it.

I used to think that people were really in my corner, and then when I found out that they were not, I use to be hurt, and that pain use to turn in to anger. Those thoughts used to turn into thoughts of revenge, which caused me to make some very stupid mistakes. I never knew when people continuously you wrong, it starts to change the person that you are.

The bible says, “Evil company corrupts good habits”, 1 Corinthians 15:33! I realized I had surrounded myself with some bad dudes, and that was rubbing off on me quick. Everyone counted me out, they saw the time that I received, and they said, HE IS DONE! When I first received my sentence, it spread across the city in 5 minutes, from what I heard there were a lot of mixed emotions.

Some were sad that I was gone, and some danced in the streets. This prison sentence has taught me a lot, I don’t know if I would’ve learned these lessons in the streets. I wouldn’t have realized that I am a better person by myself, I don’t move well in crowds.

When God has called you to be something special, he will allow you to go through things that others would not have been able to survive. Now I see why I am Still Standing, there might be storms that come that will shake your foundation, trials and tribulations that will inflict pain that is unbearable at times.

Just know that God has a plan for all the pain that you feel, all the tears that you’ve cried, and all the times that you have been hurt, there is a purpose for your pain.

I want to encourage everyone that reads this chapter, everyone is not going to want to be your friend, when it’s really time to be a friend. You are going to have to stand by yourself during times when you feel like you need people to stand with you the most. It's those times that God is going to be working on you, when you will be all by yourself! Just know that no matter what happens, no matter how you feel, YOU HAVE TO STAND UP STRAIGHT, you must hold your head up after all the mistakes, all the hurt, all the pain.

Walk into your storms knowing that God is going to be right there, open your heart and receive the message that God is going to deliver while you are going through. Make a commitment to yourself that you will stand tall even when your circumstances make you feel like giving up. The only way to get through, is to GO THROUGH!

If you don't give up, you'll be the one that they speak about while saying, everything that tried to crush him/her, didn't work. All the storms that he/she has been through made them better. I thought he/she wouldn't make it, but through it all, they are STILL STANDING!

THE OLD MAN

I was fading and fading fast, Lord please come hold my hand
Am I really supposed to feel like this, even though I'm a new man?
Is my body supposed to be tired? Is my mind supposed to be stressed?
It seems like I'm walking a fine line, but still,
I'm not at my best.
I'll pull back from the world, restructure my mind and constantly read my word,
I'll fall if I submit to the voices of sin, along

with the things I've heard.
It's good that I have a safety net, and a voice that I can trust,
It's not only for me it applies to you, and He shows that He cares about us.
The first thing I'll do is read my word; I also know I must fast,
Makes no difference I will be strong; I'll never be the man from my past.

THE OLD MAN

"The Old Man" is a poem that was written when I got to FCI Memphis, this place was gang infested. I couldn't believe the things I saw when I got there. There were so many different races and it seemed like no races got along with one another. Well, as I started to proceed across the compound, the old version of myself was in full effect. I was just getting used to walking around in a hostile environment as a Man of God!

When I saw the men with their faces balled up, I caught myself returning the same stare. I heard the old me saying, you might have to make an example early or it's going to be rough.

I wrestled with that situation for a long time. About 6 months after I got there, I was in the building with some guys I knew from my past, (BEFORE CHRIST). They knew how aggressive I was, and they couldn't believe the words that were coming out of my mouth. After I had explained to them which way I was walking, they respected my decision but, they watched me a lot to see if I was serious. It seemed like every time

I spoke about my change, I had to prove I've changed.

The test were coming from everywhere. The first test came from a young guy who was about 5 foot 5, one hundred and thirty pounds, he had a bad speech problem, so it was hard to hear what he was saying. I was in the T.V room watching an old episode of Martin. He came strolling in the room, walked right passed me and turned the T.V. Without acknowledging me or asking was I watching the T.V, that is a total sign of disrespect in the prison system. I stopped him in his tracks and told him to turn the T.V back to what I was watching, He immediately tried to say something but, it wouldn't come out and I didn't care.

I stood up and walked towards him because he still didn't turn the T.V back and he was still standing their trying to get his words out, I told myself if he didn't turn back by the time I got in arms reach I was going to try to crush his skull. He finally got his words out and that didn't make the situation and better. He was hollering and moving around really aggressive. That was always a recipe to get you an early nap/put to sleep. I was at my breaking point and I felt a calm inside of me that strangely took all the anger away.

I listened to him as he jumped around saying something I couldn't understand, I got tired of the antics, so I spoke with authority, yet I remained calm. I told myself that I would try it the way the voice was telling me to try it and see if it works, but there was still a part of me that was yearning to put this young guy in his bed early. I explained to him that I was a Man that lived by principle and respect, I would give it and demanded it in return. I spoke to him about Pride and how this T.V just put us in a position to possibly never go home to our families.

By the grace of God, the cooler head prevailed, he understood what I was trying to say to him, and he knew that I wasn't no pushover. My buddies that knew me from my past had gotten wind of what happened, and they came and asked me what was up, I hated that, when I would get into a fight, I never looked for back up, so I hated when back up came.

In prison, when a fight is about to break out it normally gets loud before the fighting begins. The commotion would always bring a lot of attention so, real men would try to calm it down and revisit things later. They would go inside a cell where you are able to cover up the door and allow Men to be Men, FIGHT! My buddies just wanted to know if it was over, and they also wanted to tell me they saw I was serious about my change.

I realized that God was giving me a moment to think about things instead of just reacting. Before I came into the knowledge of Christ, I would have never thought about it, it would have been on right there and then. God was giving me a way out of the foolishness; it was just up to me to take the way out. I encountered a few other situations, then realized after every time I would resist and old thought, it was getting a little easier to overcome.

I had come up with a strategy, whenever I felt as though I was about to lose it, I would just pull back from everyone and go read my word. "Literally fasting from people".

I wouldn't come out to eat, nothing but Fasting, Praying, and Reading. This would be my pattern for about a week, that's how serious I was about overcoming the old man that tricked me into this situation. When you are used to handling a situation one way, it is extremely hard to handle it in another way. Especially when your decisions are driven by your ego.

God showed me that I could walk away from a situation that called for violence, and still be a Man. I realized that this new plan was not easy to follow but, the results were always better, I didn't have to grab a knife and sleep with one eye open, I didn't have to worry about the police coming to get me and try to charge me with an assault. I was worry free, and after every situation my faith got a little stronger. Don't believe for one second that this thing is going to be easy, if you commit your life to Christ, your whole mindset must change. You can no longer handle situations like you want, they must be handled like God said if you want the right results, it must be done the right way, "God's Way"!

I had a struggle with worrying about what people thought or said after I let a situation go, I thought to myself, are they thinking that I am soft, do they think that they can run over me? I had to fight them thoughts often and I am still struggling at this moment. I just thank God for introducing me to a method that will help get the foolishness out of me. This is a message to those people who have to fight the old you. If you don't feed something it has no choice but to die, don't feed the OLD YOU, and He or She will die!
GOD BLESS!

LORD THANK YOU

Lord I thank you for my vision today, for the feeling of the sun on my face,
I thank you for this period of rest, because my legs were sore from the race.
That race where I ran in circles a lot, because I had no sense of direction,
Lord I thank you for your Love while I ran, because your hand has been my protection.
See a lot of us know it, and we hear that voice, but still we're dizzy from spinning,
The enemy tells encourages us to run, and he makes us think that we're winning.
As soon as you start to run that race, indeed you've already lost,
But we can start over, and run the right way, that's why he died on the cross.
All the times while running that race, and our lives will come to a halt,
That was the work of our Savior, it's His way of having his talk.
No matter what the enemy says, you can receive a Blessing, a Chance,
It's time to smile and laugh at Satan, it's time to do the Lord's dance.

LORD THANK YOU

"Lord, Thank You" was another poem to let GOD know how much I really love and appreciate Him for all that He has done for me. Thanking Him for all the times that He has saved me from myself and others.

I remember the exact moment when I wrote this poem, I was sitting in my cell staring at the sun and it was shining directly on my face, so I closed my eyes and let the warm feeling give me comfort. It felt like

God was touching me on the side of my face like a parent rubs a child's face to let them know how proud they are of them. I started to go back through my thoughts and replay all the things that I've been through.

I realized it was only God that got me through the things I survived. I spoke about this situation in SUBMISSION, you come to a place in life where you just get tired of running, and certain situations just makes you say, THAT'S IT! I just can't do this anymore.

You get tired from spinning out of control, you get dizzy from running in circles only to get back to the same spot in which you started. I look at life as a race, a race to Live and a race to Die. A race to live, because so many people try to live life on a clock, and cram everything in at one time.

Trying to see how fast they can become prosperous but, they never get there despite the pace they're running. The fast pace leaves so much room for error, when you are moving too fast you miss things you were supposed to see.

Then you have those who run the race trying to cheat life, not realizing this race could eventually lead them to Death! These are the people who live their lives in the streets, trying to make ends meet the wrong way. These people base every second of their lives around money and ways to make it. They try to sell every drug that they can get their hands on, Dope, Weed, Coke, E-Pills, or PCP just to bring in a profit.

You are just racing towards the end of your life, and what type of man wants to live an entire lifetime and have nothing to show for it. "What Profits a Man to Gain the Whole World but In Return He Loses His Soul" (MATTHEW 16:26)!

When God sits you down for a second to talk with you, embrace the time and thank Him for sitting you down and not LAYING you down. Take the chance to do good people, and never look back, start to dance in victory because it's already yours. Dancing with the Lord makes one heck of a beat, all you need to do is listen to what's being said, and you never have to worry about not having direction again.

When the Lord sits you down to have his talk, He will make you deal with those things of your past. Then He will forgive you, show you how to forgive yourself, and allow you to start over "CLEAN"! Take your time getting out of the gate, move more effective and efficient. Prosperity doesn't come over night, so embrace all the moments that it takes to get to the top. Once you get there, I promise you will appreciate it more!!!

ALMOST OVER

The days are getting long, the
nights are even longer,
The road is getting tough, so my
walk must be stronger.

The air is getting thin, so I start to
save my breath,
So when the air is needed, I'll use what I have left.
Temptations getting tougher, because I'm closer to my
end,
It's the Lord who gives me strength, so on him I will
depend.
Pushing through my past, I see the lights up ahead,
So I continue to stay in places, that my hungry
soul can be fed.
As I look at all my friends, who are fresh in their
storms,
I try to give them help, so their worldly mind
can transform.
See I'm a living testament, of the way that
God can work,
So when you see me smiling, just remember I USED TO
HURT.
Just keep your eyes on the Lord, and those things that's
promised to you,
You're guaranteed to be blessed, and those dreams will
surely come TRUE.

ALMOST OVER

"Almost Over" is a poem written in the last months of Solitary Confinement. No one told me I was in the last months of the investigation but, in my Spirit, I knew! It felt like this part of my training was over, It was time to put what God had done with me on display. Just like any other storm, when you are about to come out of it. There will be so many things that come about trying to make you stumble right at the brink of your blessing.

The devil hears when you speak but, he is terrified when he hears you speak with FAITH. I started to say things to myself that I knew God was about to bring to past. Everything I spoke upon, the enemy attacked my mind and tried to make me think the Lord would not come through.

He tried to sabotage my mindset and make me believe that I would never come out of this storm. I just laughed and kept my faith and moved forward. There were times when I would get so excited just thinking about how my future would be without the foolishness. Can you imagine living your life surrounded by so much foolishness, that you start to think it's the norm? I started to embrace a lot of stupidity because I was tricked to believe my life would not be comfortable without it.

As I sat in that cell, one day felt like two, I used to fall asleep and wake up thinking that it was the next day, only to be disappointed when I found out that I was still living the same day. This feeling went on for months, not being able to sleep because you are so anxious to see what God has in store for your new life. I didn't want anything to stop me from succeeding, but I would always get scared sometimes and ask myself, ARE YOU READY?

I used to have long talks with my inner man, trying to prepare my mindset for what was about to come. I knew I had to be real with myself and answer these questions in truth. I made up my mind that I was going to submit to change and never turn back. I was committed, no more running, no more cowering out. It was time for me to step up and step up big. The direction of my legacy would be decided by my decision.

I started to come in contact with a couple of guys that were just walking into solitary confinement, with the same look on their face I saw on my own in the beginning.

**THE ONE WHO ENCOURAGED MY DECISIONS!
(MOMMA)!**

They didn't know why they were there, and they were kicking and screaming as they were walking in their cells. No matter how much I talked to them, they were going to have to put self aside in order to see what God was trying to do/say. I knew when they saw me and heard the things that was on my mind, they were going to question my change, and question the things I was saying.

They saw me laughing and smiling inside of my cell and they would say, man you are taking this good to have been back here for 6

months. I told them the way they feel right now I felt the same way but, now that I have submitted to who I really am. I don't have to fight no more; I can be comfortable with the outcome because I knew God was in control.

Just know this people, if life has dealt you a hand and you have survived it. If you have committed to moving into the next phase of your life, right at the end of your storm things will get rough. If you have been in a storm and it is getting really tough, just know that God is about to bring you out and bless you, and the enemy is trying to make you think that it won't work, and it's not over.

Well, I come to tell you that IT'S OVER, and God is about to do exactly what He said He will do. Remember, when things start to get tough, stand tall and trust God, knowing "IT'S ALMOST OVER"!

I'M STRONG

I'm stronger than those lies, I'm stronger than mistakes,
I'm stronger than deceit, I'm stronger than envy or hate.
I'm stronger than my past, I'm stronger than those tears,
I'm stronger than those women, I'm stronger than my fears.
I'm stronger than those drinks, I'm stronger than the rain,
I'm stronger than those drugs, I'm stronger than the pain.

I'm strong because I'm Strength, I'm strong because I Love,

And how I know I'm Strong, because God said I was.

I'M STRONG

"I'm Strong" was written at 3 o'clock in the morning at my first encounter with my inner man, on July 21, 2009! I'm strong, represents how I feel right now after I have been carried through all the tests and the storms of my transformation. I'm strong is inspired by those Men and Women out there that possess so much strength but refuse to acknowledge it so they can't apply it to their lifestyle.

The only way to apply the strength inside of you is to tap into the source of the one who gives it to you, "God", through his son Jesus Christ!

He's the only one that can turn that light on inside of you, He's the only one that can give you the strength to withstand the temptation of these things. He's the only one that can make you feel like you are ten times stronger than any of these negative feelings or emotions in this poem, we just fail to realize that we are a lot stronger than the things we allow to make us weak.

We have all lied and made mistakes at one point in our lives, but we must understand that after you have failed or been a victim of these things, you have to acknowledge the strength within you and get up.

Don't lie down just because these things have held you captive, break that bind that has you stuck in one place in life. Overcome the fear of whatever you're scared of. Acknowledge that mistake and move on to never make that mistake again. Laws of man is the reason why you feel held captive.

When you live under the laws of the Lord you have mercy, and you can be forgiven for all you've done. See, the laws of Man will hold you accountable for the things that you do, and that mistake will be the only thing that they remember you by.

That negative things you've done in life will leave you labeled in the laws of Man, a lot of the good will be nullified by the mistakes you've made. I am writing this chapter to encourage you to receive this message, you are stronger than any of the things you've done. You'll get stronger once you realize why you fell to that situation. It was because you were weak in that area. Once you overcome, you should never fall victim to it again.

I fell victim to most of these things I write about in this poem, at one point I felt like I would never get back up again. I felt as though some of these things controlled me and I would not be able to exist without the mistakes of my past. I took on so much criticism and slander to the point where I started to believe I was who they said I was. I had to do a QUICK GUT CHECK and realize that God doesn't create weak people.

We become weak when we stop believing in the one who created us. We become weak when we allow someone else's opinion of us become our opinion of ourselves.

I realized God didn't give me the strength I obtain to become a constant victim of these things, He allowed certain situations to happen in order to make me stronger. Now I feel like I have the strength of 100 men. I feel like the only thing that can stand in my way is "ME"! I thank God for the strength He's given me.

I thank Him for allowing me to experience the trials and tribulations, to receive the strength that I need to survive. It's time to get up people and acknowledge/utilize the strength that He has placed inside of you, you are Stronger than the drink that causes you to sin, you are stronger than the lies, deceit, and mistakes.

You can recover from anything you have become a victim of, you just have to make sure you don't become a victim again. STAY STRONG.

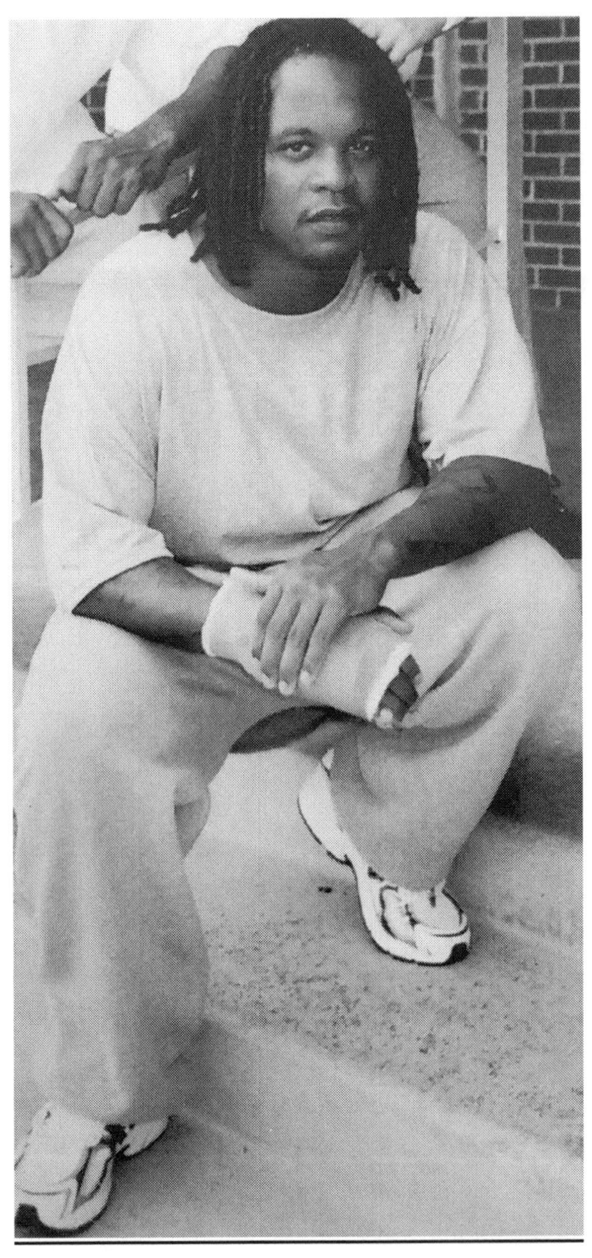

THE ONE WHO STAYED STRONG!

LADY D!

Hello Lady "D," miss puppy love from my past,
Out of all the people that I thought would write, YOU,
I thought would be last.
You brought a new dimension to me, you flew
through my life like a dove,
You opened a part that was closed to me,
which made me want to love.
I never thought I'd trust a woman, and I
vowed to judge them the same,
All because I knew they'd leave, just as fast
as they came.
But you, I knew you were sent to me, to help me
through my storms
It shows me that blessings will come, in different
feelings, and different forms.
I was ordered to give you some knowledge,
about the way you were living your life,
By paying attention to the things that count and
doing things that's right.
We thought we were meant to be a couple, but
it was meant for you to pass through,
At that time, you really needed me, and of
course I really needed you!
Even though it didn't end in marriage, I hope
that we could still make amends,
Sometimes God brings people together,
not for love, but just to be FRIENDS.

LADY "D"

This was a poem I wrote to a friend of mine that came back into my life in 2006, the first one worthy of opening my heart and doors up to again. Like I spoke about before, I wasn't going to be anything but a player when I got out of prison. I'm Not dealing with the responsibility that comes with relationships.

There's no way I'm experiencing heartache again. I was through with trying to be a good guy, I now see why people say I am done with relationships and I'd just rather be single. When you are hurt by someone it's hard to get back to a point where you trust anyone again.

You always step into a relationship looking for that person to make a mistake. If you don't forgive the person who hurt you, it will be hard to trust anyone else. I almost let what happened to me ruin my chance at love and life. If it wasn't for this woman coming into my life, I would have never and I mean NEVER, allowed a female to get close to my heart again

.She wrote me in 2006, I couldn't believe it was from her. We grew up together and we were boyfriend and girlfriend at 11 years old. Puppy love at its best!

While I was in the street life, I didn't really see Her like that, I ran into her every now and then but, we had little interaction. To open a letter from someone who I never thought would be here made me feel good. I embraced the conversations we had, and I really liked our chemistry. This was my good friend from the past, we sat on the phone and within these fifteen-minute phone calls we laughed the whole time.

I asked her to come and see me and she said she

would love too. I sent her the visiting form and she returned it in one week. I called her and told her she was approved on a Monday and she came to the prison to see me that Saturday. When she walked in, I was impressed, she still looked the same and she had a smile that could light up a room.

We hugged and laughed for the entre visit, we spoke about her kids, what she was doing with her life and what she wants to do with her life. I told her how I felt every day I woke up in the prison system and the things. I wanted to accomplish when I got home. I really needed this interaction with her because I was starting to get institutionalized.

Meaning I stopped caring about what was going on outside of these prison walls. Her presence gave me a feeling of normalcy and that's exactly what I needed. I couldn't believe the way our conversations were making me feel. To have someone going out of their way to come see me, someone who did not benefit off the lifestyle I was living. Her efforts to be in that visiting room two times out of the week was truly a blessing.

As she started to say the right things, I started to get comfortable and let my guards down a little more. She was breaking down my defenses just being herself and showing unconditional love. That goes to show you that when you try to make plans for your life God laughs and does what he wants.

We started to catch feelings for each other but, it wasn't meant for us to be a couple. God was exposing me to my gifts, and I didn't even know it. She was in a rough place in her life and she needed someone to talk too who wasn't looking to get anything in return, someone sincere. God used me to listen/counsel and motivate her to start to put herself first.

It seemed like we were allowed to cross each other's path for the betterment of the both of us. She started to pour out her feelings to me, and the things she wanted to do with her life, and I started to tell her what I thought about the things she was doing. She listened to me and I listened to God as I counseled her.

After a couple of months her life started to change, and our relationship was changing at the same time. As I opened her eyes to better ways to look at life, she started to excel. I loved the fact that she was getting better results from her decisions and better things were happening for her in her life.

God is Good, what she was doing for me was priceless. As we moved forward, I saw that He was showing us both that it was not meant for us to be an item, it was meant for us to be friends. Sometimes you overstep your responsibility and make things hard for the situation.

When you are just meant to be friends and you try to make it a relationship, you are risking the friendship. See, while we were friends, we listened to each other better, we respected each other more, we had conversations without arguing. As soon as we fell into a relationship, things changed. Now we felt that we were obligated to do certain things,

She felt like She couldn't tell me the truth about certain situations. That's when things got rough and the disloyalty set in. That was the reason why we split apart, by the grace of God we remained friends.

This is for everyone that's reading this chapter,

you must realize and recognize why people are really in your life. You can't allow them to be more then what God called them to be in their season.

You must make sure that your purpose is being filled in their lives and you are not using this opportunity to fall in love! Be obedient to what God is calling you to do and stop doing what you want to do. You can lose a good friend by trying to make them more than what God has called them to be. GOD BLESS!

STOP CRYING

As I wake up to the same thing, I really hate this place,
I get tired of what's in the mirror, is it possible to change this face.
I'm tired of this cell, the voices I hear, it's the same thing Day after Day,
I need some relief, some break in my strain,
Lord please come take me away.
I don't care where just ease my mind,
please get me out of this cell,
If you come release me, "I PROMISE", I'll never come back to jail.
I can't eat the food, the beds are hard, and the showers are even cold,
Please come get me, why am I here? I'll do the things that I am told.
I can't use the phone my visits are short, and I think that they play with my mail,
23 hours a day you stay in your room, my skin even starts to look pale.
If I knew this was jail, I would've passed those

drugs, I never would have played with those guns,
I turned myself in, man I was stupid, I had all the chances to run.
The time goes slow the jail is crowded, one day feels like two weeks,
The jumpers are small the clothes are too, and you won't believe what I have on my feet.
Man it's crazy you should see this place, I'll tell you man I'm not lying,
You'll be okay please listen to me; BOY I WISH YOU'D STOP CRYING.

STOP CRYING

This poem was written while I was in solitary confinement. This is the place where you get disciplined when you are not following the rules on the compound. I was sent to solitary confinement on an investigation for interfering with a female staff member. It didn't matter if the staff had no evidence you went to solitary confinement until they figured it out.

The cells were only made to house two people but because of over population of the prison system, they would house three men in a cell and force them to make it work. When you walk in the cell there is a metal urinal to your right, directly in front of the urinal is a slab of steel welded from the roof connecting to the floor which makes your shower.

To the left is the two- man bunk bed, up against the window is a steel stool and desk pressed up against the small slit in the wall used as our window, not a pretty/comfortable sight but you have to make the best of it.

Early the next morning the doors opened, and I

heard lot of voices arguing, pleading, and crying coming from the top of the hallway. The administration had a big shake down on the compound and locked a lot of guys up. Some guys were at the camp, (A minimum level security prison) sneaking out to the hotel to be with their ladies and got caught coming back in. I would say they bought 50 guys to the SHU, (Special Housing Unit/ Solitary Confinement) that day, on top of the 200 guys that were already in here.

I didn't think that they had room for this many people, three people were stuffed in a cell with only two beds, one guy was sleeping on the floor by the urinal, and you had to step over him while he was sleeping in order to use the bathroom, it was definitely terrible inside of those cells.

One of the guys they brought back was a good friend of mine, J.I. was a funny guy. Every time we got together, we laughed and lived like we weren't even locked up, that's the way we coped with the prison time. His security level dropped, and he was moved across the street to a minimum facility where the perks were a lot better.

You could walk your family out to their cars after a visit, you had more free time to roam around the compound, but the biggest perk of them all was you could leave off the compound to go to the hotel and have an intimate moment with your wife/girlfriend/baby-mother or whoever was willing to come, as long as you don't get caught.

J.I. took his chance and got caught coming back from the hotel, his face was tight when he walked past my cell, I kicked the door and he looked up and asked the C.O. to put him in my cell. He had a minimum-security level so he wasn't supposed to cell with me because I was a medium. I'd gained a rapport of the staff, so they let him cell with me. As soon as he walked in we laughed at each other, greeted each other like brothers do and started to question each other.

He already knew why I was in the SHU. It was all over the compound; the gossip columns are big in the federal prison. He told me he got caught coming back from the hotel, yet he would be satisfied with whatever his punishment was. After having sex with your woman after 5 years of being locked up.

I wouldn't care what the punishment was, it was worth it. Well he felt like that for about a month but, the situation started to set in, not being able to move around, watch football, or workout was starting to get to him.

He started complaining and I immediately got on him about that, I loved the guy but, he was spoiled rotten. He got his way all the time even in prison, not being able to control his situation was eating him up. We sat in that cell for months waiting on the outcome of our cases, we really got to know each other better. This time back here gave us a chance to expose who we really are.

I told him how I've lived so long hiding behind a mask, and I was tired of being someone that I wasn't. He told me how he hated living in his father's shadow, wanting to be his own man but, was struggling to find his way. We pulled our mask off inside that cell and I can truly say this brother is one of the realest dudes I have ever met. The staff found him guilty and his punishment was to get transferred to a prison far away from our region. They did that to make it hard to get visits. the day he left my cell was the day I knew I had a guy who was a real friend.

As my weeks went on, I slowly started to get use to the situation but, I hated hearing the complaints of the guys. It seemed like every time I took my headphones off someone was complaining. This poem was inspired by the crying and complaining that I heard from supposed to be grown men, Bad Boys, Bosses, Gang Bangers, Drug Dealers, Murderers! I couldn't believe what I was hearing inside those walls, I need to use the phone, the water is cold, where is my dinner tray, it's cold in here. It's funny how Men act like kids when there aren't any eyes on them.

See, this is the place where those character flaws must be addressed, where there are no rules, you can't run to the lieutenant's office and complain. You can't get on the phone and vent to someone about your problems or go out to the visiting room and see your family when you want to.

You can't eat what you like, walk around when you feel like it. If you have a problem with your cell mate you either have to deal with it physically, talk it out, or ask to be moved which rarely happens.

This is a place where you have to deal with yourself, everything that you have done will start to come to the light. I felt like God was giving me a option either I get it right or continue to get punished for doing wrong. I had to make a decision, either you stay back here for the rest of your time or get yourself together so that you won't have to deal with this situation again. They make it uncomfortable for a reason, that's why it's called, THE SPECIAL HOUSING UNIT (SHU).

When you can't function on the compound, this is where they send you. It's crazy how we can be on the compound living like we have no sense at all, drinking, drugging, fighting, stabbing, like we have no chance of going home.

One thing about this door, it's easy to get in but it's hard to get out. There were some soldiers that came back here and just said I did that, start my paper work either transfer me, or cut me loose. Then you have the ones who try to weasel their way out of it and try to manipulate their punishment.

By telling the administration about the illegal activities on the compound to get released from the SHU. When you are doing something you know is wrong, don't expect it to last long or to live that way and be peaceful. Nothing negative has a positive result for a long period of time, you will get caught.

There is nothing fun about getting caught. There is nothing fun about sitting in this cell for months just waiting to get back to JAIL, you're in jail inside of the prison, PATHETIC! We all make mistakes, there is no question about that.

Once you make a mistake you have to come to grips with the fact that, there is no right way to do wrong! When you are living wrong expect wrong things to happen. You have to expect to fail every day when you are not living right. I allowed this whole situation to be a blessing to me, I used this time to deal with my flaws, realizing the way I was living could not promise me a better life.

I will always be behind if I didn't deal with the flaws that keep me from moving ahead. I feel as though a lot of men never expect to lose when they are in the drug game, they think that they have it all figured out.

So, when they get caught, they get upset because their plan did not work. Please show me someone who can explain how you can do wrong, the right way. Then I will show you a DUMMY that will be the first one to CRY when his plan fails.

LIFE OF SUCCESS

There's so much going on in life, it seems like it's hard to fight,
It's crazy that the things you see, makes you scared to sleep at night,
It's all the visions of those days, that you really thought has passed,
Though you deal with constant hope, that this will be your last.
As you toss and turn through restless nights, with a million thoughts on your mind,
Scared your secrets are revealed to the world, the thoughts of what they'll find.
Don't worry about the mistakes that you've made, you were created to do much more,
Sometimes it feels strange, and you wonder where you've heard that voice before.

That voice is called the spirit within,

it helps if you'll receive,
Blessings you'll get, free of regret, it's
up to you to believe.

Submit to God resist the devil, you can fight the
desires of the flesh,

Don't miss that call it's guaranteed, that new life
will be a Success.

LIFE OF SUCCESS

"Life of Success" is a poem inspired by the hope that you have for your future, after you have cleaned out your closet of all the secrets and gave them to God! I realized that the sins I've committed doesn't have to be revealed to anyone but God. He is the only one that won't judge me, He is the only one that is compassionate enough to forgive me.

He is the only one who can make you great after your mistakes. Once I gave my life to the Lord, He stripped my mind of the things that I used to glorify. He allowed me to see glimpses of what He was going to do after I finished my training with him. I saw how prosperous and strong I was going to be. I saw how much of an influence
I would have in the community; I saw my life after the strife.

He allowed the visions of what I had done in my past to come back over and over again, I always had visions of people trying to hurt me, or visions of me hurting others. I wasn't concerned about these things happening in my life anymore, and as soon as I stop being afraid of these things, the visions went away. God said, "You don't have to worry about old things becoming new, stop worrying about what WAS, and start to focus on WHAT WILL BE"!

I thought to myself, how can I be so comfortable being a Nobody? How can I have so much talent and be so smart but, still run towards a dead end? How could I be so comfortable running towards Drugs, Violence, Alcohol, and Deceit, knowing the road would lead to pain and heartache. I was so confused but, once I got involved with God, that's when I chose to run the right way.

That's when I told myself I was going to be successful. That's when I said there is more for me in this world than the foolishness I was allowing into my life. I want to be successful and I was being built to do JUST THAT!

That narrow road is the hardest one to travel down, but that narrow road is the road to success, it's going to take sacrifice. Sometimes you're not going to sleep, sometimes you're going to be tired or frustrated, sometimes you're going to have to miss a lot of events, or family gatherings, sometimes you're going to have to say NO!

That narrow road of success is tough but, you will be equipped for whatever comes your way. You just have to make the decision if you want to be successful or not. The road that leads to nowhere is so easy to travel, it's long and wide, and there is no traffic. It's filled with temptation and it's so easy to make a mistake.

You don't have to struggle or think to navigate down this road, it's easy but, I guarantee you choosing this path will lead you to destruction. It's simple, if you want a life filled with promises, tighten those boots up, straighten that back up, and get to moving. Start walking down that road to success, making positive strides in the right direction.

You can do it, life only defeats those who want to be defeated, don't be the one that looks at the road and gets frustrated or discouraged because it doesn't look like fun. Understand that the Road to Redemption is not fun but, it's worth taking the chance. Don't let the small tasks of life Break You. You must be UNBREAKABLE in order to BREAKTHROUGH!

THE ENEMY

The enemy had me bound and gagged, to the point where I questioned my worth,
I almost lost it and submitted to him and fell beneath this earth.
I know I've sinned and made mistakes, but I know that I'm still forgiven,
I know I was made to do much more, IF NOT, I wouldn't be living.
Satan had me paralyzed, and doubt and fear were the cause of my pain,
It wasn't until I heard that voice, that came down and really explained.
He told me things that I heard and knew, at times the voice was loud,
That's the voice that I heard a lot, when I wasn't

surrounded by crowds.
At times when I was by myself, or stuck in a good night's sleep,
Visions and dreams would flood my mind, I could hear the words that they speak.
I paid attention to the good ones, and never the ones that were bad,
The good one's made me happy, and the others made me sad.
But God has touched me I'm awake for good, to remove this weight from my waist,
I'll trust him and keep my focus, because prayers won't work without FAITH!

THE ONE WHO FOUGHT THE ENEMY!

THE ENEMY

"The Enemy" represents the feelings I entertained that caused my vision to be distorted, I almost fell to the voices of sin and chanced never waking up again. The enemy sent thoughts to my mind that made me feel like I was the worst person in the world. He made me think that because of my mistakes I would never be loved the same.

The fear of not being loved or abandoned by your family is a man's worst fear. Well, I see that God was right, I won't be looked at the same and they will see a better version of the man they once knew. The praises will be a positive praise now, they won't be glorifying a man living a lie. The love will be more genuine, and pure, that's the love I live for now. The love for righteousness, and the love of God?

The enemy can only attack the things you speak on, that's the only way he can be allowed into your world. You can't let him in,
you let him in by the words you speak. I remember saying It's over, no more of the drug game after this last move. I got a new supplier; my plans were to buy as much product as possible because the quality was amazing.

Anytime you get good product you try your best to get as much as you can just in case it runs out. I was always told by the older soldiers in the drug game to never spend all you have on product because you never know when things will go bad.

All I kept repeating to myself was, "I'm not going to send all my money down, that would be stupid". The more I said it the more thoughts came to my mind that encouraged me to send the money. After constantly wrestling with the decision, I sent every dime I had hoping and praying everything would run smooth.

One week at a time I would go to western union and send as much money as possible, without sending a red flag with the amounts. I had a few females that would assist with putting their name on the wire transfer, so it wouldn't look suspicious if we were under investigation. As soon as I sent the last transfer, I felt like something was going to go wrong.

The operation was flawless, I'd send the money western union to a designated address in North Carolina and the product would be shipped by mail. to an auto body shop in Northwest D.C. Once I got the call, I'd go pick up the product.

I would go get the product and go to my stash house (an apartment used to store guns, cook and store drugs in) to divide or cook everything up. It worked flawlessly for about 6 months but, this one time after I sent all my money, things went sour.

I got up that morning waiting on the call, I would look at my phone to see if there were any missed calls. Checking the ringer to make sure it's at the highest volume. I was a nervous wreck for the last four days as I waited to hear back from the connect. The process usually takes three days tops but, here it is day four and I haven't heard a thing.

Around twelve noon my phone rang, I was in the shower, so I barely heard it. I got out the shower just in time to catch it on the last ring. I looked at the caller I.D on the screen and it was the auto body shop I did business with. I was pumped up and relieved at the same time.

When the package arrives, the body shop just calls my phone and hangs up, nothing is said, I already knew what time it was. This time it was different. “Hello” a man said from the other end. I was shocked because I never spoke to anyone at the shop. The package would come, I would get the call and it would be in an old car at the shop in the rear of the building, there would never be any interaction with the employees.

“Hello”, I said with a little hesitation, “Everything is good” the man said. I waited for a second and then I responded, “Okay thanks”. When I hung up, I felt a little uneasy this was totally out of the norm, I was confused and scared at the same time.

I really needed this package, so I ignored the feeling in my gut and jumped in my car to head to the body shop. I was at the stash house in Naylor Gardens in Southeast D.C, about 20 minutes from the auto shop. I was going to try to cut the time in half and get there in 10 minutes. At the time, I had a Pontiac Bonneville Super Sport, I kept a fast car because in this lifestyle you never know when you’re going to have to get away fast.

I grabbed my keys and my Glock 40 and walked out the door. It was summertime and I’d been inside all day, so the sun blinded me for a second when I walked out of the door. I got in the car and a sharp pain ran through my gut followed by the thought that something wasn’t right. I ignored it, started the car, turned the disk changer on and pulled off. I made a right on Naylor Rd and sped up the hill towards Alabama Ave.

I crossed over Good Hope Rd and made a left on 17th street headed towards Minnesota Ave. I made a right on Minnesota Ave headed towards Pennsylvania Ave. Traffic was light today for some reason, so I was meeting my goal of cutting the 20-minute commute in half.

When I got to the light on Minnesota and Pennsylvania the pain in my gut came again followed by the thought that something wasn't right. Ignoring it I rolled down my window and gave the homeless man $5, he was standing in the middle of the intersection begging for change.

I hated to see homeless people out here begging for money, then I wondered were they begging for money to get the product I was racing across town to get? The light turned and I smashed the gas headed towards 395. I was moving so fast I didn't see the unmarked police car as I flew past him, luckily, he wasn't paying attention, so he didn't see me either.

The speedometer read 60 as I looked down at the dashboard, my palms were sweating, and I was nervous. No matter how much I tried to ignore that feeling it was still there, as I got closer to the body shop the feeling got stronger. I started to get paranoid looking in my rearview mirror thinking every car was a police car, the unmarked police car was still in my rearview.

I was about 6 cars ahead of him but, I could see him. I was sweating bullets and the air condition was on high, I went into a daze as I continued to navigate to the body shop. A million different scenarios were going through my mind was it a set- up, am I about to get robbed, or were the police waiting on me at the body shop?

I pulled up to the shop slowly, my stomach was turning in knots. I was sweating so bad my shirt was wet. I felt like all eyes were on me and I was the only one on the street that day. Something told me to circle the shop one time before I got out to get the package. At the next corner on Georgia Ave I saw a black Taurus sedan with black tinted windows. I glanced out the corner of my eye as I drove past, it was impossible to see anything because of the tinting on the windows. When I got to the corner, I glanced out my passenger side mirror. I saw the chest of a man with a silver chain around his neck and at the end of that chain was a silver police badge.

Immediately I froze up. Was this the reason why my stomach was doing flips? I clicked my turn signal to make a left, when I turned on to Georgia Ave, I saw two big white guys in sweat suits standing at the entrance of the body shop. This part of the city was populated by either Jamaicans or street dudes so, they stood out like a green thumb. My phone rang again, I glanced at the screen and it was the body shop again. This was the sign I needed to confirm everything, they never call twice or say anything on the phone when I answer.

"This was a set- up", said the voice in my head as I drove past the shop headed towards Silver Spring. I broke my cell phone and dropped it out of the window in front of the Ibex. I was panicking, and I had to get out of the area fast. I pulled in the gas station about eight lights up the street from the shop. I had the A.C on but, it felt like it was 80 degrees in the car.

My mind was racing, I was looking around like a terrorist, I had to try to calm down to gather my thoughts. Tap, Tap, Tap I looked up to a guy on the passenger side of my car. He was about 6 feet 225 Lbs. wearing a tank top, he didn't look like a police officer at least I hoped he wasn't.

I cracked the window enough for him to hear me, "Can I help you" I said. "Yeah you could move your car if you're not getting gas" He shouted angrily. I looked at where I was parked and pulled away from the pump. He looked at me crazy and walked off mumbling something under his breath.

Right now, I couldn't entertain this guy but, Lord knows I wanted too. I got out the car and used the pay phone to call my business partner to let him know what was going on, when he picked the phone up he already knew. "Someone tipped the feds off about the shipment, lay low for a minute. Don't worry about it, whatever we lose the connect will replace we just have to wait about 30 days for things to calm down".

I couldn't tell him I went against his advice and went all in on this trip, I didn't even have gas money. I had bills on top of bills, not only mine but I had to make sure my women and their kids were straight. For the next thirty days, I was putting the press on everyone that owed me money trying my best not to look desperate but, I was.

Thirty days went by super slow, when I got the call that another package had arrived. Relieved it was here but, not looking forward to starting from scratch. It seemed like every time I got close to the number, I set for myself I would take a huge loss and have to dig deeper to get it back. I wanted out but, I couldn't see myself being able to survive without having a good cushion as far as my finances.

The enemy's job was to make sure I stayed in the game until he devoured me. If he could keep me in the game, he could keep me away from the life I really wanted to live. I don't care what no one says if you're in the streets, you really don't want to be, if you could make a nice amount of money, start a business, buy a house and start a family you would be satisfied. We want the life that a working man lives, yet we don't have the patience to work to get it, we want it fast and reckless.

I'm constantly on my knees thanking God for His grace and His mercy, if He didn't love me, He would've let me die in the streets. No matter what the enemy did/tried God always blocked the worse outcome. I would pay for a bad decision but not like the enemy intended. It's a blessing to be able to share my story with you, I'm proud to be a survivor.

It seemed like as long as I continued to listen to the voice that told me to go left when I was supposed to go right, I'd find myself in a deeper hole. I fought against that voice my whole life, doubting myself, doubting others, and making a lot of bad decisions and I paid for it. Please learn from what you've read in this chapter and apply it to your life, remember everyone doesn't get a second chance.

COME HOME SON

Hello Dad, how's it going? You sound like
you're tired from working,
Hello son, and I am tired, and my body is

constantly hurting.
Dad is something wrong, besides your pain are things alright?
Yes son, but I'm slowing down, and I feel like
I'm losing the fight.
Come on Dad, YOU'RE STRONG, keep them
arms up never stop fighting,
I know I depend on you for money and things, but
regardless I'll never stop writing.
I really appreciate the letters son, believe me they
help me a lot,
Because you know how I feel after Momma died, I
feel like you're all I got.
Son, I know I wasn't there for you, but
everything happened so fast,
Dad I want you to listen to me, I LOVE YOU
despite our past.
I know son you told me that, but it still doesn't
excuse my actions,
When I look back on the life I've lived, I wasn't
adding always subtracting.
But Dad look who you're talking to, you push 5
to answer the phone,
I was far from an angel a rebellious child; it's been years
since I've been home.
I know son it's been a while; I hope I'm here when you
finally come back,
Come on Dad you're fading again, and I hate when
you talk like that.
Just look at it, and picture this, you'll get millions if I
happen to die,
Hold on son it's the other line, when he clicked

over, I started to cry.
I'm back son, are you crying boy what's up with those tears,
Because you talk like you're leaving tomorrow, and that's the worst of my fears.
Dad you are getting older, but that's something that we call wise,
Son, I'll tell you for the last time, I hope you're here when I close my eyes.

COME HOME SON

When a father and son sit down and settle their differences the conversation can go one or two ways. They can fight about the past or be adults and talk it out and work on establishing a relationship. My dad and I sat down and came to grips with the fact that life isn't perfect, and we aren't either.

The conversation we had answered a lot of questions and healed some wounds. Men go through a lot in the process of becoming a man, especially when he has no role model to follow. Generational curses destroy families, but I refused to allow it to destroy mine. Thank God for the conversation my dad and I had.

When my grandmother passed it hit my pops very hard because he was truly a momma's boy. He loved his mom and he never wanted to leave her house, he stayed there for years to be with his mom. After she passed on he started to get sick and gained a lot of weight from stressing.

At one point he was hospitalized for two weeks, he had multiple things going on with him because of the way he was living. He consumed a lot of alcohol then he killed his only means of exercising when he retired from his job, which made matters worse.

I told him when he quit his job, he would get old, he just didn't want to fight anymore. I heard it in his voice every time we spoke. All he talked about was what I would get if he dies. I hated to hear him speak like that, he sounded like he was defeated, and I knew he was a fighter. God allowed me to minister to him and tell him that he had to "GET UP" and start to fight again. I didn't care what happened in our past, I would never dislike him to the point where I would rejoice over what I would get if something happened to him.

The enemy was using my grandmother's death to destroy my dad, I started to pray and ask God to keep my father strong until I was released. If he passes while I'm away I would not be the same, it would be hard to forgive myself for being here when I lost one of my parents. I was not going to allow the enemy to destroy my pops, as long as I knew how to pray, I was going to pray against the enemy's attacks and get my father back on track and that's exactly what happened.

He just kept speaking about death and what I would get when he passed on. I told him that money would not replace him, the memories we had, the pain of him passing, and me not be able to be there to say goodbye. Money could never compare to the love I have for my pops, so I would check him every time he would start to speak about death and money. It was like he felt so guilty about not being there for me in the past. He would make himself feel better when he thought about the money I would get when he passed.

He felt as though it would make up for the years of his absence, I didn't care about the money. All I wanted was a chance to make some new memories with my dad and my son as a unit. I don't know about anyone else; I'd rather be broke spending years with my family then be rich and alone. So, from that point on I wrote to him every day. We worked on our relationship through mail and phone calls, God allowed me to fix a lot of relationships while I was in the hole, that was a place of awakening for me, a place of healing.

It's crazy how you can hear so much when you're in a quiet place, you realize what really matters. There was one phone call that showed me that God was moving in our relationship. I called and told him that they were shipping me to Memphis Tennessee. When he heard the news, he cried on the phone.

That's how I knew that the spirit was working, prayer started to show its results. God was showing me that He was healing the situation as we were speaking. I started to notice that every time I would call, my dad would say I love you or did I need anything before we hung up the phone. God was really doing it, he was working on my dad just like he was working on me. GLORY BE TO GOD! This man started to send money before I would even ask.

I was loving the way my dad and I communicated, He still would fall into a state of depression and start to speak about him not being here when I got back. I used to have to check him and get him back in line because I refused to allow him to speak like that in my presence.

I learned that whatever you speak into your life, will be the things that you allow in your life. I had to stop him from speaking negative so, we wouldn't have to worry about the negative. Life and death is in the power of the tongue, so we made an agreement to only speak positive things out of our mouths. We would no longer speak anything that was not what we wanted in our lives.

My father then started to speak like a fighter, and He got up and got another job making good money and feeling like he was back on his game. To hear the joy back in his voice was a good sound to hear, He is back in the swing of things because of Prayer and Positive speaking. See, when you think about what really matters in life you don't allow anything to come between you and the people you love, whatever is in the past stays in the past.

God wouldn't allow it to happen to you if he thought that you wouldn't be able to survive it. At times my father would speak so bad of himself and I would have to remind Him of my failures. I had problems and I also added to the problems that we were having in our relationship.

Sometimes healing begins when both parties accept where they are wrong, I accepted my flaws while forgiving him for his, thank God for the spirit of truth!

When I call Him now, He says I am doing fine and feeling good, that goes to show you that God always uses the right people to do the job He wants done; He chose me to save my father.

This chapter was just mainly about how generational curses can plague the relationships within your family, and how God allowed my father and I to break the chains THROUGH FAITH!

I just wanted my father to know that I loved him enough to forgive him for not being at the basketball games, the football games, for saying he was coming to get me and didn't come. I loved him enough to ask him to forgive me for anything that I've done, and that I was no better than him.

We both made mistakes that could have been avoided. We stood strong while we were apart, but soon we'll be able to stand strong TOGETHER!

Love You Pop's, and YOU ARE FORGIVEN!

FATHER'S DAY

Hello Dad, it's me, your son who's thinking of you,
Who worships the ground that you walk on,
and loves the things you do.
This is the day that we thank you, for the food
you put on the table,
Because when problems arose and I needed
to talk, you made yourself available.

A loving father and example of man, who always played by the rules,

No matter the job you maintained it well and managed to put us through school.
I want you to know we're thinking of you, and your work doesn't go unnoticed,
Not only did you warn us in life, you always took the time to show us.
I want you to know we're pulling for you; you know we're your biggest fans,
I'm working hard to ease your pain and take some of the weight off your hands.
I also want to say that I'm sorry, for the times I sent stress your way,
So accept our apology, and accept our praise, because you surely deserve it today.

FATHER'S DAY

"Father's Day" is a poem I wrote to those hardworking men out there who are truly holding the torch and being the fathers that your children need. This poem represents the man I plan to be when I get home. I don't have no doubt in my mind, I will be that father that does everything in his power to make sure my son sees the positive example of a man.

I now know what it takes to be the man that you want your son to follow, I realize that it's going take more than just words to get this thing right. There are so many fathers out there that are doing exactly what a father has to do, and not getting recognized for it. From getting the kids up in the morning taking them to school, from trying his best to do his daughters hair.

From doing his best chef impersonation, to setting the example for his son and showing his daughter what type of man she should allow in her life.

This is the type of father that I salute today, men if you never heard it from anyone else, you heard it from me today. You guys are the reason why the name father was created. Way to stand tall “MEN”!

GOD BLESS.

A FALLEN ANGEL

A fallen angel, a tarnished soul, a person who made mistakes,
A saint who fell short of the Glory of God, by not standing strong on his faith.
A man who submitted to the voices of sin, that was repeated in the back of his mind,
Someone who couldn’t focus on the things ahead, but what mattered was the things from behind.

A goodhearted man with goals to achieve, and with constant steps to the light,
With submission to God your vision shall clear, you’ll conquer the enemy’s plight.
Can’t do it alone you’ll need some strength, and some help from the spirit within,
Ask for forgiveness and he’ll make you clean, and he’ll show you where things will begin.
For the scripture says many are called, but

surely only a few shall be chose,
But the few that he called to shed light amongst men, I'm sure only God really knows.
He chose some men who fell from grace,
chasing Money, Cars and Clothes,
But what profits a man to gain the whole world, but in return he loses His Soul?

A FALLEN ANGEL

"A Fallen Angel" represents the men who tried to do things on our own, by chasing a promise that was given by the biggest deceiver of the world. SATAN! We've all fallen victim to our own understanding and came to a shocking halt in our lives, wondering why you can see the door but can't walk through. I think the reason why we can't get in the door is because we are using the wrong key. The only key that opens the door to a prosperous life is our Lord and Savior Jesus Christ.

We run out on our own thinking that we have all of the answers to each and every problem that we encounter. Question, how can you have the answer for something that you can't see coming? You never have the answer for unknown trials and tribulations, that's why when they hit, we crumble.

We chase so many things that were really of no value, money, cars, clothes, and jewelry. All these things are possessions that will never be ours, and they will leave just as fast as they came if they are not gained honestly. It's like we start out chasing these things, and once we get them, we want something else, not paying attention to what we lose in the chase? Ask yourself this, who did you have to lie to, deceive or manipulate to receive these things?

I look at it like this, anything that you gain in the drug world, you had to do something wrong to get it. You had to cross someone, you had to lie, or deceive someone. These things will happen when you are living an unrighteous life. Who did you have to give your soul to in the midst of all of this? Did you give it to the enemy, or did you give it to God?

If you've given your soul to God, you're at peace right now, things are happening all around you but not happening to you. Now if you have given your soul to the enemy, the love of these things are driving you crazy.

The need to have these possessions has you neglecting the things that you love, and the people you love. It's a known fact, when you are living for God you will do your best to make sure your family is good, and the people around you are good.

There will be no distractions or worries. The only thing that you must worry about when you are living for God, is how you are going to handle all the blessings he gives you! Can you imagine a life like that, to get up in the morning and the only thing you're worried about is what am I going to do with all the money, or the airport am I flying out of today?

The things that you gain when you are living a good life, can't even be compared. I don't know about anyone else but, I don't want a life that can't Promise me Peace. I don't want a life where I have to constantly look over my shoulder, in fear of my possessions are going to be taken. I just can't live a life that has the ability to make me lose the only thing that God gave me to protect, My Soul!

If the love of these things and the need to have these things are ruling your life, you have to get out of that life. You cannot Serve Two God's, no matter what you say or do, God is not going to allow you to be at peace with this lifestyle. You have chosen these things over God and once you do that, God will take everything away from you that you put before Him.

So I encourage each and every one of you that is reading this chapter, worship the one that will give you the blessings that will bring you Joy, and Peace, versus worshiping the one that will make you think that your possession is a blessing, and it turns out to be a Curse.

When you feel like your possession is causing you more stress keeping it, it's because it came from the wrong source. My people, if you have fallen into the old possession trick, and lost the core of your life chasing it.

Get on your knees right now and tell the Lord that you are sorry. You want to be a part of His family. Tell Him that you don't want to lose your soul and that you are willing to conform to his laws for your life. I tell you this, I thought that as long as I had these things in my life all my worries were over.

I came to find out that the things that you obtain in the drug game comes with a lot of stress. Trying to hold on to these things consumes most of your life. I let the enemy trick me into thinking I needed these possessions in order to have a good life. I then realized I didn't need these things to have life. I need life in order to have these things. I am just glad that the life I chose, is the life that God wants me to live!

GOD'S BLESSINGS

When God sends a blessing to you, make sure that your eyes are open,
He'll send an angel to speak to you, so listen to the words that's spoken.
We walk through life confused, not conscious of the people we meet,
Thinking our feelings are hid from the world, but to God they're never discreet.
We walk through life in search for love, in places we never should be,
The blessings of God have opened my eyes, so now I definitely see.
I see that I have a blessing of many, that the world would love to possess,
So I thank my God for the woman he sent, I see God really gives his best.
Now I thank you for your sacrifices, you're a blessing I never thought I'd have,
Can't wait for the day to be in your arms, and I am happy you crossed my path.

GOD'S BLESSINGS

This poem was inspired by the situation I chose to be in while I was incarcerated. I never thought that we would be in a relationship. If you would have asked me why I chose to be in this relationship in the beginning, I would have told you I didn't know.

Then I looked at the things that this relationship has taught me, good or bad, I can see that this whole situation was meant to teach me some things that I didn't know, strengthen me in areas in which I was weak, most of all, provide me with the right person that I needed in my season.

God is just so clever, he put two people together that never were interested in each other and molded their hearts to make them say," I LOVE YOU", and really mean it. He knew what we needed at that time, and He knew what kind of people we needed in order to help each other out of their season. I now see that you can have zero feelings for someone, and God can touch your heart and make you love a person.

I used to look at some couples and ask myself "Why are they together"? They don't seem like they would even be interested in each other. When I experienced it for myself, I understood that God has made someone for every season of your life. Whether they are meant to stop through, or they are meant to take their shoes off and get comfortable inside your life.

A lot of times we miss the lesson within our seasons, good people come into your life and you allow them to walk away because you try to use them for your short- term benefit, instead of seeing that they are there to teach you something that will benefit you in the long run.

God's blessing can come in a person, a place, or even in a tragic situation. We just have to make sure we don't miss it when it comes. He sent a woman to me that invested time in me.

She loved me and made me feel like there was hope. People really can have a sincere love for you, this woman really picked up the torch I was about to let burn out. I didn't think I would ever love a woman again. I didn't think I would ever trust a woman again but, God showed me when he wants something done, He'll use people that will make you say "I knew that had to be God."

I can't lie, there has been two women that have come into my life since I have been in prison, that has really made me understand that God loves me. He loves me enough to put people in my life to help me through this storm. This thing isn't easy, and situations like this can really destroy someone, because prison is a place where you will see betrayal at its best.

People that should be there won't be there, people that said I love you, lied! People that benefited from the lifestyle that led you into this place will be the first ones to leave. To look up and see these two women coming into the visiting room when they have no reason to be here, was definitely a blessing from God?

No matter how these situations turn out, I can really say that I really appreciate the love that was given, I appreciate the lesson that was learned. I realized that two people that are total strangers and not even attracted to each other, can be a blessing to one another.

God is a good God. He will always send you love from places you never thought they would come from, in order to get you to a place that He wants you to be.

We have to stop looking for love in places that we know that we should not be looking. It's very important we look to God for the love we need.

That's when He will send the one that you need, and not the one you want. Be careful of the people you look over; they might be the one who helps you get through GOD BLESS!

GOD'S GIFT TO MAN

The greatest gift God gave to me, was a lady of my own,
When my days going bad, I get nothing but joy
when I hear your voice on the phone.
I'm sorry that I can't be there for you, to
hold you on, this day Always know that I
Love You, no matter what they say.
Baby I've made decisions in life, that surely made me stumble,
You're the only lady that can cross my mind, that will surely make me humble.
Sweetheart you are my everything, My Heart, My Soul, My World,
I'm happy my baby turns 14 today, Happy Birthday to Daddy's little girl.

GOD'S GIFT TO MAN

This was a poem written for a brother of mine I met

while I was incarcerated in Memphis. It was his daughter's birthday, and he wanted her to know that she would always be the most special girl in his world. See, when you are behind these walls, you get to a point where you are so consumed with survival, that you tend to neglect the people that are waiting on you to come home. We lose our relationships with our kids because we fail to stay focused on our fatherly duties while we are away.

I don't care what no one says, you can still be a parent inside of a place like this, it starts with communication, if you stay in your child's ear and listen to them enough, you will find out who they are, and who they're becoming.

You will be able to hear them grow, instead of seeing them grow. Parents that are out there in the world, they don't have time to really sit down and listen to their kids, everyday life consumes them, and they only set aside a little time to speak to their children. On the other hand, we have the time to speak to our kids, and make them comfortable with talking to us.

We can get things out of them that the parent that's there every day, will never hear. We must stay focused on our duties, the small things like this will make huge a impact on our relationship, keep the communication lines open with your kids, sending them a card, or a letter, something they can read over and over again. The only way you lose them, is when you stop communicating with them.

When you are in a place in your life where it feels like it's too rough, and you are about to snap. Allow your mind to drift back to the memories you have with your child, allow yourself to think about the New Memories that you are going to make.

I guarantee you that if you have any love left inside of you, the thought of loving your children will always calm you down or bring you back to earth. I know this works from experience, whenever I am at that point, the only thing that calms me down is thoughts of being with my son.

I WAITED

I waited for you and prayed for you, for 6 to 7 years,
Through all those empty nights, and all the lonely tears.
As I waited for you with patience, with hopes of your return,
I thought we could heal our friendship and salvage some things that were burned.
I never thought I'd endure this pain, from the absence of you for years,
I never thought that I'd see the end, because my eyes were flooded with tears.
As I take long looks in the mirror, I thought "RED" was the color of my eyes,
I never felt this pain before, when the depths of your soul cries.
I hope that these words reach you, and I hope that you're still listening,

I feel like I am incomplete, because a part of me is missing,
You're the part that's missing, the part that makes me whole,
I never thought I'd feel like this, I thought I had control.
I'll snap back eventually, because God has made me strong,
I waited for you patiently, but I just can't wait to long.
Don't miss your chance at happiness, this moment will make you a wife,
Don't pass up this moment of greatness, don't miss your chance at LIFE!

I WAITED

I wrote this poem for an ex-girlfriend. I wanted her to know how long I waited for her to be who she said she would be to me when I left. I met her when I was in the streets and most of those women are temporary, it's just that simple. Some people come into your life for a reason, and a season. I found out that I was brought into her life to encourage and motivate her to go to school and stay focused on herself before anyone else.

I taught her a lot, both good and bad, some things that we experienced forced her to grow up fast. She came into my life after a bad breakup and I really needed someone like her at that moment. Cynthia encouraged and consoled me when I was in a terrible mood and constantly made me feel like a king.

This is my second time going to prison, and I already knew I would not be able to do this long stretch with a girlfriend. When the judge handed me my sentence, I told her to go on ahead with her life. She was young, smart, and had a whole life to live. I didn't want to hold her back from becoming the woman she wanted to be, she deserved better!

I knew how loyal Cynthia was, and she would have tried her best to be right there until she couldn't take it anymore. I knew she was making a promise that she was not going to be able to keep, so I told her to go on with her life and just promise she would always be my friend. In the beginning she would argue and fuss when I told her to go on about her business. Then after a few times of her coming to the visiting room and seeing other women there, she gladly moved on with her life.

That wasn't the way I planned it, but that's the way it all went down. Sometimes God allows people to hurt you for you to let them go! If you don't know, let me tell you right now KARMA IS REAL.

Whatever you do to people will always find its way back to you. If you are out there disrespecting your girlfriend/boyfriend who is being good to you, believe me it's coming back and coming back when you least expect it. God was allowing me to receive what I was putting out into the world, it didn't feel good but, it was needed.

God stripped me of every woman I thought

really cared about me. He removed those who laid down with me and lied. He also taught me how to appreciate a woman by keeping them from me. I didn't understand His method, but it worked.

I was really going through it when I wrote this poem, mainly because I expected her to continue to be supportive of me as a friend. That was not in her plans, and it wasn't in God's plans either. It didn't matter how many poems I wrote, or how many times I called and caught an attitude, she was gone, and I knew it, but it was for my own good.

Through all the situations I have encountered I learned how to appreciate women, respect their feelings, and how to be real with myself. I asked myself if a woman did those things, I did to them in the streets and I found out, would I have stayed even as a friend?

People don't be like me. If you are not going to be faithful to the one that you have in your life don't commit. I don't care what excuse you try to tell yourself, learn from my mistakes, or get prepared to learn from your own. Be real with yourself, you know if you are ready to be in a relationship or not. Don't get into a relationship and then decide that you want to be with other people.

I'm telling you, when it comes back around it doesn't feel good. You are going to wish you would've just stayed faithful.

This was one of the main lessons God had to teach me because this has always been my struggle, staying committed to the person who's in my life. Love the one that you are with and appreciate the love that they give.

Don't let your DISLOYALTY, be YOUR LESSON!

<u>IT'S NOT ABOUT US</u>

I send my blessings to you my lady, the mother of my child,
Even though things are shaky right now, and the conversations are wild.
I refused to fuss and fight with you, cause there's better things to say,
If I'm angry or things don't sit right with me, I'll express it another way.
I know we're separated by a million miles, and conversations aren't very long,
I'll take the weight for our disagreements, but really, we both were wrong.
I know I'm not there to help ease your pain, and cast away your fears,
The best I can send is encouraging words, that's something you'll need to hear.
I'll put away the kid this time, I promise you'll definitely see,
These are the things I've promised you; will you keep your promise to me?
Both of our lives are crazy right now, but we don't have to make it any harder,
Because at the end of the day it's not about us, in reality it's about Our Daughter.

IT'S NOT ABOUT US

This poem was written for a friend of mine that I met while I was in Memphis. We used to sit down and have talks about what was going on in our lives and the problems that we were having within our relationships. He was constantly going through it with the mother of his child and he asked me to put a poem together for him.

He wanted to see if it could help her understand how he felt. Parents, we must realize that when we have a child, life stops being about us, it starts to be about our Child. We must be conscious of what we say and do when we are around our children.

We can't be arguing and fussing at each other, we must come to an understanding and move on. If you are paying attention, look at your child's face when the two of you argue. Pay attention to the things that they say when you argue. She/he will pick up on the fact that you only talk bad about him when you are mad, or she gets on my nerves when you are mad at mommy.

In this situation, someone must step up and be the bigger parent, and realize that life is no longer about being an item. If you guys can't get along as a couple, you will have to learn how to get along as parents. That's it and that's all!

You must realize the more you fuss and fight, the more Love you take out of the child's life. You two can be mad at each other forever, but that should never involve the baby. Now I want to speak to the men. It's time for us to stop arguing back and forth with the mother of our children and start to do more listening.

If we listen more men, we'll be able to hear where the real problem lies within the argument. There is something else wrong 90 percent of the time, it doesn't even have anything to do with the current situation you're arguing about. It's usually something old.

Men remember, we are that child's father, and women, remember you are the mom, so start seeing him for who he is, and stop letting your feelings get involved. If you guys used to be madly in love and it doesn't work out, then move on with your life.

Don't try to hang on to something that causes so much confusion, you can move on and still be great at Co- Parenting. It's time that we put a stop to what the enemy is trying to do inside the household. He just wants your child to think it's cool to argue and fuss with their mate when they get older.

He wants you two to continue to be mad at each other, which will affect the way you show love to your child as a unit. In order for our children to make it these days, you have to be a UNIT OF LOVE. Not just love coming from one side, it must be a UNIT. When the love comes from both sides, the child starts to reap the benefits of the VILLAGE.

When the two of you stop telling your parents bad things about the other, they then will be able to get involved and be the grandparents the child needs. When the two of you are constantly arguing, the parent will eventually take sides, and the mom will eventually start to keep the child from the father. Which keeps the child away from the Grandparents.

Which in turn deprives the child of the love they need from the village. NOT FAIR AT ALL! We both must accept responsibility for the part we played in the reason why we are arguing. Men, if you are not stepping up being the parent that you are supposed to be, then accept your responsibility and do better. That just might stop the arguing. To the mothers, if you are constantly arguing with him because he has a new girlfriend and they seem to be happy, CUT IT OUT.

Don't be the petty one that causes confusion in his household because you are not a part of it anymore. Same thing goes for the men, it works both ways, when it's over and she finds a man who's good to her and the child. Embrace the fact that she has chosen someone that can add to their lives instead of subtracting.

I know that it's a hard pill to swallow, but it's all about being a man. REAL MEN MOVE ON! Men, we also must realize that when we live a life that leads us to prison, you have to accept the temper tantrums. When she looks up and has to pay a bill that you used to pay, when she turns over at night only to feel the cold side of the bed.

When she looks at the calendar and realizes the man she loves, is not going to be back in her life until she flips that calendar 10 more times. When she has to answer the same question a million times, "Mommy where is daddy, and when is he coming home"? Or when she meets a guy, she likes but, doesn't want to deal with him because she loves you so much, or when she has to come to see you and get touched up and down by a stranger in order to get in.

When she has to calm the child down when they leave, because all she hears for the 5-hour ride home is, “I WANT MY DADDY”. Sometimes men, she is going to lash out, she is going to have her moments when she wishes that she NEVER MET YOU. Pain makes people think about a lot of crazy things. It also makes them say things they really don’t mean, that’s just how it works.

Parents, you both have played a part in the arguments you’re having. When you really sit back and analyze what the argument is about, I guarantee you can see where you played a part in the decision that you guys are now arguing about. STOP IT, and be the parents the child needs, if you want your child to have a healthy relationship with their mate/people when they get older.

Don’t let your problems plague your child, get it together, if not for the sake of PEACE but, for the sake of the child. In all reality, WHAT REALLY MATTERS?

HEALING

I came to the Lord wounded, no one knows the pain I feel,
He let me know that He can make me well, but there’s somethings that must be revealed.
I fought strenuous battles with the enemy, he left me with scars to bare,

Then the Lord said, those scars are healed, but first you must cut your hair.
I heard this message for months, but the battles in my mind I fought,
I tried to run and resist it, but there was no peace outside of this thought.
I'll trust in the Lord's direction, ignoring the feeling deep in my gut,
His message was loud and clear, How can I heal if you keep it covered up?

HEALING

"Healing" is a very strong poem; It represents a time in my life where I was wrestling with revealing my scars that I had accumulated over the years. When I was young, I got a bad haircut which left scars and irritation in the back of my head. I was always self-conscious about these scars because I lived my life caring about what people thought about me. When I was out there in the streets getting money,

I really didn't care about the scars being visible, I don't know why but, I just didn't care as much as I did now. I started to grow dreads so that my scars couldn't be seen, I will be honest though. I was really going through it about people seeing these scars on my head. When I came into the knowledge of Christ,

He started to deal with me about this situation, He started to put me in places where I had to expose the scars but, I would always get around that with a head covering or something. Then I got to Memphis, and He kept sending this one guy that kept telling me that God said I needed to cut my hair.

Not only did he bring the message, he brought scripture with him. You can't argue with scripture when it's presented to you, it's up to you to accept it or reject it.I wrestled with cutting my hair for about a year, then one day I got up and I went to the barber shop and I cut my hair. I was so scared, look at this, 235-pound half gangster, worried about what people are saying about him. WOW, the things that we don't know about each other.

I walked around for a couple of days with nothing on my head, I used to do my best to block it out but, it was extremely hard. Then one day, God spoke to me," HOW CAN I HEAL YOU, IF YOU KEEP IT COVERED UP?"

I thought that He was talking about making the scar go away but, he was talking about making the fear of the scar being seen. Or worrying about what people were saying. God wanted me to expose the scar so I could get healed on the inside, I didn't understand what He was talking about until I matured enough to receive what He was saying.

Then it got a little deeper, God said "There are plenty of things that you have hidden to the world, I know you've done them, and the people you have hurt know you've done them.

You lie about the things that you've done because you don't want people to know that you did them, in fear of what people might say or think. There were a lot of things that I have done in my past that I am extremely remorseful for; I would always be so hard on myself for being responsible for doing such things. Being disloyal when I should have been loyal, lying when I should have told the truth. Laying down when I should have stood up, being an enemy when I should have been a friend.

Every time I had a chance to accept what I have done in my past, I used to ignore it and keep it moving, "Hidden Scars". God said, "You will never be healed of any situation as long as you keep hiding behind it, you have to endure the pain of people knowing in order to move on with the situation". Until you deal with it, this situation or things you have done in your past will control you.

You will always walk into a room and be worried about what people think or what they are saying as long as you hide behind a lie. I thought God was just talking about MY HAIR, and the scars that my hair had hidden. God was talking about everything that I tried to cover up, these things needed to be exposed so the wound could be healed.

A lot of us hide behind a lie so our mistakes won't be exposed, we do that so we can always remain perfect in the eyes of others. In Christ you have to know that there is nothing perfect about you. You have to understand that the more you hide behind a lie, the longer it will take to heal.

God can't heal what you try to cover up, and at some point, you must be mature enough to let yourself grow up. Or you will become a slave to those things you hide. You will walk into every room wondering, are they talking about me, or do they know about my past? Give that thing to God, and however He heals you embrace the process.

In some cases, God will not give you time to prepare, He will just expose you and guide you through the healing process.

I just want to encourage everyone reading this chapter, there might be some things you're hiding that God already knows about. This thing has you living in Fear, or has you not wanting to be in certain places or around certain people because of your Failures. You must give that thing to God and Move on with your life, don't let the mistakes of you past control the things you want to do in the present.

God wants you to get to a point where you can hear about the things that you have done in your past, and not even worry about what's said. He wants you to hold your head high and move through life with an assurance that you are forgiven. Remember, GOD CAN'T HEAL, WHAT YOU KEEP COVERED UP! Sometimes being transparent is the best healing.

PARTING WAYS

Sitting back thinking about the name I used, as I was running wild in the streets,
I'm no longer that child that used to run wild, wearing the mark of the beast.
That was Grandma's game that gave me the fame, but I'm truly not the man from before,
I had to realize that it was my disguise, I can't be called by that name anymore.
Thoughts come with it, the way that I lived it, but those things were just for show,
I had a talk with a man that blessed my hand, he said son it's time to let go.
I tarnished that name, I got in Grandma's game as she pushed me around in that stroller,
So I have to part ways with what Grandma gave,

because life with that name is OVER.

PARTING WAYS

"Parting Ways" is a special poem that I wrote about my nick name, (GOOCHIE) that turned into my street name. It's sad how we can get a name from our parents with a significant meaning behind it, and then attached so much negativity to the name when we start to get older. My name came from my mother tickling me a lot when I was young, and my momma saying, Goochie, Goochie, Goochie, in that baby voice, so my mother said why don't we call him Goochie?

I thought that my grandmother (MY MOTHERS MOM) gave me that name my whole life. When I read this poem to my mother, she told me that she gave me the name. So, when you see Grandma in this poem, it's supposed to say Momma but, I wrote it before I knew the truth, Grandma sounds better in the poem.

I remember growing up being a so-called lady's man, and a Bad Boy, I loved to fight and play sports. I loved to see people face light up when they saw me coming, it was either the girls, or either the little dudes that were scared of me. As I got older, that name started to bring a lot of trouble my way. Some guy would hear that I love to fight, or that I was good at fighting, and be the first one to try to start a fight in order to get a name for himself.

Enemies were created before I even met them. Females would have a look of lust in their eyes when the saw me, either it was because of what the females said about the encounters they had with me, or the Bad Boy reputation that came with my name.

It's crazy how a name can carry a lot of lies, and you can dislike a person without even laying eyes on them a day in your life. There are good and bad things that come with having a popular name. A GIFT AND A CURSE!

I used to hate when I walked into a barbershop or a club, and automatically a dude would be looking at me crazy. I would always wonder why; it wasn't until I came into the knowledge of Christ that I finally understood what was going on.

People will carry a name as far as they can take it, they will put their own spin on a guy's name, and make it seem like a person is a God, or the worse person in the world and the result of that would make people envious.

I used to love walking into a club and see the ladies huddling up in a corner, and when they saw me. They come running and screaming "HI GOOCHIE", that used to make me feel like a million bucks. I used to love the attention; compliments would fuel my little boy ego all the time.

When I came to prison, I used to love the way the guys respected me, and I loved the way that they treated me, but I soon realized that they were respecting the wrong things about me. Nothing about the man I was deserved to be respected, I was a liar, a manipulator, a deceiver, and a womanizer.

I surrounded myself with guys who could not be trusted, which turned me into a guy who could not be trusted, so it's safe to say I accepted a follower's mindset. So many people respected the leader in me, they didn't see that I had a little follower in me as well. God wasted no time with his request for me to remove that name, then a process of removing the spirits that came along with the name.

Sometimes I used to walk into a room and just automatically think that I am the meanest, toughest guy in the room, then I started to get into a lot of fights with guys I never said or did anything too.

I knew it was because of what they heard about me, and I started to get tired of fighting for no reason. I got tired of being used because of my aggressive nature. It would be the guys that couldn't fight at all, that would surround their selves with guys that could fight.

They would talk as much trash as they could because they knew they were surrounded by guys that carried a reputation. Most of the people reading this book has either heard something good or bad about Goochie.

Well, that's the reason why God told me I had to let this name go. This name was attached to the memories the enemy allowed me to create. A person's name goes along way, it can either get them ahead in life, or it can be the reason why they don't go anywhere at all. God said, "Son, it's time to start over, you must change everything, there can't be anything left of that lifestyle or that name. You must start all over and you must go by the name I gave you, John Edward Bell Jr"!

No more Gangster, no more Ladies Man, no more Drug Dealer, no more Fighting, no more "GOOCHIE"! The only way you get rid of your past, you must delete everything that comes with it. I wrestled with letting the name go for about seven months.

Then God started to show me there were so many negative things tied to this name, and I needed a fresh start. Old things have passed away, and all things become new (2 Corinthians 5:17).

I finally let go and moved on with my life, so after you read this poem and chapter. If you knew me as Goochie, please delete that out of your memory. My name is John Edward Bell Jr. Please try your best to call me by the name that God gave me. Remember, in order to move on with new things in life, you have to let some things go. It's okay to START OVER!

He Chose Pain! "2006"

He Chose Peace! " 2014"

IT'S ALMOST OVER!

Made in the USA
Middletown, DE
05 May 2019